Charles Allen Sumner

Notes of Travel in Northern Europe

Charles Allen Sumner

Notes of Travel in Northern Europe

ISBN/EAN: 9783337207595

Printed in Europe, USA, Canada, Australia, Japan

Cover: Foto ©Andreas Hilbeck / pixelio.de

More available books at **www.hansebooks.com**

HARBOR OF GOTHENBURG.

IN

NORTHERN EUROPE.

BY

CHARLES A. SUMNER.

WITH VIEWS, PORTRAITS, MAPS, AND PLANS, ENGRAVED EXPRESSLY
FOR THIS BOOK.   A. L. RAWSON, ARTIST.

NEW YORK:
ANDREW J. GRAHAM, 744 BROADWAY.
1886.

COPYRIGHTED, 1885,
BY
CHARLES A. SUMNER.

TO MY WIFE

AND TO

MY DAUGHTER ESTHER,

MY COMPANIONS IN THESE

JOURNEYINGS,

THIS VOLUME

IS

AFFECTIONATELY INSCRIBED.

CONTENTS.

I.
From London to Gothenburg.................................. 11

II.
First Objects of Observation................................ 19

III.
Public Institutions... 29

IV.
The Gotha Canal.—Trolhattan................................ 37

V.
Trolhattan to Venersborg.................................... 53

VI.
Venersborg to Stockholm..................................... 62

VII.
Stockholm to Stromsholm Castle.............................. 79

VIII.
Monktorp to Kolbeck... 87

IX.
In the Kolbeck Parish....................................... 101

X.
The Stromsholm Vardshus Family and Neighbors................ 113

XI.
Stromsholm to Vestanfors.................................... 122

XII.
At Smedjbacken.. 134

XIII.
Delecarlia.—Smedjbacken to Leksand.................. 141

XIV.
Leksand to Mora.. 152

XV.
At Mora and Utmeland..................................... 166

XVI.
From Mora to Falun.. 182

XVII.
At Falun; and thence to Westeras........................ 190

XVIII.
A Week at Westeras.. 203

XIX.
To and in Upsala... 218

XX.
At Stockholm.. 236

XXI.
King and People.. 260

XXII.
From Stockholm to Malmo.................................. 274

XXIII.
Copenhagen.. 298

XXIV.
From Copenhagen to Stettin............................... 310

XXV.
A Glance at Berlin... 316

XXVI.
Berlin to Dover. A few Notes at Dresden, Cologne, and Paris. 331

List of Illustrations.

	PAGE
Harbor of Gothenburg. *Frontispiece*	
Steamship "Alaska"	12
Hotel Christiania	19
The Bourse and Ostra Street, Gothenburg	24
Statue of Gustavus Adolphus	26
Mauritz Rubenson, President of Board of Practical Education	40
Sidney W. Cooper, U. S. Consul to Gothenburg	45
Canal Locks, near Trolhattan	48
Trolhattan Falls	54
Venersborg	59
Vadstena Castle	71
Gotha Canal, near Borenshult	73
Brunneby	74
Cloister Church	75
Soderkoping	76
Grave of Baron von Platen	76
Mem	77
Horningsholm	78
Strengnas Cathedral	80
Stromsholm Castle	81
Charles IX. Statue	84
Landlady of Vardshus	121
Skansen Locks	126
Leksand Church	144
Mora	153
Cottage Scene in Delecarlia	157

LIST OF ILLUSTRATIONS.

	PAGE
Mora-Kulla	162
Gustavus Wasa's Concealment	173
Monument of Gustavus Wasa	177
Rattvik Church	181
Ornas	189
Falun.—View of Market, Cathedral, and Copper Hill Range	191
B. V. Norstedt	193
The Stoten Abyss	195
Map of Southern Sweden	202
A. P. Erickson, Keeper of Westeras Castle	205
Interior of Westeras Cathedral	208
Statue of Gustavus Wasa	216
Skokloster	221
General View of Upsala Castle and Cathedral	223
Upsala Cathedral	227
Upsala University Library	232
New University Building, Upsala	233
View of Hasselbacken, Stockholm	246
English Church, Stockholm	250
The Royal Palace, Stockholm	252
Riddarholmen Church, Stockholm	255
Interior of Jacob Church, Stockholm	256
King's Theatre, Stockholm	258
National Museum, Stockholm	259
Gustaf Adolph Square, Stockholm	265
Bird's-eye View of Stockholm	269
Norrkoping Public School	275
Linkoping Cathedral	277
Prof. Victor Hugo Wickstrom, of Lund	279
Lund Cathedral	280
Crypt of Lund Cathedral	282
New University Hall, Lund	283
Malmo Castle	286
Malmo City Hall	287
St. Peter's Church, Malmo	289
Kockumska Hus	290
Flat and Side View of Swedish Bread	292

LIST OF ILLUSTRATIONS.

	PAGE
Costumes in Skane	294
Our Malmo Entertainers	297
Map of North Germany	299
Plan of Copenhagen	303
Stettin	315
Kaiserhoff, Berlin	318
Royal Palace, Berlin	327
Berlin and Vicinity	329
Central Portion of Dresden	333
Bruhl Terrace	336
Helbig's Restaurant	337
The Belvedere	338
Old Bridge and Cathedral, Dresden	340
Grosse Gardens, Palace, and Lake	344
Royal Museum and Theatre	351
Zwinger Court-yard	352
Rev. H. R. Haweis	355
Great Choir and High Altar, Cologne Cathedral	359
Main Aisle of Cologne Cathedral	361
Arch of Triumph	364
Tomb of Napoleon Bonaparte	366
Palais Royal, Paris	368
Grand Opera House, Paris	369
Grand Stairway of Opera House, Paris	371
The Seven Bridges of Paris	373
Steamship "City of Berlin"	381
Cliffs of Dover	382

NOTES OF TRAVEL
IN
NORTHERN EUROPE.

I.

FROM LONDON TO GOTHENBURG.

Thursday, the 21st of June, was a foggy, drizzly day, in London; such a day as Englishmen appear to delight in calling "nasty." The walking in the streets where the mud was about the composition of the inside of an average loaf of London baker's bread was declared to be "beastly." [You must not say that you have been or are liable to be seasick; you must not employ that term when speaking in "society" in the metropolis; you must or may admit that you are not a good traveler; but "nasty" and "beastly" are words frequently used by ladies and gentlemen in conversation at a fashionable dinner-party. The former is pronounced with a breadth of accent on the "a" that is of itself at first almost medicinal to a stranger from Yankeeland.]

We are glad to get on board the *Belle* at 6 o'clock at night—out of the rain. And such a long carriage-ride as it is from Russell Square to the steamer-landing; no end of streets, and ever-changing variety of trades and inhabitants. The incomprehensible immensity of this tremendous city again fairly oppresses us.

The Göthenburg steamer starts from Millwall Docks, London, at 1 o'clock in the morning. You are requested to be on board not later than 9 o'clock the evening before sailing. And we found that most of the passengers were at the supper-table, which was spread at 8 p. m.

The *Belle*, Captain C. A. Petterson, is of 1400 tons register and a thousand-horsepower, capable of making 300 miles a day in good weather. What further is to be properly recorded in this connection should be the fact that the vessel is very neat, and the food most excellent in material and cooking, and the service "all that could be desired." We could not refrain from mutual confessions of a sense of "cramped conditions,"—though in no manner or degree complaining—after our accommodations on the mammoth "Alaska."

THE "ALASKA" AT SEA.

You have a suggestion of Swedish proximity before the supper-bell rings; you are invited to help yourself at the side-shelf or smorgersbord, on which is spread a plentiful supply of bread and cheese, and cold fish and cold meats, cooked or cured in various forms. Admonished by the experience which Du Chaillu so vividly describes, I tasted with great caution, lest I should bite a morsel that required an educated appetite before it became entirely palatable. But I found everything not only eatable on first acquaintance, but decidedly delicious. O, what a blessed change from the pasty bread and unsavory meats of the London restaurant! I do believe that the true genealogy of the New-England kitchen, as I knew it in my boyhood, is to be traced not to our Plymouth forefathers' hearths, but to the ovens of the Scandinavians, who, in a still somewhat undetermined century preceded the Mayflower immigration to the coast of Massachusetts and Rhode Island. Precisely how this happened can not be told; but there are strong grounds—such as are called in philology "inherent"—for this sincere conviction or faith.

We are welcomed by the Captain himself, saluting in his native tongue, and then speaking in that charming broken English for which his kinsmen—and more especially his kinswomen—are renowned. And when he learns that we are from California, he comes again to us from the fore-hatch, where he had been watching the stevedores load his vessel, and talks rapidly and earnestly with us about "the land of gold," and inquires respecting his people there.

He says he never had any inclination to quit his native land for good. In fact, he never leaves her shores without a pang of regret. He has mingled with the inhabitants of many nations; gone among them in their own homes as well as in their places of domestic trade. He has seen nowhere that mutual love and affection that is always to be observed, he says—and he utters this in a very pleasant, kindly way—in his dear old Sweden. He thinks that it is well,—in truth, he knows that it is well—that multitudes should leave Sweden to settle in America; and he rejoices that there is such a country for them to go to,—under the circumstances. But he always looks with pity upon the poor emigrants, who must go far, far away from their beloved kingdom. All this he says without ostentation or the slightest sign of affectation. He means what he says; and he does not intend to offensively disparage any other country. His frank, straightforward manner of speech, and his entire freedom in it are delightful, to the point even of being deserving of the title of charming.

In his intercourse with his officers and men and the passengers, throughout the voyage, he endears himself to us all; and as we came in sight of land the last day out, his "guests," as he called them, caught each other halfway in expressions of regret on account of our separation from such a master—"Just what I was going to say." If you should ever chance to make this trip, my dear reader, I advise you to seek a passage on the new ship that is being built under the orders of this model and "popular commander." His new and larger boat will be ready in October, 1886.

At two o'clock Friday morning we are aroused by the noise of departure. Looking out of the cabin-window we appear to be sailing down the center of a street. We are, in fact, passing through the basin that connects Millwall Docks with the Thames. At six o'clock we are at the mouth of the great river. We pass close alongside of two wrecks "of recent manufacture" as one of the sailors explained; and a steamer with a shifted cargo, signaling for a pilot, is seen as we turn the corner of the British Kingdom, and begin moving up in the direction of Yarmouth. But we are not going to hug the shore so far up as the home of Peggotty and little Em'ly. O, for even a brief telescopic squint at the veritable fishing-grounds of Ham and his guardian.

The offing is crowded with sail: we counted thirteen steamers with the prows pointed toward London; and the brigs and schooners are literally uncountable. Nor does the cluster thin out rapidly; but up from the vasty deep new incomers seem to rise, for some time after we had "northered," almost as fast as the score of crafts we met at the mouth of the river descended from our sight. We were disappointed in not meeting as many vessels as we expected to see near Liverpool; contrariwise, we are content on this side of John Bull's dominions. It is a busy part of the Earth's surface; these waters are daily vexed at every angle.

The sea is not rough at the beginning of the voyage, and it grows more calm and smooth as we approach the Swedish harbor. All proved to be "good travelers" on this trip. There is a party of four Englishmen and Scotchmen on board, under care of a professional guide, J. G. Bergquist, who are "programmed" for Norway and Sweden, and perhaps a part of Russia. They go from Göthenburg to Christiana, "and so."

"So," simple "so," declaratively and interrogatively, is a favorite expression with the Swedish population hereabouts, for "That is so," and "Is that so?" At first I imagined that it implied incredulity. Not so. "So," *solus*, may, with a heavy emphasis or sharp rising inflection, indicate great surprise at your words, but has no signification of disbelief. At times it appears to convey, and I am confident it does mean, hearty satisfaction and profound gladness on account of that undoubted statement which you are making—about America, for instance—to your Scandinavian friend.

We hugged the English coast up as far as the line of Harwich, when we turned and pointed for the northern cliffs of Denmark. As the land fades out of sight I count the sail within our horizon, and find that we have the goodly company of twenty-three vessels. Although the sea is smooth, and it is not an uncomfortable occupation to simply sit on the bridge-deck and watch the motion of the boat, and listen to such bits of conversation as drift toward you, we feel anxious to get a closer acquaintance with some of our fellow-passengers,—knowing that that can not be a difficult task if we once set aggressively about it.

We have for one of our companions a gentleman of about 60 years of age, whose benevolent countenance would be a passport into cheerfully inclined company anywhere. He opens communication with the youngest member of our domestic circle, and at once establishes relations of a most cordial character. It transpires that he is a Scotchman,—a practical mechanical engineer. His card shows us the name of J. Jackson, of 27 Walbrook, London. He very shortly improves the occasion to announce himself an uncompromising Liberal, an ardent admirer of Gladstone and John Bright, and a missionary for free trade. He can quote at length from Bright's recent speeches at Birmingham, and is never tired of speaking of Gladstone as a wonderful man, a wonderful man, a wonderful man.

He asked me about the general feeling in America on the Irish land question; and when I assured him that the large majority of our people deeply sympathize with the peasants, he said with vehemence that they ought to,—that Ireland was most outrageously oppressed.

On the second day out the passage was like a trip up the Hudson or the Sacramento River with respect to the smoothness of the water and the motion of the steamer. During the entire voyage we were rarely out of sight of sail. As we approached Jutland the number of vessels in sight rapidly increased.

Denmark land is seen at 2 p. m. of the second day from London on this trip; and it rises and lengthens out until we swing around its northern promontory.

We pass by and in among scores of fishing-boats in the vicinity of the upper lighthouse, and the boys in their skiffs hold up specimens of their catch for us to examine. They spread their nets on steamer-days with a view of getting the benefit of a "scare" toward the shore, created by the beating of the screw.

Sunday was Midsummer-day; which would be only restating a fact of the calendar for the northern hemisphere in any other country but Sweden or Norway. Here it im- implies a great deal; here this is the red-letter day of all the year, as may be noted from one item in my diary:—

"On Board Steamship *Belle*, Sunday Morning, June 24, 5.30 o'clock.

"We are on the bridge deck, looking through the Captain's glass for land. The second officer points out where the lighthouse will "stick up his nose" when we shall have arrived at the point of the globe where it can be seen by the incoming traveler. The air could not be clearer. It is so pure that it seems as though you could look very far beyond the line of the horizon of the sea,—far away into the illimitable sky before us. Now we will try our eyesight again. * * * One of our English fellow-passengers has just cried out that he has detected the yellow speck that must mean, being properly interpreted, the sail of a pilot-boat. The discovery is confirmed by the officer on deck, and he immediately told us where to look to see an unusually white perpendicular line on the edge of the ocean. His vision is keenest after all. And this is the first taper that by night, or this is the first object that by day is beheld by the visitor or the returning Swede, who comes on this path to this northern country. * * * The little shaft-cloud rapidly developed into an unmistakable pillar of stone, and the coast-line has risen up beneath and round about it. And this is Sweden! — the ragged edge of it, at least — that we have read and dreamed so much about, and so often and so devoutly wished to see.

"One year ago to-day a good Scandinavian friend asked me where I would be twelve months from date, provided a certain thing happened; and I jokingly replied that I would be in Sweden. I have not thought of the pleasant prophecy from that time to this hour. And here I am about to enter the harbor of Göthenburg, — a most unexpected fulfillment of jocose, conditional foretelling. The pilot has just come on board, direct from the pilot schooner, and not as with us transported to the ship by a small boat. * * * We are in the archipelago — in an intricate channel between barren, rocky islands. We are meeting many gayly dressed little steamers, crowded with people, who greet us with cheers."

Not without a dry vein of humor is Capt. Petterson. Several passengers, in an eager manner, without due consideration for his proper devotion to his still remaining duties of watchfulness, — although the local pilot is in navigating charge, — began exclaiming in the Captain's presence, and with an inquiring inflection, with respect to the little treeless and sodless islands on either hand. As we passed along up the narrow channel the Captain is evidently bothered somewhat by these interrogating remarks; but he does not "bluff" any one, and seeks to avoid showing any annoyance. He finally replies, in a most natural and genial fashion, "Yes, they are entirely barren, but that is not the peculiarity that distresses our folks the most." So he starts a curiosity that works on the minds of a half dozen men and maidens with increasing torment. They appeal to other native Swedes on the bridge. "What is the peculiarity to which the captain refers?" No one can tell; or if they have ever heard—as I think some have heard, judging afterwards from the quiet smile that appeal begets on their countenances—they will not tell; they evade the question. Finally the anxious inquirers *must* be appeased: although by this time it is evident to all on board that the master would not be disturbed with impertinent or unnecessary questions.

"What is the peculiarity about those Islands that most distresses your people?" With a bow and a most benignant expression of the eyes and face, the commander responds, "They are harder than the bottom of a ship." The questioners turn aside and take sweet counsel together over that revelation,—admitting that this information is good,—very, very good.

With cunning piloting—and an expert steersman is required, no doubt—we wind into the buoyed haven of Göthenburg, and at 8 o'clock Sunday morning our boat is fastened directly alongside one of the granite wharves of the city. The custom-house officials are polite, but very thorough, in their work of examination. They go down to the bottom of the trunks, and they sift the "duds" of the passengers—as one English lady called her clothing—with great deliberation and care. But the ordeal is not a very severe and lengthy one, and in half an hour after our vessel is tied up we are on our way through the streets in the omnibus of the Christiana Hotel.

The passage-price, including your cabin accommodations, from London to Göthenburg by this line is £3 3s; half-fare for children under 12 years of age.

II.

FIRST OBJECTS OF OBSERVATION.

The drive up town from the Stora Bommens Hamn, where our gangplank is put down, is through the principal street of the city — the Stora Hamngatan — in the center of which is the Stora Hamn Kanal, and on either side of which are elegant three-story and four-story stone and brick edifices.

HOTEL CHRISTIANIA.

Your first impression of Göthenburg, or Göteborg, is very pleasant, and I can now say that the favorable opinion you take on the hotel 'bus, on the morning of your arrival, is augmented by all your subsequent walks and rides through the city. It is cleaner than London, far; even cleaner than that much belied town of Liverpool; as neat, in every part, as is our own beautiful New York City, in the neighborhood of Union and Madison Squares, in the month of May.

The two principal hotels, of which the "Christiana" is the lesser, may be said to be situated on a square formed by the intersection of the Sodra Hamngata and Drottningtorget. Haglund's Hotel and Gota Kallare are one and the same institution. The rooms here are commendable for their neatness, and their heavy, massive furniture,—including single beds all around. I have observed that the accommodations are in all respects about the same in the two or three hotels mentioned, while the "tone" and high prices are at Haglund's. Both are kept, of course, on what is known among us as the European plan. Everything in the way of accommodation and service is separately charged for; and even as far north as Sweden the much-talked-of imposition of an item for candles, whether burned or not, is on the daily rendered bills—at some hotels which friends have visited.

The service up stairs is exclusively by girls. In the restaurants we find at each place one "English boy" on whom you must frequently expend more trouble, for the purpose of making understood that which you want, than when you are left to extemporized deaf-and-dumb signs and the compendious phrase-book.

The first peculiar article that requires investigation is the porcelain stove that sits in one of the corners of each room. It reaches from the floor nearly up to the ceiling of rooms that are fully eleven feet high. Some have very handsome cornices, and many are adorned by statues, or busts, or figures of reindeer or bears. On our corner furnace is set the bust of a lady, which I take to be the representation of Dido—head-dress and all—just before she mounted that funeral pile of which our schoolboys are reading. At this moment, at 10 o'clock p. m., she is looking down upon me with a countenance that sometimes seems to shape itself into one of inquiry; which I fancy asks me now and then what I think about this writing without the aid of artificial light at this hour of the day. And she will insist, I can imagine, now and then, on an answer—a mental consideration of her query, and an inaudible response, at least.

In the center, half-way up, in these porcelain pillars for fire, is a cupboard with thin brass doors, in which you can place anything that you wish to keep warm or hot during the day or night. The fire, of hard wood, is kindled at about a foot and a half from the bottom of the stove-shaft, which is about two feet in diameter; and it is said that two fires will last abundantly during twenty-four hours. The doorknobs are egg-shaped—a decided improvement on the round handle.

The face of the buildings on the principal streets is mostly of a light-brown color. The roofs are all covered with tiles, which are reddish, or black, or yellow, according to the taste of the owners of the different buildings,—which seems to alternately and it might be said fortunately change, and so give a pleasing and regular variety and relief, so to speak, to the complexion of the housetops. A few houses, like the Gota Kallare Hotel, have flat roofs; and in such instances the structures are usually of that woodboxy description so familiar to us in the architecture of some of the hotels in San Francisco.

As soon as possible after our arrival we hastened to the Cathedral, where services were about to begin. The building is cruciform in construction, and will hold probably over 2,500 persons. There are four galleries, exclusive of the organ-loft. The organ is a magnificent instrument,—nearly the size of the one at St. George's Hall, Liverpool.

Of course this is a Lutheran cathedral, but it is also an Episcopal cathedral,—the Swedish church differing in this respect from the German Lutheran. There is an altar, with the communion-bread upon it; and back of the altar is a large, richly gilded cross, with cherubs in gilt flying round about it. On each side of the altar is a full-sized angel, with enormous wings,—disproportionately long wings, I thought; one angel pointing down or pointing in a presentation way at the sacred elements on the altar, while the other points upward toward the cross and the skies.

Half-way down the building from the chancel, on the northern side—and so situated as to allow the preacher a view of all parts of the church—is a pulpit, with a sounding-board above it. In front of the pulpit is a gilded protrusion of cherub-head, lion-head, and ox-head, surmounted by an eagle. The whole of this "ornamentation" looks very tawdry,—like a great molasses-candy medallion daub.

The church was well filled when we arrived; and we stood at one end of the main aisle, in which a number of short benches were placed crosswise, and occupied by elderly women,—from 60 to 80 years of age. It was a remarkable sight to see so many aged females together, —all appearing to be in excellent health, and all very attentive and devout in their actions.

At 10:30 a priest came on the altar. He wore a gown which I could not distinguish from the Roman Catholic priestly garment,—it having a large cross on the back, splendidly illuminated. He read the exhortation and confession and several prayers, and gave out one hymn, or indicated that the singing of the hymn was to take place. Several psalms were sung meanwhile. The numbers of the hymns were posted at different portions of the church,—brass numbers being hung upon pegs set at proper intervals on small blackboards. Then the preacher ascended the pulpit; the youthful priest retiring from the chancel.

The preacher read a chapter from the bible, read many prayers from a large flat book, preached a sermon an hour and a half long on the subject of rearing children in the nurture and admonition of the Lord, and deprecating undue levity on holidays, especially when a holiday happened to be on Sunday; and concluded his portion of the day's hard ministerial work by receiving from the sexton's hand a dozen different sheets of paper and announcing births, marriages, and deaths that had taken place during the last week, and proclaiming for the first or second or third time notice of intended matrimony between members of his great congregation.

When the services were about half way through, a lady unlocked her pew and bade our party enter. The narrow seats would keep any man awake who struggled to impinge upon them; and while I appreciate the kindness and courtesy of that lady, I wish she had been impolite or thoughtless enough to have allowed me to stand until the benediction.

In the afternoon we visited a private park, which is kept somewhat after the style of Woodward's, and where we heard excellent music. The admission-charge to this park is ten ore, or about two and a half cents. The charge of admission to the splendid observatory—almost equal, in dimensions and variety of plants, to the great tropical planthouse at Kew Gardens, London,— is twenty ore, or five cents.

An American soon becomes accustomed to the money issued here, as it is of decimal basis. And you are not snapped at and snubbed if you confess or apologetically explain that your hesitation in making change is due to your being a foreigner. The copper coinage is one ore, two ores, three ores, and five ores. Precious metals are in the 10 ore, 25 ore, and, of course, the kroner. The bills are from five kroner up to 100 kroner—5, 10, 25, 50, and 100. Most of the bills are about half the size of our greenback,— the 50-kroner bill alone, though of different shape, being nearly as large as our paper issue. With the exception noted, the bills are about one third as large as a Bank of England note.

Near sunset—that is, about 8 o'clock—in company with a Swedish acquaintance I met on board the *Belle*, I visited the old round tower at the rear of the city, known as the "Lion." A trooper who was on guard admitted us to the structure; for that purpose unlocking a small iron door at the north side. From the ground-floor—which covers a spring—we ascended three flights of stairs. There were portholes and casemates on each floor. At one side there is an angle pushed out from the circle, in which was the kitchen of the garrison. The Lion is about forty feet in diameter, and about the same number of feet in hight. It is on a sharp natural eminence, and it completely overlooks the city. From it you look directly across to the twin tower, known as the Crown,—situated on the other side of the city, and distant about a mile and a quarter.

The trooper was indignant when we offered him money for his trouble. I am out of England!

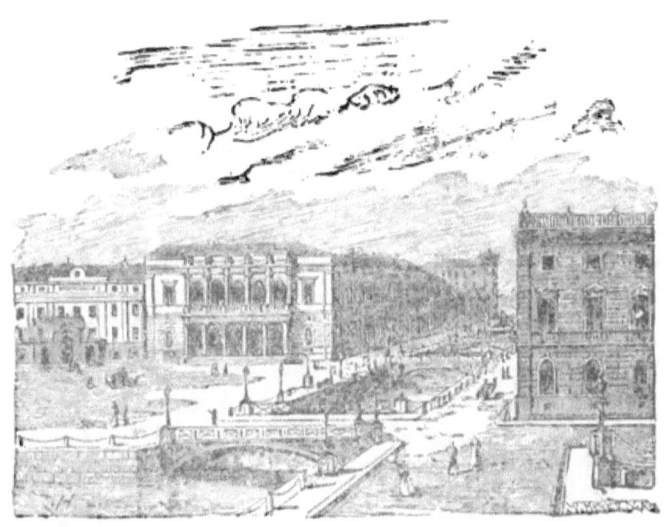

THE BOURSE AND OSTRA STREET, GOTHENBURG.

On this same eminence once stood the fortress Galberg, renowned for its resistance to the Danes when its Captain, Martin Krakow, was wounded, and his wife took command of the garrison and made a successful defense. She poured down on the heads of the assaulting parties pailfuls of boiling pitch and tar. The enemy became discouraged and disgusted on account of this unusual and irregular mode of warfare—as they termed it—and without making any breach in the walls, they contemptuously quit this district for more hospitable climes.

Looking over the city from any one of the many commanding edifices that rise on either one of three sides, it is difficult to realize that Göthenburg contains a population of 76,000 souls. It is very compactly built, and I have yet to see the first house that is for rent. The Vice-consul says that it is a city inhabited mostly by business people: if you seek pleasure, he says, go to Stockholm.

There are three lines of tramway recently constructed, leading to the southern, eastern, and western ends of the city borders: fare 10 ore.—half the sum we pay in San Francisco. These city railroads were built and are owned almost exclusively by English capitalists. Advertisements are blown in the glass of the street-car windows. Hack-hire here is one kroner-and-a-half an hour (or 39 cents), and the drivers do not attempt to overcharge or in any way exact more than their prescribed fares. Most of the hacks and carriages that stand for hire are owned by a company, and the drivers themselves get one kroner and a half a day. When you give them ten ore extra they are profuse in their thanks, but I am told that they never show any displeasure if you do not fee them. I wish a few of them could be exported to London, and properly advertized. The hack-drivers and street-car conductors are uniformed and numbered.

The wages of the common laboring-man here is one kroner and a half to one kroner and three-quarters per day. Women who work in the field get 80 ore. There are 100 ore in a kroner, or 26 cents.

Sailors from this port going on long voyages receive $16 per month. Cooks in the hotels and steamers—mostly women,—receive as high as $18 per month. But, then, they can cook. They must have served an apprenticeship of three years or more, and have passed an examination.

Street-car conductors are paid 65 cents a day; steam railroad car-conductors get twice that sum.

You can telegraph from one end of Sweden to the other

for a kroner—twenty words. I sent a dispatch yesterday a distance of nearly 600 miles for that sum.

There are two other large parks adjacent to this city, where music is to be heard, of the best order, from 8 to 11.

STATUE OF GUSTAVUS ADOLPHUS.

The statue of Gustavus Adolphus in the principal square of the city, immediately before the Governor's house, is a noble figure, and will at once suggest to many Americans our own Gen. W. S. Hancock. The likeness is very striking.

I have not seen a drunken or a disorderly person since I have been in Göthenburg. All look sober, and appear to be industrious and happy. Over several small gardens and entrances to restaurants I have noticed the name "Good Templar." Göthenburg has a peculiar license-system, which has recently been imitated by the authorities elsewhere. All the liquor-licenses were bought up by a corporation; and this corporation rented or established so many places where liquors are to be sold. The person dispensing the drinks has no pecuniary interest in the sales; and from the profits of the sales that are made the company pays to the city authorities all but five per cent of their investment. This plan is said to have resulted in a great reduction in drunkenness and crime. Beer and other malt drinks are sold in a great many places, and they are of the most excellent character. You have the clear, agreeable smell of the malt when you come near to a bottle of freshly opened Swedish ale.

The police are a fine-looking body of men. They are very polite and obliging,—as it will be agreed all policemen ought ordinarily to be,—and make every effort to inform a stranger. They advise you gratuitously. We are not in London. They wear a handsome blue uniform. Their frock-coat is three or four inches longer than the coat of our New York or San Francisco guardians. They have a blue cloth belt covering a leather strap, on which they hang their clubs at night. They do not carry clubs in the daytime. They wear a glazed cap, which fits close on the head, being skull-shaped from the back of the head to the crown.

During this holiday-week, and for two weeks to come, the militia are in camp, undergoing training in all three branches of the service. There are six companies on the hill immediately to the south of the city. This service is compulsory on all able-bodied men between 21 and 25; that is, for the space of two years out of the four. These youths are called bevärningar. Their uniform resembles the American soldier's dress in most particulars. The artillery and cavalry boys have a leather back to their pants, from the waist to the feet. Their jacket is single-breasted, with small brass buttons. The officers are very much pleased by a visit from a foreigner,—especially from an American. When you say "from California," they exclaim, as everybody else does in this region, "Oh, California! Oh, California!" and they then apparently redouble their efforts to be courteous and entertaining. Their tents pitch close down, being tall and having an unusually sharp incline from the roof-canvas. It is, perhaps, needless to say that we found everything in "apple-pie" order when we "inspected" quarters.

Immediately in front of the parade and camp ground is a large new brick house,—fully as large as the Occidental

Hotel, and not dissimilar in appearance. If you put some turrets—sprinkle a few along the front—of our principal Montgomery Street inn, you would have a close copy. This building is the property of a widow lady. I have heard her frequently spoken of as a very nice woman, good-looking, and fond of the military.

If you wish to make any inquiry in this city, and have not your interpreter with you, you can step up to any passer-by and ask in Swedish if he or she understands English. If he or she does not speak English, as will probably be the case, you will not be merely met with a negative, but you will be requested to stay where you are until he or she brings some one to you who can speak English. He or she will cry "Nej! nej! nej!" if you offer a fee for their services.

We are not in London,—where, if you stand on the street and look doubtingly two ways, some one will come up and propose to show you the way,—often immediately thereafter demanding or begging two pence, although you have been posted in the premises, have not even replied to their offer. Of course you do not object to pay for a street-corner guide, when occasion requires such a person; but you find from experience that these pointers in the English metropolis frequently give you wrong directions. The London police will misdirect you in two cases out of three, and they are frequently very offensive in their appearance and actions when you apply to them for information as to localities. The best practice there, is to double your payment to the shoe-blacking boy, when you will probably reward merit and will surely not be misinformed. The members of the shoe-blacking fraternity in London are as well acquainted with the streets there as the hansom drivers. There are no shoe-blacking boys in Göthenburg.

The water here is soft and pure. The price to manufacturers is about one-fourth of what is paid in San Francisco. There is no charge for water for household or domestic purposes. Gas is supplied at a little advance on the London price. Swedish coal is not as good as the English, and the latter is brought to this port for steamer and domestic cosumption.

The poorhouse is a two story and a half building of brick, 300 feet long, situated on the east side of the square or plaza; facing which are also the two principal hotels of the town and the station of the railroad that leads directly to Stockholm. The very poor are well taken care of here. Their food and bedding is excellent, as we can testify from personal observation.

III.

PUBLIC INSTITUTIONS.

I had the good fortune to make the acquaintance this day of a member of a Practical School-board, Mr. Mauritz Rubenson, and in his company and under his guidance, I made the rounds of the city institutions, so far as time and other considerations would permit. It is vacation in all the public schools of southern Sweden at this time, and my friend much regretted that I could not see the classes.

Fifteen years ago a rich man of Göthenburg died, leaving a will which provided that out of his property or estate 1,500,000 kroners, or about $375,000, should be set apart and put at interest. At the expiration of every nine years after interest had begun to run, the Board of Trustees having the matter in charge should proceed to use the accumulated interest in the erection of such public buildings and the endowment of such institutions as the city of Göthenburg could not properly provide for the benefit of its citizens,—for their education, recreation, comfort, and happiness.

Unlike the usual course of events in some other quarters, under similar circumstances, there was no contest of the will; and the bulk of this good man's estate was not divided up among lawyers on the ground that the deceased was crazy when he wrote or dictated his testament. And hence it is that the people of Göthenburg, and, you may say, society and men and women in general, are enjoying the fruits of his life of industry and economy and of his benevolent disposition. The Board of Trustees have exhibited unusually good judgment in the disbursement of the funds so left under their direction and disposal, as most readers will concede when I enumerate the plans already made and carried out in the name and with the power of this great charity. I do not speak of them in their order of accomplishment, but I believe I embrace them all.

A public bath-house was erected in a most eligible situation, and supplied with every convenience. It will accommodate, in all its departments, three hundred persons at the same time, —men and women. Here, at a ticket charge to the public that is annually fixed at the lowest sum consistent with the cost of the management and care of the establishment, the best of bathing-rooms are to be had—plain baths and baths Roman, and Turkish and Russian and plunge. From hence, also, bath-wagons, with every appliance therein contained for such a bath as may be desired, are dispatched to the homes of the sick, and especially to the dwellings of the poor. On proper application the latter are so supplied without price. We walked through this immense establishment, and noted its neatness and thorough modern furnishing. Nothing is lacking, and the tariff is nominal as compared with strictly private houses for the same entertainment. For twenty-five ore, or about six cents, an ordinary hot and cold bathroom is rented: for thirty-five cents a Russian or Turkish bath is given. We entered the oven of the latter. There was no wanting in hight of temperature. We inspected the cooling alcoves. They are luxuriously furnished. Here, also, the very poor, on due recommendation from a medical man, have free access and complete attendance.

Connected with this establishment is a washing or laundry department for the poor. Here twenty pounds of soiled clothes are thoroughly—I ought to say artistically—washed for twenty-five ore, or about six cents. The work is done almost entirely by women and girls; and a cheerful row of laborers they seemed to be, as we walked along their courtesying ranks. The mangles are driven by steam, and the amount of work turned out in glossy smoothness is surprising. Nothing is ironed here, except the linen surface of shirt-bosoms and the like. People express great surprise on learning that we have not their custom of taking out the creases in the clothing after a wash by pressure. They exclaim, "No wonder your table-linen wears out so quickly." They say this in Swedish, but I have it interpreted into English for the benefit of my readers. But the amazement which doth set upon their countenances on the occasion referred to, could be interpreted by any person who understood what the laundry folks were listening to. They are very much pleased to see visitors, especially from America: more especially—as before observed elsewhere—from California. We have it again and again: "O, California! O! O!"

This bathing and washing establishment, occupying a block of ground, is immediately in front of one of the beautifully shaded city promenades. Two thickly tree-lined avenues are in front; and alongside of the hard-graveled highways benches are placed, at short intervals and at different angles. "Sometimes," the good matron told us, "those benches which are nearest to the bath-house are occupied exclusively by waiting customers,—mostly people of the poorest class."

From this bathing establishment we proceeded to the Business College,—a splendid structure, with every possible appointment of classroom, sales-halls, exchanges, book-keeping offices, apparatus for instruction in natural philosophy, etc. This also came from the dead man's hand, whose will was not contested.

Then we visited a drawing-school,—a school for student labor in sculpture and design. Every convenience and opportunity here. And masters in the art are here encouraged from many different nations. No tuition-fees; everything free. Also the outcome of the generous giver's funds, and the kind consideration of the lawyers, who did not illustrate their ability by inducing legal tribunals to declare that the noble donor was a lunatic. Thanks.

And now we visit a practical school for girls. The course is two years and a half—thirty months. The number is limited to thirty, six in each class. In a handsome two-story-and-a-half building, covering probably an acre of ground, the academy is located. This institute is intended for the education of girls whose expectation is to remain in the servant class in life, and who wish to be and are by nature fitted to become first-class servants. The first six months is devoted to attendance in the nursery department. Women who are obliged to or who desire to go out and work during the day, can bring their children here, and for 10 ore—two cents and a half—have them properly taken care of by the pupils of the first term, under the supervision of the experienced matron. We saw eighteen little boys and girls in their cribs— just waking from their afternoon nap, as we walked into one of the wards. Healthy and bright and ruby-cheeked were they. Some of their mothers could not go out to work at all if this keeping was not had; and with many others it would be a loss of half a kroner to a kroner a day if the little one was with them.

Of course we did not fail at this moment to speak with pride of similar institutions in California, conducted by Catholics and Protestants, and in San Francisco more particularly. Nor did we miss the opportunity to inform our friend of the practical School-board of the magnificent bequests of James Lick, and express the hope that some portion of them might be put into practical benevolent operation—before we die. We had to acknowledge, however, that Mr. Lick was forewarned of the consequences of a mere will-distribution; and that even his dedication, in his own lifetime, of his vast property—or a large share of it—to scientific and charitable purposes narrowly escaped complete overthrow. We had to confess this, for, from some intimations dropped in a casual and very friendly way, we had reason to believe that the facts in the premises were not hidden from our guide's recollection. So we made the whole story of the matter plain, and saved all the credit that we could for our people in general and our saints in particular, with respect to this item.

The second six months in this practical school for girls is occupied by the pupil in learning to wash, starch, mangle, and iron. To this house the richest people in Göthenburg send their soiled "fabrics,"—for here the work of cleansing and glossing is most excellently performed.

Then comes the baking department. The specimens of all kinds of cakes and bread, and tarts and confectionery, testified unto the palate that the business here was as near perfection as can be reached with the recipes of this kingdom. One of the women in charge was bereaved because the time of day had gone by when she could have shown us what her girls could accomplish in the way of doing a piece of meat to a turn, and mixing a gravy that would be just right and not a bit greasy. This is about the way we understood the conversation.

Standing down in front of the brick oven was a handsome girl—pretty as a picture—watching a batch of bread and cake. We stayed by persistently until she pulled out some kringlors. Ah! how crisp and delicious!—for we tossed one in our hands until it was cool enough to taste. This blushing maiden courtesied to us a great many times and said she was flattered. That was my understanding, at least. I did not intend to flatter.

The table cooking, the meat and vegetable cooking, it should be understood, is a separate compartment from the bakery. Another six months of tuition here. We were conducted into the kitchen proper by the matron in charge, who had been with us also in the bakery.

During the Winter season many boys who come to Göthenburg to attend the gymnasium or other academy, board here at a charge of only fifty cents a day. And in cooking for them and for other boarding patrons, the pupils in this department acquire their art. Of course we did not see any broiling, frying, baking, or stewing, actually going on in the kitchen; but we did see the bright pots and kettles and gridirons, and all that sort of evidence of good housewifery; and in the cold meats shown there was sufficient evidence of the skill of the girls who "did it."

Time is also here set apart for special instruction in the best manner of taking charge of the bed-chambers; and instruction is given in that kind of needlework which will be most required at the hands or fingers of the perfect maid-servant.

We were introduced to the chief matron, in her parlor chamber, and met with a most cordial welcome. "Americans? O, very glad to see you. What, Californians! O! O!" And we were shown everything in the way of stitching and crocheting from the hands of the girls who had passed under her teaching during the last fifteen years. How proudly she exhibited the mementoes which she had of their skill as pupils and their personal affection for her. An album containing a photograph of each graduate is also shown to the visitor.

Why cannot we have a similar institution in San Francisco —as well as in New York city?

For every graduate from this institute there are a score of applications coming from the best families of Sweden. "But many of them get married pretty soon: for they will make the best of wives and mothers in the laborers' cottages," remarked the lady Principal, as we closed the album and proceeded to take our leave. "Many of them have become the wives of gentlemen," she added, as we said good-bye. This she said in a way that made us suspect that she had reserved the information for a reply to an expected question or remark from us.

Immediately in the rear of this practical college for servant-girls is a home for incurables, recently built and endowed by a wealthy gentleman of Göthenburg. Not far away—about two blocks distant — is a building that on the outside looks like a chapel; but is, in fact, a kindergarten school, of which there are several in the city.

Three blocks distant, to the southwest, is a large building which provides a suite of rooms—a kitchen, bedroom and sitting-room—bedroom and sitting-room in one—with gas, water, and every appointment, for aged people who have been in good circumstances, but who, through no immorality, have lost their property. Seventy-two families are so kept, and they are supplied with all the necessaries of life. Another similar establishment is in the block near by. In one instance all the beneficiaries are in one large edifice; in the other, provision is made for fifty families in a dozen cottage buildings,—three or four families in each building.

Deaf-and-dumb and blind asylums are here; lying-in houses and hospitals for consumptives are pointed out as we drive along. Within the past fifteen years rich men in Göthenburg have given over $3,000,000 for absolute and for conditional charges, as they are called; that is, for the founding and maintaining of institutions that are entirely free in the dispensing of benefits, or that have a small fee attached to the services thence rendered and the gifts thence in part bestowed.

We were driven past many blocks of houses erected for workmen,—most of them of recent construction,—where two rooms, with two closets in each and a fixed range in the kitchen, are provided on the ground-floor, and two or three rooms partitioned above. The dimensions of the separate buildings are about 20 by 20 or 25 feet; the ceiling is ten feet. There is a back yard of at least 20 feet in width, with 15 feet of depth. In one of these rear yards—a specimen, we presume—we saw a bed of vegetables and a neat little arbor with a table and seats arranged for a tea party of from four to six persons. These buildings rent for $13 a month; and at the expiration of eighteen years they are the property of the continuous tenant. In a house where our companion took us, a mother was sitting in an easy chair singing to her infant, that was almost asleep, she said, when we came in. She was unmistakably pleased at the intrusion, for which our conductor apologized. "Not at all, not at all! Glad to have them come in and see how nicely we are situated. What, Americans? O, Californians! O! O!"

Göthenburg is literally founded on a rock. It is all one continuous rock down at the near bottom. You soon strike bedrock. Nothing but rocky eminences round about constitute the preëminently commanding peaks. And between, and on lower hights, are pine-wooded ridges covered with thickly clustered evergreens. Dipping into bowls and troughs, is the figure of the country just beyond the borders of the city proper on the south and southeast; while immediately to the north and northeast are meadows that have been drained within the past few years, and thus changed from unhealthy, miasmatic swamps into fruitful, grain-bearing fields. No wonder that this place is rapidly growing in population and business. Added to what contributes to the latter, in the way of outside traffic and foreign commerce, here is a great home of advancing civilization and comfort. A noble, generous, Christian people, are at the head of the management of all affairs, municipal and social, in the city of Göthenburg, in the kingdom of Sweden.

The workingmen have a large building, containing within it a hall capable of seating 2,000 people. Here they hold their great assemblages, at which they consider what is for the best interests of their class. Here was recently held an immense mass-meeting to protest against the unjust competition of convict-labor; and in this meeting they had the sympathy of the entire city, so to speak,—as our latest acquaintance told us. The protest has been partially met already, by obedience to it; and the sure promise is that the labor of prisoners will soon be confined to branches of industry in which they shall not conflict with the honest breadwinners of the land.

The workingmen have a society here by which they take care of those who are out of employment, partially or entirely supplying their wants and the needs of their families, as the necessities of each case may determine. One of the dwellings in which the unemployed reside was shown to us. It was a building that deserved the term "elegant," and was situated on a Nob Hill eminence immediately overlooking the entrance to the harbor. I would respectfully venture to commend to our people a study of the rules and regulations of this fraternity of laborers. I had the pleasure and honor of conversing with many of the representative men among them; and I shall never lose the impression which I have received of their intelligence and honorable sentiments. It would seem as though they understood their rights and privileges, and their needs as well, with a thorough good sense of appreciation. Of their advantages and enjoyment they spoke with gratitude and pride: of that which they believed they lacked, and should enjoy or possess, they spoke with reasonable and sober wish and expectation. I shall cherish my memories here, and in this very particular. I think that no miscreant demagogue will rise to eminence or power among these bodies of workingmen. And I think their condition of service will rapidly grow from good to better and best. So mote it be.

IV.

THE GOTHA CANAL.— TROLHATTAN.

It is probably necessary, as well as appropriate, as a preface to an anywise satisfactory sketch of a trip from Göthenburg to Stockholm via the Gotha Canal, to put in a short compass the data of planning and of construction labor on this remarkable work.

Bishop Brask of Linkoping, whose cathedral town was situated a few miles south of Lake Roxen, is the first known or recorded suggester of the "idea" of connecting by canal lakes Malaren, Roxen, Boren, Vettern, and Venern, with the Gotaelf. But it was not until 1716, fully two centuries after the wise and far-seeing prelate had proposed the scheme and urged its undertaking and accomplishment upon the attention of Kings and nobles, as well as upon brother Bishops and priests—who, it seems, in those days took a deep and practical interest in the commercial affairs of Sweden—that a serious effort was made to carry out the project. Two civil engineers, Svedenborg and Polhem by name, in 1715 mapped out a feasible or possible route, and under their direction work was actually begun on a system of locks and dams at Karlsgraben and Trolhattan. Their plans, somewhat changed and simplified, were afterwards taken up and labored upon under the superintendence of Engineer Viman, in 1753-54. In 1755 the working of Viman and predecessors was destroyed by a "jam of logs," as it would be described on the Ohio or St. Lawrence, or one of their tributaries; and the project was then pronounced wholly abandoned, until 1793. In that year a company having a million of rix dollars, or about $250,000 for capital, "went bravely to work," as one chronicler says, to construct locks around the Falls of Trolhattan, and brought their often-derided labors to a successful termination in 1800. It then remained to connect Lake Venern and Lake Vettern, and open a continuous navigable passage between the latter and the Baltic Sea. This was done between the years 1810 and 1832: the result of repeated and persistent efforts, sometimes separated five or six years by a period of enforced idleness: the successful plans being wrought under the personal supervision of Daniel Thunberg, Baron Von Platen, and Thomas Telford,—Telford being an English civil Engineer of already established and high renown. The cost of this work on this section was five million of rix dollars, or about $1,250,000. The above sums of course scarcely represent one-third of what the work would actually cost at the present time, notwithstanding all the modern advantages of vastly more effective blasting material, etc.; unless, indeed, the companies in charge of the construction pursued the plan of the beneficiaries of the people's donations to the Central Pacific Railroad Company, and rejecting the labor of white men, imported Chinese slaves to do the digging at rice-diet wages.

The section between the two great lakes is called the Vestgota line, while that portion which connects Lake Vettern with the Baltic is called the Ostgota line—both, however, coming under the general title of the Gotha Canal.

You are continually informed in Göthenburg and out of Göthenburg that that city is "quite modern,"—that is the exact phrase. In fact, you are told that Göthenburg is only 250 years old, or some such matter, as it stands. The inhabitants appear to take great pleasure in assuring you of this

recent origin, and tell you something about an old town—
or if it were now in existence, a village that would be an old
town—that was situated somewhere in the neighborhood (it
has been pointed at, or towards, for my benefit, so many
times, from so many different corners, that I am much con-
fused with respect to its exact location), that had rather a
hard time of it in the way of suffering sieges, etc., a matter
of some eight centuries ago: and which may perhaps be considered the lineal forerunner, as it were, of this flourishing,
latter-day settlement. And I have noticed that some good
Swedish people who live in admittedly older places than
Göthenburg exhibit a touch of amiable contempt in their
speech about this new city; on account of its freshness on
the page of history. I do not precisely appreciate how this
is, but it is so; and as all parties concerned seem to like it I
cannot complain, and I will forbear to make further comment on it. When you come to Sweden via Göthenburg, my
dear reader—as I hope you will one day—I beg you to improve an early opportunity to form the acquaintance of some
stranger on the streets, by inquiring as to locality or distance, and see how many seconds it will be before you are
told, in substance, "Göthenburg. I suppose you are aware,
is not an old city. O, bless you, no, no: it is only about 200
years old. There was a city or a town that was huddled up
(they have a word that sounds like this), about in that direction (pointing, as we reporters are often compelled to most
ambiguously interject); but, bless you, that place was
knocked to rack and ruin, pretty much, several centuries ago.
You will find our city, for a young city, quite a pleasant and
enterprising and creditable place."

Ancient or modern as it may be, or as you may choose to
call or consider it, it is with a sigh of profound regret that
we contemplate our departure from it: regretting most sin-
cerely that we have not had another week to spare in visiting
this section of southern Sweden. And we think and say
that, as Liverpool is generally passed quickly by travelers
who have no business connection there—treated as a "jumping-off place" in very word and deed—thus missing or de-

clining a stay in a city that is well worth a week's time of observation on the part of the sightseer, so Göthenburg—most unmistakably rapidly rising into importance as a commercial entrepot and as a community whence proceed sug-

MAURITZ RUBENSON, PRESIDENT OF BOARD OF PRACTICAL EDUCATION.

gestions and illustrations of the highest practical value along the line of the civilization of our age—is given the slip by the tourist, has bestowed upon it only a hasty glance of the student who does not sufficiently observe and reflect for himself when he first outlines his travels, or when he reaches a point that marks itself—on due consideration, in spite of the guide-books—as a place of abounding interest.

But a little antiquated in some things, a little behind the times in some things, as we in America would judge it, Göthenburg certainly is.

Its railroad stations are admirably located, every way appropriately easy of access and conspicuous by their adapted architecture. But its steamboat offices are hard to find, even after the most diligent search by the stranger under the direction of the official city dictionary and accompanying maps. And yet there the office of our canal boat is, absolutely facing the quay from which the steamer is to start. But when you do not know precisely where the steamer lies, the word "opposite" is of obscure and doubtful signification. We were told where to go several times with great and kindly emphasis of speech and finger-pointing, and we missed the place with almost as much accuracy as if we had been threading the streets between the Strand and Oxford Street in that mighty metropolis on the Thames. However, it is, of course, not worth while to dwell on such a small matter any further; at least not any further than to say in reply to a suggestion that would naturally come up, "Why didn't you call a cab and be taken to the office," by stating that we did that very thing, and were taken to the wrong building twice before the driver himself "guessed" the spot.

For a first-class passage to Stockholm, via the canal route, occupying two days and a half, you pay $6.25. This includes your cabin accommodations, but not your meals: it amounts to about two cents a mile for your carrying, after deducting a proper allowance for a room as a lodging apartment.

Our steamer, fully dignified by that name, is the *Venus*. This little goddess is of 200 tons burden, 75 feet long by 22 broad. Her Captain is an old sailor, who has sailed the Atlantic and the North Sea over these thirty-five years last past, as man and boy; and his name is O. R. Samsioe. He and his mate—a smart fellow, as we Yankees would call him, who has gone in and out of Philadelphia many times on a sailing packet—are the only ones who wear gold cap-bands; taking their turns on deck as first and second officers, and maintaining the jolliest relations as between themselves and the steersmen, and the passengers of every class. Another boiled-dinner party on a steamer on this Swedish excursion! We are fortunate.

The *Venus* is handsomely fitted up in cabin and dining-saloon. Plenty of red-plush cushions in the former, and convenient tables of beautiful wood fastened near either side of the paneled wainscoting of the latter. All the crockery is stamped, and all the spoons and cutlery engraved with the name of the vessel, in high-hotel style. And the Captain sits down the first morning out at the head of the left-hand table and incidentally mentions that he left New Orleans just before it was vacated by the Confederate forces in 1862. This is a voyage of coincidences.

The *Venus* starts at 11 o'clock at night, and you are expected to be on board by 10. You may be on board by 8, it is suggested at the office, and begin your affiliations in the forward saloon by taking a delicious cup of coffee in gossiping company with the fine old lady who has charge of the eating department of this institution.

Sweden is noted for its excellent coffee, and the *Venus* and its companion boat have a special reputation of superiority in this very point of Java flavor. The aroma from the urn spreads out through the atmosphere that surrounds the dock of the Lilla Bommens Hamn. this evening in question, as our party is promenading up and down beside the steamer; and, on motion, we vote unanimously to go down and take a cup of the best.

Eleven o'clock at night and light enough for me to make a memorandum of several pages, as I sit on deck at the time of departure. I see the waving of white handkerchiefs when we have backed several hundred feet away from the landing point, and I can even distinguish the color of the scarf in a young gentleman's hand, as he stands on a rope-peg at the corner of the Hamn, and flourishes it rapidly in adieu to a waiting-maid on board, that—well, we do not blame him for admiring.

I notice that the habit here is to wave "good-bye" until the last fraction of distance is reached within which a fluttering cloth can be seen. A national custom, is it? Illustrative or indicative of that ardent affection here existing, which the Captain of the *Belle* referred to and boasted of with honest pride?

Prompt to a minute, at 10:45 the whistle blew; at five minutes to 11 the bell rang; at 11 the boat pulled its nose out of the slanting space it had occupied at a neighborly angle with other crafts lying at the same wharf.

Already familiar with the scenery for several miles up the Elf, and knowing that we must be on deck at a very early hour if we would see the first of the seventy-four locks on this route to the Capital of Sweden, our party is not tardy in getting in bunk, after the signal has faded from the range of sight.

Baedecker, the best, and, generally speaking, most accurate of guides, is certainly in error when he intimates that the sleeping quarters on these little steamers are uncomfortable, or not as agreeable as could reasonably be expected. We all say that we must write to our favorite and highly esteemed author—guide and friend, indeed!—and gently remonstrate against his discouragement to travelers who would naturally come this way; testifying that our first and last nights' slumbers on board were of the most refreshing character.

At 4 o'clock the sound, unusual to our ears, of the dashing or "swashing" in the first lock is sufficient to rouse us, and jumping up we see that our cabin windows are darkened by the closeness of granite walls, and we know at once that we are boxed up in the first trough of the passage. Although we dress with all speed the boat is "up" before we are on a level with the plane No. 1 of the line of the Gotha. We are in a short canal—the Channel of Ström—a section that passes to one side of the rapids that are first encountered.

You may be sure that advantage has been taken of this fall

of six or eight feet, inclusive of the grade surmounted by the second lock, by an enterprising mill firm; and a village of 200 or 300 inhabitants—Lilla Edit—has grown up around the forges. For a distance of five or six miles above the second lock we steam on the river Orelf, whose channel has been regained, and then suddenly turning to the right we face the lower series of locks that girt the Falls of Trölhattan.

Baedecker says that the traveler's patience here will be sorely tried by the "numerous dealers in photographs and other small objects;" but such was not our experience. We were, however, very much distressed to find that our little company of passengers was altogether insufficient to give employment to all the boys who came in upon us with proffers of guidance. But a selection had to be made, of course, and a hard thing it was to decide between the applicants. By a concerted distribution of small coin among the rejected or disappointed competitors there was much relief—on all hands. Again we dispute the assertions of all the trip manuals; and declare most positively—for the benefit and warning, even, of all who may come after—that guides are required on this short but devious way, or rather along these crooked paths—in and out the ragged edges that border the falls. Give the boys a chance; their services are needed, and they are good boys, who, having earned their agreed fee, are tested by an exact payment. They go away with thanks, and are unmistakably surprised when they are recalled for an extra 25 ore, which each separate company bestows upon them. May they all retain their present guileless character, and may some of them become hansom drivers in London—without changing their nature.

And here, as most readers will understand, we are not making a boast of our great liberality; but as a German gentleman said, we felt that the lads were entitled to a larger sum than they asked. And here let us not fail, as in duty bound, to protest against the lavish, wasteful, and, by its example and encouragement, most iniquitous, practice of some travelers—especially Americans—in the matter of throwing large gratuities to any person who does them a service under any employment or volunteering along their routes. It is not a pleasant thing to publicly express or renew this protest; but the habit ought to be deprecated on every available occasion. Those who have not been abroad as travelers may, and

SIDNEY W. COOPER, UNITED STATES CONSUL TO GOTHENBURG.

probably will, criticise this continued or repeated objection to what they will consider a generous and altogether decent custom. But experience will bring all or nearly all to the same judgment in the premises that is set down on this page.

It *is* outrageous: the extravagant manner in which some of our people toss their small change about among those who have to do with the stranger, as servants or attendants; fostering a spirit of greed and rapacity that is painful in its effects upon those of the same nation who come after with moderately, or, if you please, meagerly furnished purses. It is not alone, indeed it is not frequently the case that the truly generous, the actually benevolent ladies and gentlemen, indulge in this pernicious practice. On the contrary, it is usually the coarse, vulgar men, whose wealth has come easily through dishonest trade or professional trickery— perhaps sprung from bounties jumped or lobbied out by themselves or their agents, or acquired from fraudulent railroad contracts made with themselves, whereby they have robbed the individuals or Government that intrusted them with funds for a special purpose, or gave them gifts to be sacredly devoted to the first cause of a great public enterprise. These creatures create or stimulate a disposition for extortionate demand upon the traveler in Europe that you, my good friend, who may be now inclined or disposed to lightly consider this notice, will suffer from, if you pass over many of the prescribed lines of journeyings in Britain and on the Continent. Perchance you will thank me one day for joining in this protest, which is calculated to check this habit, or fasten against it, at least, a rising sentiment of reprobation. Intelligent, thoughtful rich men and women, who have honestly gotten their wealth, are not often guilty of the practice to which we refer.

The boat turns sharply from the river Orelf to the locks. You personally then turn with equal abruptness and take your path in another direction: to the eligible points of view along the cataracts. The way seems plain and simple at first, and you may be at the outset reminded by this appearance of the declaration of the prejudiced guide-book writers. "Guide superfluous;" but you will soon be convinced that within your allotted time for observation you could not have found the "sites-for-seeing," as they are called, and made good use of the limited period for beholding, except our little friend had been with you.

In "seeing the falls," you lose the opportunity of seeing all the old canal locks—the ruins of the work that was done under the first effort to surmount this obstacle in the way of navigation on this line, and also, of course, are deprived of the gratification of beholding the first and the larger successful work of locking, around this great ascent. You must choose between the two, and of course nearly every one who makes the passage once takes in preference his one passing glance at the greater wonder, at the marvel from the hands of nature; though the evidences of the struggle of human genius at the beginning of this combat for a watercourse of commerce are every way worthy of a prolonged observation and study.

I applied at the office of the Canal Steamboat Company at Göthenburg for a stop-over ticket, such as we are accustomed to obtain in America, such as our own courteous railroad officials are accustomed to sanction in behalf of any tourist who has a mission as a seeing and recording traveler. But, no; the rule was inflexible: you must go through in the same boat on the same trip-time, on each starting. If I had thought it was of so much consequence as it was afterward disclosed to be, that more time should be had at Trölhattan and Vadstena and Motella than is afforded on the straight-through schedule voyage, I would have bought a ticket from place to place. In that case I should have had three days at Trölhattan and vicinity,—a space of time which I now know is not any too long for instruction and entertainment. I mourned my inability to examine the deserted locks and the working of the granite jaws which succeeded and superceded them. But we did see the falls; and I did afterward make such representations in various influential quarters that I am confident a stop-over period will be agreed upon in the chambers of the Board of Gotha Canal Steamboat Directors, and due advertisement made accordingly; for which I shall be entitled to credit, which some Americans will surely hereafter mark on the pages of their diaries,—and, perhaps, engrave on the walls of some of these boulders!

Well. Too much introduction for the volume of the book? Too much exordium, too many preludes for the body-speech or narrative? Perhaps so. In fact, I admit and confess, and beg pardon, and—come to business.

CANAL LOCKS, NEAR TROLHATTAN.

And strictly in the line of proper description of this visit to this remarkable series of rapids and falls, I should declare and testify that they are a well regulated succession of river rushings and cascades, in the matter of comparison and climax. There is no mistake in the order of gradation of these wonders. They "rise" upon you in every sense of the term. To make a homely illustration, or one that will be very widely understood. I will say that it is like "progress of events" in any of the Kiralfy Brothers' spectacular pieces, or like the unfolding of one of their settings for a transformation scene. First comes the ordinary, old-fashioned, long-ago familiarized, hackneyed procession of spindle-legged girls in spangles, for a ballet performance that our grandmothers yawned over.—" Well, if this is all there is of Trölhattan Falls, I wish I had stayed with the Captain on the deck of the *Venus*."—" Wait a moment, my dear sir. The curtain is rolling up, and there is a shift of scenery behind the first dance and drill hall, and there is a procession coming that you have not seen, and that has not occurred to you before." Then picture after picture, pantomime after pantomime of superlative beauty is displayed in rapid succession! So commonplace rapids at first, and then! ah, then!

Still abiding by the theater for hint and suggestion of effect produced, let me tell you of a man from Virginia City, with whom I once journeyed from Reno to Chicago. We became very well acquainted on the road, and he was evidently anxious to remain in my society as much as possible until the hour should arrive when we must part at the door of an Eastern railroad station. As we approached Chicago on one December evening, he looked over my shoulder at the newspaper I was reading and inquired if I wouldn't go with him to see a comedy. The name of the comedy and the names of the well-known actors who were to appear in it were pointed out on the page before me. It was an attractive play, and the comedians were of our best. But I replied that I had noticed that Edwin Booth was to play "Richard III." at McVicar's that night, and I had fixed my appetite for that very performance. My esteemed acquaintance labored to dissuade me, so that I would go with him under the invitation and at his expense. But finding that I was firm in my determination with respect to the little matter—though I hope I showed him that I was desirous of pleasing him where I could consistently—he finally said in a manner half joking and partly quarrelsome: "Well, if the mountain won't come to Mahomet, Mahomet will go to the mountain." And so, too loth to quit company for the sake of suiting his own excited taste for amusement, he went with me to witness our great tragedian in his masterly presentation of that masterpiece of Shakespeare, "Richard III." Repeatedly, immediately after his first announcing—in most sullen phrase—that he intended to accompany me, he spoke of his resolution to go and endure the play at McVicker's for the purpose of having an opportunity of talking to me between the acts and at the close of the performance. His conversation on this subject was, of course, in an indifferent tone of raillery; though now and then he would express his serious surprise at my preference for such a "stupid bore of a tragedy." And after the first act was over, though in a modified way, he indulged in similar remarks and reflections. But, there came the second act, and a sobriety of countenance was gradually developed—I can use no other word so fitting—by the Washoe miner at my side; and presently he began to draw long breaths and rub his hands together at intervals, in a sudden, nervous manner, that attracted the attention of many who sat adjacent—old tragedy-hardened theater-goers,—whose rather compassionate gaze in no wise disconcerted or troubled my friend,—if he noticed or was conscious of it. And by and by, when some lighter passages were being read, he whispered, but without turning his head, "Young man, I am getting your money's worth";—which I take it was one of his strongest current sentences of commendation. And when Booth, as Richard, wheeled around and snarled at the Queen, "I hate you;" and turning again, exclaimed, "If that don't kill her, I don't know what will;" I was slapped on the back by my companion—who had never taken his eyes off the stage—as he muttered, "My God! what an infernal villain that fellow is!"

On our way back to the hotel there was no frivolity—no hilarity—in the conversation of my friend. With quiet earnestness he asked about and talked about the character of Richard III—about the record of his times; inquired about the best historians of those days; dwelt with solemn imprecation on the traits he exhibited; and finally, with great gravity and impressiveness, thanked me over and over again for compelling him—those were his words—to go and listen to such a play. I recalled and meditated on this as we moved along by the side of these rapids and over the waters of the six falls of Trölhattan.

No long, precise detail of description will you expect or I attempt. Such a description at my best, and however independently written, might prove to be but a poor paraphrase of the guide-books that assume to present the measurements and comprehensively the arithmetic of the scenes.

It is true that some of the lower falls are higher by foot-rule calculation than others that are situated farther up the stream: but still the truth of my assertion remains: that the interest and the reason for an excited feeling of awe and admiration increases at every upward step.

"Falls" not always; not often literal cataracts, here abound. I have not counted them. The books that I have seen have undertaken to fully or exactly number them. Eight feet, and twenty-three feet, twenty-five feet, forty-two feet, are respectively set down for the Stampestrom, the Gullo, the Helvetes, and the Toppo falls. But I dispute the assertion that they signify grandeur, or sublimity, or beauty, in proportion to their elevation.

As I have probably, with sufficient tax upon the attention of my readers, indicated and emphasized, there is in the enlargening, the lengthening or broadening, the changing view of hight or depth, gorge or chasm, with the tumult of water within and around and beneath,—the building, by stronger and stronger forces, of an enthusiasm of rapture, until it seems as if you would reverently exclaim before your Maker, as an old translator has a scripture: "Lord, this magnificence doth fill and satisfy; yea, it doth inspire my soul, until I can bear no more." And this cold endeavor to intimate what are the sensations that are begotten within the chambers of the mind by the glories that are here displayed seems almost like a sacrilegious mockery of the tremendous experience. Not Niagara, with its incomparably grander distances and voices, can surpass this spectacle of granite hillside and plunging waters,—in the touching, and rousing, and thrilling, of the finest chords for music that answers unto music in the human breast.

Rescue these scenes, also, from the "enterprise" of the millman and the manufacturer—as New York has done for her superlative wonder. Yes; although here there does not as yet appear to be a gross or despoiling intrusion by the hand of utility.

Of such things you may have spoken before; and you may talk of them hereafter. Of these things you will not think, you will not tolerate consideration, until you shall have passed beyond; and the charm and enchantment of the perspective of rapids, and fountains, and cascades, and verging steeps of rocky precipices and woodland, with the many-keyed Anthem of the thunder of the floods, shall have faded from actual sight and sound, and become one among the transcendently glorious memories in your bosom that shall never lose its power and vividness in ministering to your enjoyment.

From a point just below the Giant's Caldron, the most extensive and comprehensive view can be had:—except, of course, the scene from the tower,—which is not, after all, so pleasant, and which you will wish you had taken before the one recommended, in order that the latter might be the last in your recollection. But from the swaying bridge that reaches from the left bank to the Island of Toppo, you have the vision of visions! Behold It! With what a sharp and indescribable pang of regret do you hear the warning call for a return to the shore, and to this rough, matter-of-fact world again!

Surely this was well named Trölhattan—the gathering place for witches of old. See! this is not an insensate torrent. This is a vital, living, human intelligence, that is moving before and beside and beneath you! It is more. Look! How majestical the waters come over the summit immediately in front of you! It is not simply volatile matter. It is the assumed shape and the stirring form of one of the Northmen's gods that is here; it is Old Thor, lying prone at your feet, slowly nodding his forehead with the dignity of Deity, while ever and anon there is tossed in your face from his long, flowing, yellow beard great drops of the frosty dew of an Artic morning.

V.

TROLHATTAN TO VENERSBORG.

Some of the guide books appear to make a studied effort to dissuade travelers from taking the Gotha Canal line to Stockholm from Gothenburg; one referring to the Falls of Trolhattan as "not worth the trip;" another remarking that they are of "comparatively little account," etc.; but Baedecker, with characteristic candor—although he, too, has considerable to say in disparagement of the route—admits that in one respect the falls are "unsurpassed in Europe," and "that the enormous volume of water makes a spectacle extremely imposing." That which in his judgment detracts much from the "effect" of the principal falls —namely, the islands in the middle of the stream—is, I think, justly to be regarded as enhancing, as it certainly greatly diversifies, the interest and admiration which they excite. Suppose a river of clear water at some angles, or in many of its pitchings tinged with a saffron hue from the color of the rocks beneath, or the reflection of the banks— a river of the size of the Hudson at Albany, or of the Sacramento as it is within its bed at highwater mark at our Capital, flowing as described over successive declivities of twenty-three and forty-two and twenty-five feet. The entire descent of the falls proper is 112 feet, with a great number of eddies and rushings and side caverns and mid-stream fountains between and beyond, in a distance of a quarter of

TROLHATTAN FALLS.

a mile comprising a succession of cataracts, cascades, pools and rapids—and you have, I think, without further description or suggestion, assurance that the "spectacle" is indeed beautiful and sublime.

The very disappointment which you at first undergo when you leave the foot of the locks and are on the watch for scenes of unusual magnitude or picturesqueness in the movement of the stream and the surroundings of the country, tends to make your delight the keener as the "vistas" from the bordering pathway open up before you.

Of course, as compared with the Niagara, these falls are of dwarfish dimensions; nor is there here that reeling sense of grandeur—although at one or two points there is something akin to it—that you may have or are likely to feel in looking down from some great altitude into the Yosemite valley. But abiding, awe-inspiring results, as well as a peculiar charm and a fascination for the immediate moment of beholding, are to be experienced here by all who are capable of receiving such emotions and disposed to cherish them in the mind and heart.

Trolhattan itself is an insignificant appearing town or village, situated at the head of the falls; and the statement that it contains three thousand inhabitants makes you wonder where all the people who claim to be or are set down as residents have their homes.

Close to the head of the canal is a mill in which pine wood is ground into a pulp and converted into paper; a thick, dark, very serviceable kind of wrapping material. On the doors and in some of the windows of this manufactory—in which the work is mostly performed by women—are signs in different languages and in invariably bad grammar, inviting you to stay outside, and forcibly announcing to you that you have no business in these premises that the proprietors are aware of; and the intimation distinctly is that they do not wish you to venture on any inquiry on the subject. The posted literature on this point becomes formidable in your eyes as you pass around the main building on your return from a walk to the opposite bank, and you involuntarily examine your breast pockets to see if you have your passport with you.

The women who stood at or who came to the large door of the establishment and stared at us, were not only as dirty as their occupation required—poor creatures—but they had the lines of suffering from extraordinary care or overwork stamped indelibly on their countenances. It was about our first observation of women at hard labor in Sweden; and the sight was shocking to some of our party; who declared that they would have preferred to forego the pleasure of a visit to any falls in the world rather than to be compelled to see at the same time or in the same hour such an exhibition of wearisome, slavish toil, and its consequences as marked on these wrinkled countenances.

There is a hotel at Trolhattan where muddy coffee or sour beer can be had at memorable prices.

And in this connection I will state that I inadvertently omitted to mention that there are photographs of the falls and vicinity to be had at the Tower, from whence you have a complete view of the panorama, at a charge not to exceed three times as much as you can buy the same pictures for in Gothenburg or Stockholm. There is something here that reminds you of Chester and London; where—in the first instance—views of the old Roman wall can be had at King Charles Lookout for double the sum asked in the galleries where they were printed; and where—in London—in and about monuments and sacred edifices, even, you can pay big bonuses for indifferent photographic copies of inaccurate drawings and dauby sketches, made by artists who, as you are somehow assured, have as yet gone unwhipped of justice.

There is a deaf and dumb beggar at Trolhattan, who salutes you repeatedly. He has no memory of your first two givings. He has a ghastly smile and a military gesture that is simply irresistible. It was some time before any of us knew what his malady or infirmity was, although he had a sign on his cap that told the whole pitiful story. The difficulty was that you could not read it all at one time; and it was actually by comparing notes that we first ascertained the nature of the affliction. Some of the passengers laughed outright on this very account, and then poured a handful of coppers into the unfortunate man's hand, as if in a generosity-provoking fit of shame over their levity or hilarity in such a presence.

In front of the hotel there appears on dress parade a man with a gold band around his cap, on which it is written that he is the "Chief of guides;" but what his precise functions were we could not learn—we could only suspect. The German gentleman remarked that the liberality of tourists would probably be much reduced in the matter of extra fees and donations to the boys, if this cap put in an appearance at the other end of the locks; and he hoped that we would all write to our friends who were coming this way and tell them to give their gratuities to the lads on the sly.

In spite of the great and lasting pleasure of the view we had just seen—and let nothing of this present, immediate record detract from whatever of promise and stimulant in favor of this trip there may be to any reader, in what has been set down before in this same correspondence—we were glad, as the German gentleman phrased it, to "trollelol away from the town of Trolhattan." When he was glanced at for this, with a sort of Pinafore no-never look he said he had acquired some vicious habits in America—and passed on.

From Trolhattan the steamer, by river and by canal, alternately passes through a farming section of country; the valleys in which these waters flow having a strong resemblance to the New England landscapes, as some on board agree in testifying. The season also seems to be advanced to about the same degree as that to which we were accustomed in Massachusetts. But, of course, there were striking dissimilarities and novelties in the pictures.

Here we began to feel that accelerated sense, which was more completely developed as we rode from Motala to Berg —a sense of riding in a chariot with noiseless wheels over dustless roads, over verdure-clad and flower-sprinkled fields —literally pushed over the green sward and meadows by some unseen but powerful hand. Sitting in front of the pilot-house, and looking at the country on either side, or far away in front, you forget that you are on the water, and take in the whole scene as from a carriage window, undistracted by noise or jar of any kind; and there was a very thrill of romance in waking up, as it were, to a consciousness of threading your way along a narrow channel defined by grassy banks that always appeared at the distance of a few rods in advance to be too close together to admit of a possible passage of the chubby vessel on the knob of whose cover you are sitting. Why, this is a little fairy toy-boat, and we are playing "ride a rocking racehorse right to Boston town:"—so thinks the little child on board, and so say we all. But it is not to Boston town, but to Venersborg that we are going. Here is a town of 5,000 inhabitants lying at the first point where the Gotaelf flows out from Lake Venern. It is situated on an island, though you would not know that fact from what you can see from the boat. The hour and a half that we would prefer to have had at Motala or Vadstena is given here, by the grace of the canal boat proprietors; and we go off and up to visit the town, of which the captain correctly says that there is a church and a market place, and a water-tower that can be seen from the outside.

Long before you reach Venersborg, (where we had hoped to visit a manual school,) the spire of the church and the high, round brick water reservoir is seen staring at you with a severe "What are you coming here for?" kind of significance—as you approach their base.

Our German friend comes up behind us as we step on the wharf. He is laughing. (He usually laughs by a process of grunting starts and fits.) What is the funny thing now? He has Baedecker in hand, and with the exclamation, "Best thing yet!" points to this sentence: "The town has been frequently burned down, and now consists of unusually spacious streets." Evidently Baedecker does not like this route. The captain—good, amiable soul that he is—says that it is his opinion that Baedecker was not treated as well as he ought to have been on his journey up the canal. That is all he says about him.

There is a market—closed. There is a church in the midst of a little grove-plaza or square—also closed. No janitor in sight, though I think he could have gained at least a half-dozen kroners in the aggregate if he had put in an appearance with his keys and opened the portals of his sacred edifice. "Show us the inside of any house and we will pay you for it," announced Herr Wrangel, speaking voluntarily to the invisible guardians of the place, but speaking authoritatively, nevertheless, for all the parties that straggled along before or beside and behind him.

VENERSBORG.

A little girl sat knitting on one of the benches in front of the kyrka. "What church is this, my pretty maid!" inquired a lady in the party of the first part. "Lutheran Episcopal Church," was the reply, in an excellent English pronunciation, and in such a musical tone of voice that every one within hearing distance began to comment upon it and to try to enter into a conversation with the little maid; beginning simultaneously to speak prophetically of another Christine Nillson—and all that sort of thing. The girl blushed and bent over her half-finished tidy and replied no more. She had evidently exhausted her stock of English, and was annoyed if not offended by the attention—somewhat rude at times, I thought—that was paid to her. Afterwards, when we came back this way, a Swedish lady addressed this maiden again, and obtained from her in her own language a long account of her family and situation.

We looked into the windows of the church as well as we could. Some one of the party put our little child on the window-sill at one end, and got her report as to the interior. Strange what a morbid curiosity there is in human nature with respect to something or anything that is locked up or has "No admittance" on the doorpost! There was a gilded cross over the altar ; there was a huge organ ; there was a mid-corner pulpit with a sounding board ; there were most uncomfortable pew accommodations for about a thousand attendants, and standing room for about five hundred persons? What more of importance could we have learned if we had seen the interior from the interior, and paid twenty-five ore each for the privilege? Come now! And yet we would all have been glad to have made that deprecated bargain.

As we ascend the main street we pass by a restaurant, which is called a Masonic Restaurant, and which has on one of its doors a sign similar to those Masonic emblems of high degree that are planted in a rock by the side of one of the cascades that we have recently visited. We are tempted to go in and see what sort of fare the Templars provide within for latter-day pilgrims. But a slatternly housemaid makes her appearance in the dining-room as we are about to enter, and in a voice that is not at all musical, but quite the reverse, shouts to some other housemaid — we presume — (whom we are glad we did not see,)—to the effect that she must hurry with the work in hand so as to attend to cooking for the customers ; and, as the German said—borrowing from "Bleak House" this time, evidently—"We are floored again."

We visited the outside of the water tower, a new, round brick structure built in 1881 ; 30 feet in diameter, we guess, and 60 feet in height. Herr Wrangel tried the door, and put his jack-knife under the windows. He then said "———." One of the party pinned his visiting card above the keyhole.

Retracing our steps, the conversation referred to was had with the maid in the grove. She was an orphan, and had two sisters dependent on her for their support. She received the contribution that the janitor perhaps might have had.

In all this time and during all this march from the vessel, occupying half an hour in leisurely sauntering and hesitating—our party going a distance of fully half a mile—we saw not a solitary person, save and except as hereinbefore noted. "In the name of all that is Swedish, and by all the gods of the Norsemen's mythology, what sort of a town of 5,000 inhabitants is this?" finally burst out our friend of the meerschaum—with his native brogue exemplified in the utterance of at least every other word. And he laid his velvet-tasseled cap down upon a cobble-stone and walked around it and picked it up. Then asked for a loan of a companion's opera glass and took an observation with it all around the horizon; then uttered his favorite exclamation, with the addition of "Not a soul!" Then he walked, with unusual rapidity for him, in the van of the wandering troop to the steamer's plank. Thereon he stood and shouted to the captain, "Vat sort of a sleepy hollow is dis, Captain Petersen, dot you empties us into for an hour und a half?"

"Didn't I tell you there was nothing to be seen?" replied the Captain.

"Did you?"

"I did."

"Vell, you vas right, O, I forgot dot leetle girl. Dot vas one good ding we did see. I vill give her dot restaurant in my vill."

And under the evident impression that this was a great joke, our German tourist gruntingly laughed deep and long while on his way to his seat on the pilot-house deck.

VI.

VENERSBORG TO STOCKHOLM.

Almost quiet enough to be the actual abiding place of the Sleeping Beauty of the fairyland or garden, of which we have all at one time credulously read and in which we have all taken delight; having a solitary living representative in its central grove that was worthy of being adopted as the slumbering enchantress herself; a pleasant village with architectural features of interest, old and new; situated in the valley and at the lake-bordering, island-made end of a plain of surpassing loveliness: that is about what we have to say of Venersborg in a passing, comprehensive and farewell paragraph. While we regret that we did not have as much time as was given us here at Venersborg, to visit other places where there was more of immediate interest to be quickly seen, we by no means intend to leave the impression that there was not much enjoyment derived from our stroll through some of the "spacious streets" of this most sedate and noiseless of Swedish towns.

We came to the conclusion that a large share of the population who dwell inside of the village were at the hour of our visit at work in the fields adjacent or in the workshops that stood a little way off from the main cluster of houses. So, mounting our canal coach and resuming, with our excellent traveling friend from Germany, our stations for observation, we saw Venersborg recede as we had seen it draw near to us—such was the sensation, rather than that of an approach, on our momentum—with audible expressions of unfeigned sorrow. As Herr Wrangel said—(the landlady of the steamer called him Herr Wrangel,)—it was a debatable question whether we should or should not have ventured into that Freemason's tavern and bought a voluble and probably intelligent and gossiping acquaintance, whatever the expense in silver and otherwise might have been.

Here is pointed out to us Mount Halleberg, 435 feet high; and also Mount Hunneberg, 490 feet high, which is said to be completely surrounded with charming little lakes and picturesque cascades. Both are said to be well worth a visit; the former having, among other attractions, an "attestupa," which is interpreted to be a place from which old and infirm persons threw themselves in ancient times, to avoid the supposed ignominy of dying in their beds.

We are at the foot of Lake Venern. This lake is a little over 100 miles long and 50 miles wide, and is 143 feet above the sea level. Its average depth is 359 feet. Thirty rivers are emptied into this lake, and often it is raised in flood time 10 feet above its ordinary level. You are warned by all the guide books that storms frequently occur on this great inland sea, and may be experienced at any season of the year; and if you are liable to seasickness you can have as severe an attack on Lake Venern as in the mid-Atlantic —other things being equal. But nearly as smooth as our canal highway, was the passage we made across the lower half of this beautiful lake. Soon after we enter upon its waters we lose sight of land on our east, and are ten miles distant from the coast or shore on our right.

It is sixty miles from Gothenburg to Venersborg, and it is eighty miles from Venersborg to the point where we enter upon our canal track again—at a place called Sjetorp; but the distance is made in the one case in twelve hours, and in the other in less than eight. Our fat little steamer is here put on full head and best-go-ahead behavior, and we are conscious of the fact that we are bumping along at a goodly rate of speed. Although there is little swaying, there is that pounding jar that was rendered so familiar to our ears and —I was going to say our hearts—on the Alaska.

It is during the trip across this lake that we may be said to have formed an intimate acquaintance with the master of the vessel ; for while he watches on his 14x12 feet deck, we, at his request, sat in front of the pilot-house and listened to his biographical and geographical conversation. He talked well. A short inquiry winds him up ; and you will, doubtless, get nearly as much as there can be edifyingly said in regard to a given locality in the neighborhood of our voyage, if you will only come this way and put your interrogatory and hush and listen.

In particular he dwelt upon the attractive features of the hill of Kinnekule, whose outlines he showed us through his glass, just after we had passed the latitude of Lidkoping and rounded the isle of Kolandso. This hill of Kinnekulle is 916 feet high, is 12 miles long by five miles broad, and is composed of six distinct geological formations. There are granite, sandstone, alum-slate, limestone, clay-slate and trap-rock. There are scores of grottoes ; there are high cliffs, from which fine views are to be seen in every direction. And a portion of the hillside is very fertile ; and on a portion the trees are the largest known in Sweden. Extensive granite and slate quarries are on the west side ; and the water, pure and soft, is often "tapped" by a blast, and bursts forth as though struck by the wand of the old leader of the children of Israel. Wild apple and cherry trees, with fruit that rivals the cultivated European species in appetizing qualities, are to be found on all portions of the hill, or range of hills, that come under this name. In short, so enticing is the description of this section of the country that we have from the captain, that we join with our German friend in the proposition that the *Venus* be headed for the shore, and leave given us to stop over in this vicinity until the next boat ; and when, as a matter of course, this simple proposition is met with a nay, we join again in the chorus, when our spokesman sings out, "Vell, den, Captain, we don't want to hear no more about it ; because such dings is an aggravation under de circumstances."

Captain C. Reinhold Samsio has been going to sea over thirty years, but cannot swim. He went to a swimming school when he was a boy, as boys are accustomed, and, indeed, are compelled to do in Sweden ; but, before he had gained the requisite confidence, which is the main element in the business, his teacher became irritated at his relative lack of proficiency or daring, and gave him such a "long ducking" that he was constrained to play truant towards that gymnasium ever afterwards. But, notwithstanding the fact that he cannot swim, he is not afraid of the water. He has been overboard twice in the Atlantic ; once rescued by a fellow seaman, and once saved by a piece of timber that was thrown after him.

We pass between the islands of Thorso and Bromo, which are inhabited principally by fishermen, and the boats of some of the net watchers come close alongside. The little lighthouses on the islands are curiosities in their way. The lanterns are often set in the sides of the cottages, sending a gleam in only one direction. They afford abundant illumination for the household as well as a safety-flash for the mariner. Those that stand as light-houses, separate and alone, look like a short, corpulent woman in a full-flowing white skirt.

The path from Thorso to Sjetorp is indicated by small sticks—hoop poles we would call them—and the inner channel is very devious. In the night, or when it is foggy weather, the boats take an outer track.

As far as our eye can reach along the line of the shore, after passing the northeast bay of Thorso, we see what appears to be a small sail ; and such we suppose it to be for some time, until the mate, who has now come on deck, informs us that it is the lighthouse to the left of the canal entrance at Sjetorp. A few scattered houses constitute all there is of the hamlet. Here we make our first entry by a lock, and begin the third stage in our journey.

There are twenty locks between Sjetorp and Lake Viken ; and I walked fully one-third of that distance by the side of the canal. From the Venern to the Viken is about twenty-one of our miles. Along this portion of the route we met a great many girls and boys with birchen baskets filled with wild strawberries; which delicious berries they sell for ten ore (or about two-and-half cents,) a quart. It is probably unnecessary to remark that they find a ready and stock-exhausting market for their goods.

Nosegays of wild flowers are also offered for sale at the vakt houses by the pretty barefooted daughters of the lock-tenders; and the cabin and dining-room of the *Venus* is soon laden with the richest perfumes that Nature can yield. The sailors are very fond of roses and forget-me-nots; and every one of them has a bunch of his favorites fastened in his cap before we have passed the third lock on this section of the canal.

The supply of milk which the people along this line have for sale is also speedily purchased; and by getting in advance of the steamer one or two locks we can see the maids and men hastening the milking operation, or beginning that operation in advance of the usual hour—you cannot "hurry" that job very much?—so as to have their jars, in which they offer the rich, pure article for sale, full to the brim, when the boat shall have arrived opposite their dairies.

We should judge that there had not been much foreign travel this way during this season as yet, even if we had not been explicitly so informed by the Captain and others on board, for the children and maids gathered around us with curious and inquiring looks at every watchhouse, and took great delight in feeling of the hat and dress of the child who walks in our party of passengers. But there is nothing forward or impudently intrusive in their manners. They make friendly advances after the communication of trade, in a way that is captivating by its delicacy; and they are so much gratified when you interpret their wish—unexpressed in words—to take up our little girl, that they cannot repress an exclamation of joy that is, or would be, understood without a dictionary anywhere. The elderly inhabitants are very reserved, and some of them have an almost austere and sullen aspect of countenance.

When the steamer approaches a lock she whistles—a distance of a half a mile or more—and if she is not in sight of a watchman, by reason of a curve in the canal, the signal for coming ahead for a clear lock or for waiting, is given by a shrill police-whistle response. If the steamer officers can see the gateway that is far ahead, the signal for "coming ahead" consists in the waving of a red flag by a woman or little girl. I have seen this flag displayed more than a score of times on this trip, and invariably in the hands of a female.

Here again we ascend to the hurricane deck and renew our charming ride through and apparently over the meadows. The hay and grain look well. The crop is said to be "sure of abundance" in this part of the country, and the close-at-hand and the distant scenery is all enchanting. O, my friend, when you come to Sweden next summer, or the next, you must take this trip. Let no man prevail upon you to pass another way.

What is it that gives such a special charm to this landscape? That something which we have always attached to it when we have looked at pictures of it in days gone by? Here it is, just like a picture; "pretty as a picture!" All the still life of the canvas and the engraving is here. Faithful engravings you have in your drawing-rooms of scenes like these. What is it that makes this so precisely the copy rather than the original of what we have actually beheld before? All of a sudden it flashes upon us: *What is it!* Why, it is the red tiled roofs of these large and small houses and barns, sheds and cottages.

We must introduce red roofs into the United States. We must have a law passed, if necessary to accomplish the object: providing that from and after the passage of said Act, in every city and county, every housetop cover, cornice and roof, shall be as crimson as gore! Then we shall have sometimes, approximately, the picturesque scenery of this old country. Oscar Wilde's knee-breeches may remain an unsettled proposition for revival during a century to come, without any serious detriment to the taste of the cultivated classes in America and the enjoyment of all mankind; but *this* decree ought to be on our statute books before another decade is passed. Let the law first be enacted in California, and begin to take effect on Nob Hill.

The locks are 112x24 feet in size, and often the steersman points the boat into one of them without touching either side. Then the Captain or the mate will sing out "Bravo!" and perhaps will clap his hands. A fine of 500 crowns (or $125) is affixed as a penalty for touching the gates with the prow of the boat. Last year a steamer poked its nose through one of the gates and caused such damage as to stop through-navigation for the space of a month. The company owning this careless craft had to pay 16,000 crowns damage-money.

The waiting-maids on these vessels receive $2.50 a month as wages from the company. The chambermaid and the cook receive 12 kroners a month. The Captain gets 300 kroners a month—about $75—and the mate receives $50. The deck hands receive $8 a month.

While on deck, and approaching Toreboda, our party diversified their conversation by reference—first made by the German gentleman—to the Consulates at Gothenburg and Stockholm. It is agreed that these ought not to be places for rich gentlemen, or "billets" for war veterans who have no special qualifications for such a place. The former, as experience has shown, will not attend to the duties of the office, and the latter cannot do so with credit or justice to the Government represented. Nor should any man be appointed to a consulate in a nation of his nativity.

Toreboda is a place of considerable importance, as is shown by the amount of freight that goes off at this point. A large invoice of petroleum is rolled up the gangplank at this landing. A few oil wells have been discovered in Sweden, but their value is as yet said to be problematical,—the quality so far being very inferior. The United States still supplies this burning fluid to the people of Scandinavia. The principal business of the Vice-Consul at Gothenburg—which taxes his intellect and strength to about its uttermost capacity—is to certify to the Custom-house at New York or Philadelphia that so many barrels are *bona fide* returned as oil-holding barrels from Sweden to the American republic. It is not necessary that the American flag should be displayed every time this exhaustive work is done; which is one of the reasons that we have had assigned for not displaying it at all over the door or house of the Consulate on any occasion. All the logic of this hinges on the matter of oil importation; a large deposit of which, I should say, was made on this trip, from our steamer, at the wharf at Toreboda.

Something has to be lost to sight in a sixty-hour trip—continuously made—and therefore withheld from memory dear, on this voyage; because tired nature seeks and must have repose:—"sleep that knits up the raveled sleeve of care," "balm of hurt minds." Well, if you had heard our German friend drop into poetry, and especially into Shakspeare, about bed-time, you could not have kept this much of paraphrasing and quotation out of your diary, except by such special and painful effort as would have been too costly a price for the exclusion.

We wake—having passed through Lake Viken and the Bottensjo—to witness the landing at Karlsburg. We swing around a corner from the canal to touch at the wharf at this point: at the end of the second canal-section from Gothenburg and on the shore of Lake Vettern. You see very little of this place as a "fortress;" in fact the uncompleted fortifications are so far distant from the little bay into which the steamer runs that not much more than a tower, about 100 feet high and 25 feet in diameter, with a flag floating therefrom, is obtained in your glance on this journey as at present regulated. As between Karlsburg, Vadstena and Motala, a delightful three days stop-over, at least, should be spent by the traveller. Karlsburg is intended to be a "great railway point and place of refuge" in case of invasion.

Vadstena is situated diagonally from Karlsburg,—across Lake Vettern, an hour's ride from the fortress. Close to the wharf is a castle which Gustavus Vasa built in 1500 and something; still in a good state of preservation.

We begged the captain to let us have an hour's time in which to visit the Abbey of St. Briggita; the only remains of the Monastery of Vadstena, which was constructed in 1395, and which is old enough and sufficiently full of memories of Romans and rascality and religious consecration to satisfy any searcher after the ancient abodes and haunts of warlike, brutal men and devoted Christian women. But, certainly, this was an unreasonable, impudent and ridiculous petition; and while every one of the passengers had encouraged our German friend to brace up and make the request, all but three persons of real principle, including two ladies, treacherously deserted him in his hour of snubbing and defeat. He took his rebuff philosophically, however. He merely used a Lig, big D, and glared at the individuals who perfidiously and exasperatingly remarked in the hearing of the Captain, "Of course, such a thing could not be expected;" and then he, and all of us, went to see the castle. We had ten minutes for that purpose, and we agreed to keep close together, so that if the Captain went off before we returned he would make a wholesale business of it. I attended a little to the covenant on this arrangement myself, but after we left the steamer and were on our way to the castle gate our German friend privately showed me an English bull-dog revolver, which he had concealed on his person informing me in a phlegmatic tone of voice, "I fires ven the first man runs."

Over the door of the castle—which was formerly entirely surrounded by a moat, and which is now partially girt about by water—is a coat of arms, and the end sides of the building and the roof immediately above are adorned with medallions and figures and statues that may have been intended originally to represent somebody, in all seriousness, but which now approach the grimly grotesque in their appearance.

This castle, which is now reported as "restored" is used as a granary—when it is used at all. Most of the immense chambers are vacant, though there is a smell of the rye—new rye—in most of the rooms. In one of the halls on the first floor we found a man engaged in sorting and sacking the staple grain of the realm—(the only sacking now allowed, our German friend explained,—with a grunting demonstration)—and he gave us all a sample and took a few ores with an obeisance that was of itself worth the money. It was a kind of a dodging bow, as if he was about to butt us, ram-fashion, and was getting quickly

VADSTENA CASTLE.

into the proper attitude. I saw that our German friend enjoyed it; he took two samples and feed the miller twice.

In one large chamber of the second or third floor, we noticed the remains of rude frescoing, and on the sides of the window-openings and on the face of the opposite wall there were portraits of warriors clad in mail and pages dectorated with ribbons. This must have been a dining-hall for there was as additional suggestive, circumstantial evidence,—a kitchen close at hand.

We were shown the window out of which one of Gustavus Vasa's sons, the imbecile Prince Magnus of Ostrogotha, leaped on one cold night; jumping into the waves, as he supposed to meet a Nyad of the Vettern, who was, as he described it, almost insane with love for him. It was a long leap of at least forty feet (if we were shown the right window), and we could not do otherwise than sigh and repeat the story to each other, as well as feed upon it—according to the measure of our respective credulity.

Just then, and when we were getting into a romantic state of mind, the steamer whistle blew fiercely and there were indications of a stampede. The German put his hands behind his coat and shouted, "Gentlemen, the first man that runs gets there last." The whole current of our thoughts was changed. Several members of the party stole the copyright on the big D. In the confusion that ensued, in spite of every military effort at discipline, we lost our way. One lady thought she had sprained her ankle in going down one of the stairs (the stone steps were very much worn), and had to be carried the rest of the way to the steamer; where and where upon she proceeded to walk about as lively as ever. When we regained our exit-line we marched in pretty good style, and the Captain, who had no idea of our bonds, said that we came out of the portcullis and across the drawbridge like a squad of infantry. Whereupon the German, who was not to be surpassed nor yet superceded in the dry line, spoke up and informed the Captain that the artillery was where General Heintzelman after the first battle of Bull Run is reported to have jokingly but with decided injustice said he always wanted to have it when raw troops went into battle

—in the rear. Here and thereafter we had occasion to express surprise at the familiarity of the average woman with the history and popular gossip of our civil war.

At Motala, a half-hours ride distant from Vadstena, we turned into the fourth section, and thence to Berg; passing over or through that which is undoubtedly on the most beautiful division of the route.

The water at Motala is so clear that you can see the bottom at a distance of fifteen feet as well as you can see your hand when held flat against the opposite side of a pure window-glass. Such transparency of water I never saw before, nor yet dreamed possible.

A Swedish man and wife who had lived three years in Michigan here left the *Venus* and took the cars for her

GOTHA CANAL NEAR BORENSHULT.

father's home. These were the first acquaintances we made with any returning Swedish immigrants. When they started for their old home they were very homesick; but we believe that we shall meet them in California.

Ten miles below Motala is Motala Verkstad, a flourishing manufacturing village, where 2,000 hands are employed in iron factories. The works are said to be driven by one water-wheel, turned by the water of the canal on a fall of thirty-eight feet. On a "through trip" there is not time afforded for a satisfactory visit to this place, though visitors are gladly welcomed.

Soon we reach—walking ahead of the steamer—the famous locks of Borenshult; five locks that let the vessel down 49 feet into Lake Boren. The scenery hereabouts could not be surpassed in loveliness. And after we reach Husbyfjol, which we do in an hour after entering the lake, we pass into a canal, where we sail and steam along for four hours through a land of enchantment. The grounds adjacent to the canal are well described by Baedecker as "park-like in character." A party of French gentlemen who came on board at Motala, following the advice of the guide books, and who departed at Norsholm, and who were evidently men of much travel on the Continent, pronounced this ride the most fascinating that they had ever enjoyed. I use their word of emphasis, but I cannot give by any description an adequate indication of the animation which they imparted to their language by their gestures and their beaming countenances. One declared himself *blasé* as a tourist, but vowed that he would return to this trip on his way back from Stockholm, although he had planned his journey far differently. Imagine a canal running from San Mateo to San Jose, through a country as finely cultivated as that in and immediately adjacent to Menlo Park, and you have some faint idea of the marvelous delights of this passage.

BRUNNEBY.

The beautiful village of Brunneby, with a quaint old church is now passed, on our right. At, or rather near, Berg —for the boat does not go within two miles of that town—

there are seven descending lock steps into Lake Roxen. By
the side of this monstrous giant stairway we sit, while the
steamer is approaching through the locks above;—a full two
hours of waiting, but which seems scarcely half that time,
so enrapturously ab-
sorbed is every one in
silent admiration of
the scene of the
meadow and lake at
our feet, and the far
away plains on the
shore and wooded
hills in the horizon's
edge, and the sugges-
tive and curiosity-pro-
voking old church

CLOISTER CHURCH.

towers on our right—distinctly to be seen in the general
utline, yet too dim for architectural inspection. This to the
human eye is the very perfection of nature. Of other views
bring aid to our recollection through the art of the painter
or the photographer, but let these pictures alone in the gallery of memory.

At Norsholm we pass again from lake to an artificial
channel. Here our French tourists and several other most
agreeable passenger companions bid us "farewell," including our Teuton friend who had endeared himself to everybody on board, in one way or another,—an intelligent,
kind-hearted, jovial gentleman, whose conceit over his own
attempts at humor was always pardonable and sometimes not
without justification by positive merit. May we meet again;
may we have the pleasure of welcoming him to San Francisco.

It is eleven o'clock at night—and light enough to read a
paper without the aid of a candle—when we leave Norsholm. Early next morning we wake to find ourselves on the
Baltic sea, sailing between the little islands that thickly
cluster along the shore line, which we are to follow on our
way up to Sodertelje. Asplangen, Hulta, Snovelstorp,
Klamman, Venneberga, Karlsborg, Marichof, Soderkoping
(which, with its old buildings, and its new and mammoth

hydropathic establishment, is another great argument for a stop-over passage) and Liljesta, are passed in the very early morning hours; and we have to mourn again on account of the

SODERKOPING.

recurring evidence of our mortality—that which Alexander sighed over, and for which Sancho Panza gave great thanks.

Every record of this kind should state the fact that after the seventy-fourth lock is passed, three from Soderkoping, there is to be seen a marble slab, set in the wall of the canal, on which is engraved in Swedish these words: "Except the Lord build the house, they labor but in vain that build it."

GRAVE OF BARON VON PLATEN.

We thought of this most appropriate passage of Scripture, as quoted in the guidebook, and repeated it aloud as we stood beside Baron Von Platen's grave in Dufvedal, and cast some sprigs of green on the slab that covers the remains of the chief engineer of this tremendous enterprise. And we could not help comparing him and his co-laborers and supporters, as we have read their histories and studied their characters, with the men who received our Government

Pacific R. R. subsidy loan and gift of lands, and took a noble engineer's outline of a transmount railroad and built an iron highway upon it; and while so doing conspired with each other to obtain four to six times the cost of their road, under the false pretense of *bona fide* expenditures. O, what a desecrating juxtaposition of comparison is that! There is only one mode of excusing and justifying such joining of names and biograpies—a momentary toleration for the moral of contrast and execration.

MEM.

"The domain of *Mem*" and the story of the hiding of the silver statues of the twelve apostles, by one of its former proprietors, Cal Bagge, are at the headings of the Captain's entertaining talk. At this point we pass near the picturesque ruin of the Castle of Stegeborg. Narrow is the channel and crooked is the way along the shore of Sweden from Gottenvick to Sodertelje. We counted 23 islands on one side and 12 on the other at one time. "In and out and cross lots," we hear some cry; and we find that a sailor has learned an appropriate English song, which he habitually sings—or attempts to sing—whenever this part of the trip is reached. At Safenud lighthouse we stopped and took on a basket of sea perch, which very much resembled our Lake Tahoe trout externally and by their flavor.

The chateau of Horningsholm, on the site of an old castle, is an edifice about the size of the Metropolitan hotel in New York, two stories less in height and with a red-tile roof, but otherwise decidedly like the great hotel on Broadway.

The Sodertelje that faces the sea has nothing of interest to show this Sunday to the passer-by save the outside of its half dozen of hydropathic hotels. But the Industrial School for boys near by sends out a small army of swimmers to give us a hurrah of welcome from the docks of that establishment.

As we pass around the canal that leads to Lake Malaren, we hear the sounds of the church bells in the city of Sodertelje proper, joining or clashing in summoning peals.

At Motala there was no escape on the part of the lady passengers from the lace merchants, who sell the "genuine, home-made article" at very low prices, we are told; and at Soderielje (where there are a number of steamers from Stockholm that have just disembarked crowds of excursionists) neither man woman nor child can escape the importunities of the women who sell "kringlor" and "papparkakor" of their own baking on very moderate terms. Several passengers, who have no hint as to the quantity of these kinds of cake that a kroner will buy, find themsevels loaded down with gingerbread—for that is what papparkakor is—and proceed to wasteful indulgence in pelting each other with pieces of their superflous, crispy provender ammunition.

HORNINGSHOLM.

Up Lake Malaren, a two hours passage to the Capital of Sweden! We anxiously watch for the first view of the city that is to be had from the pilot-house, and we have it in a sight of the scaffold-circled tower of Clara Kyrka, now undergoing "reparation." Then we notice slowly moving windmill fans of enormous dimensions. Then, suddenly, and just as we become assured of our object and get a stout "yaw" from the steersman in response to our inquiring ejaculation, "Stockholm?" the tall, slender iron spire of Riddarholms Kyrka topped with a golden cross that flashes in the midday sun, is set in the heavens; and the whole central picture of this jewel of cities is before us, reposing beneath this holy sign and between loftier ridges that rise on either hand at the same time inclose and form a part of this well-named, wonderful "Venice of the North."

VII.

STOCKHOLM TO STROMSHOLM CASTLE.

I think that most travellers in Sweden will be surprised at first—however much they may have read beforehand in modern books descriptive of the life and the homes of this people—to find such large tracts of country that would come under the designation of "rolling land" in America. Here, for instance, is a view that nearly makes a horizon-bound plain on one side.

There is a slight eminence, of perhaps fifteen or twenty feet, in the centre of the landscape to the North and West as seen from the cavalry ground beyond Stromsholm Castle, and still beyond the ground is gently rolling; but for the most part from Kolbeck to Quicksund and from Westeras to Monktorp, it may be said that it is one valley. Through the middle of this nearly level reach of country passes the Stromsholm Canal; which extends from the Malare Lake at this point up to the mines of Dalecarlia; and the vessels that are to be seen constantly making their way up or down on the mirrory surface of the channel that has been prepared for them in the midst of the meadows, lend an additional charm to an exceedingly beautiful picture, which nature had already provided.

The trip from Stockholm to Quicksund, which is about six miles from this castle, can be made by rail or steamer, but the latter is much preferable. The little steamers are of 40 tons burden, and their quarters are, of course, very contracted. But they are really very comfortable; large enough for the the trade which they are intended to meet; and they run like race-horses. The fare for first-class passengers is one and a quarter cents a mile.

The scenery on lake Malaren has been so often and so extensively described, that I hesitate to give it here even a passing comment. It has not been over praised in any volume that

I have read. There is a sufficient variety and peculiarity to make the five-hours passage between the points named delightful and memorable.

Perhaps the most remarkable feature for record is the *mirage*. Along the route you often behold the painted vessel upon the painted sea. And oftentimes at this season a score of little islands that lie between you and the sun's horizon will seem lifted up above the waters—"Isles of the blest" floating in the sky.

But in the narrow way that you must frequently sail along, through the woodland and mountain declivity close beside you, the vista of lake and border before and behind is marvelously

STRENGNAS CATHEDRAL.

lovely, and is entirely worthy of the much abused descriptive word "exquisite."* There is nothing grand or in that sense or direction impressive about the views presented; there is a pensive serenity in all the prospect, a combination of pictures that begets a feeling of quiet pleasure which it is difficult to more than hint at, and which it seems the function of poetry alone to approximately describe.

We stop a few minutes at Strengnas, an Episcopal town, where Gustavus Vasa was elected king, and Chas. IX., Sten Sture the elder, and Admiral Stenback are buried.

Over three hundred years ago a castle was built at Stromsholm by Gustavus Vasa; who, it appears to me, is worthy of

STROMSHOLM CASTLE.

the title—among others—of The castle-builder of Sweden. He made a present of the structure to his wife Catherine Stenback —a lady who was some forty years his junior. And she spent the years of her widowhood here; dying at the age of 92. After the old castle was partly destroyed and, in the course of nature, had partly gone to decay, Queen Eleonora, wife of Charles

X, constructed a residence here which retains the name of "castle." The building is not a fortified edifice. But the indications of the fact that this place was once occupied by a strongly guarded council, are to be seen around and below. It is completely surrounded by water; the Kolbacksa being divided a short distance above the castle, and an equally distributed stream flowing on either side. Here was doubtless a moat; and draw-bridges were provided on the front and at the rear. Such is tradition—if not history. From the cellar, subterranean passages have been traced, which lead out—deep under the island and under the channels of the stream—and which, it is believed, once afforded means of escape for a beleagured garrison.

The present structure—200 years old—is a 3 story building, with a high basement, and with a cupola nearly in the centre, and immediately over a chapel hall. And there is an additinal story in the four square-cornered towers. The whole edifice is about 200 feet square. It is of brick and stone; the body being painted a light yellow, with white pillars and black roof. Altogether it has a quaint appearance; and it would do very well for the main "location" of a novel. Indeed I expect that on this suggestion several romances will be worked up, with Stromsholm as a focalizing and radiating point. In fact, I have almost outlined one myself, in spite of an effort of will against it.

The immediate surroundings are charming. In the rear, across the stream, are two broad avenues, a quarter of a mile long, lined with beach trees, with a margin of gravelled path. The space between these avenues, which are shaded by trees of two centuries growth, being a lawn about four hundred feet wide—extending from the stream to a thickly planted grove, in which the reservation for this royal residence terminates on the East. In front there is a regularly shaded park; and a road, straight as an arrow, that leads from the castle door to the house of the superintendent of the estate, which is a half a mile distant, and situated, as before observed, on a piece of ground that is slightly elevated above the adjoining country.

For twenty years last past this castle has not been occupied as a home for the royal family or any of its retinue; though up to the date of the death of the last king—who, by the way, was a very popular sovereign—this was a regular summer resort for his "majesty." Twenty years ago, and prior to that time, since the castle was built, this was a dwelling for the nobility, or for some distinguished representatives of royalty whenever it was not the abiding place of the king and of his own household. For nearly or quite two hundred years, this has been the scene of domestic life in which men and women who were born to a title were the principal characters. Now it is almost exclusively devoted to the use of officers in attendance upon the riding academy, which is situated near the house of the superintendent of the farm lands of this district. Six royal apartments, besides the dining room, are still reserved as "His majesty's drawing rooms and bed chambers;" and these are shown to visitors by the very urbane porter, who imparts all needed information about the pictures; etc., at such length that it is evident he is not pressed for time or accustomed to this kind of demand for his services.

The royal apartments face to the East and to the North and South; the rooms in front are and always have been occupied by the officers of the king's guard. The tables and chairs in the large drawing-room are arranged as they were left, eleven years ago, when the last royal card parties gathered here for a season of social enjoyment. The satin on the chairs and sofas —each set of different shade and pattern—is much worn and faded; and notwithstanding the evidence of some little care in keeping the rooms free from or relieved from dust and moths, the whole of the cloth and tapestry and paper covering has a frayed and dilapidated appearance.

There is a blue bed-chamber and a red bed-chamber; and on the couch in the latter, where royality has often reposed, I laid me down to test the ancient mattrass. We have better beds in California, in every country hotel. If this is a specimen royal couch—and I was assured that it was—no wonder that some heads that wore crowns lay uneasily in palace-chambers. Better a blanket on the green sod. And I am convinced that a pile of the boasted feather-beds on such an oval basis would rather aggravate than improve the situation. The thick curtains, stiff with needlework and goldbands and gimp, when allowed to fall together, absolutely shut out the light and fresh air, and were sufficient to have stifled a king of such prodigious breath as Charles XII. if they were in place about him for the space of an hour. I am satisfied that he did not patronize this establishment very much; or if he visited it at all, he had his hammock swung under one of the beech trees in the grounds behind the castle. I have seen his bed-net elsewhere, and know that he was in the habit of taking a siesta in it. So I pass into these simple suppositions.

Here is a large life-size portrait of Queen Eleonora. She has the countenance that is generally painted on the ladies' royal canvas in this country, so far as my observation goes; the exceptions to the rule for queenly beauty being rare and noticeable. There is the long face, with flat pasted or plated hair; and a dress very much after the style that our own dear grandmothers wore in New England forty years ago. I have a high opinion of Eleonora, as a lady of gracious qualities, and I am sorry that we have not a

CHARLES IX: STATUE.

good Morse photograph of her, as she really was in form and features. And here is Charles X. and his family. Here is Charles XII. The latter somewhat resembling King Henry the VIII. of England. This painting being evidently an attempt to actually represent on canvas the lineaments of his majesty's face, bull-dog tenacity and voluptuous desire are prominently indicated in his physiognomy. Over the doors leading into the red bed-chamber are two paintings that have considerable merit; and I wonder that the present king did not order them sent to his country residence near Stockholm —along with the greater portion of linen and plate that he had removed shortly after his brother died. They are scenes among ruined temples—(Lakes of Baalbeck or Palmyra?)—and the artist deserves mention in the future catalogues of art.

All the rooms have closets, the doors of which are even with the walls—some of them not being seen by the visitor unless his attention is specially attracted to them. Two or three of these closets connect with stairways that lead to the cellars beneath, and thence afford access to the underground galleries already spoken of. They are supposed to be convenient passages down stairs for the butler and wine vault keeper; but of course *we* know already that these were roads by which our assassins came in and went out, as will appear in our future "Revelations of the Mysteries of Stromsholm"—revelations, perhaps to be begun in the next chapter and continued in our next, and in our next, etc.

The frescoing on the walls of the dining-room is of comparatively recent date; and is in good taste and appropriate pattern. By "recent" or "modern" on this side of the Atlantic you are always to understand something constructed or done within a couple of centuries last past,—as already indicated in the case of the founding of the city of Gotenberg. Here is indeed a "banquet hall deserted."

The present king deigns not to visit this once beloved country residence of royalty. He has not crossed the threshold since his predecessor died; but in 1883 for the first time since his coronation, he came to the riding school by the early morning boat from the capital, and returned to his palace at night. Various causes are assigned by the peasantry living round about, for this desertion by the king and his immediate retinue. Some say that his wife does not like the place, and that he has a degree of respect for or obedience to her inclinations that constrains him to allow her to appoint their summer home. Others say that he is disgusted with the way in which the crown estate in these parts has been managed, and that he is determined to divide up and sell out all the royal patrimony in this neighborhood at the earliest practicable moment.

Whatever may be the true reason for his neglect or avoidance of this castle, in the way referred to, it is certain that the people here-abouts mourn his absence and speak with great intonation of sorrow about the "good times" they had when the favored monarch and his equally beloved queen were in the habit of spending a full fifth of the year at Stromsholm.

"O! the good times we had when the king and queen attended service in our chapel!"

We go into this chapel and sit down in one of the pews. Shades of our pilgrim forefathers! your torture benches are here. Ah! but go up into the royal gallery;—or, more exactly, imagine that you go up into an open cupboard—which immediately faces the pulpit. There is cushioned comfort for you! Here we take up a prayer-book dated 1701. "Modern," of course! Well, the print is as clear and distinct as if the impression was made by Bacon & Co. day before yesterday. Indeed, it is plainer reading than the average of such pages, in smaller type, from the press of Stockholm, of the year 1880.

We compare line for line on this particular examination. The broad face of the head letters is jet black, after 183 years of service in conveying psalm and hymn and prayer to the eye and heart of the worshipper in this little attic chapel of Stromsholm Castle.

VIII.

MONKTORP TO KOLBECK.

I WRITE in the shadow of one of the oldest churches in Sweden,—the Kyrka (pronounced chyrka) of Monktorp. As the name indicates, this ancient structure was left by the monks, who built and occupied it; laying its corner-stone some time in the thirteenth century; their ecclesiastical successors leaving the premises shortly after the coronation of Gustavus Vasa. I must confess that I have enjoyed walking along its aisles and sitting on its altar stairs and reading aloud from its pulpit, almost as much as I delighted in indulging in much more limited but similar liberties at Westminister. This has little more space than the famous chapel of the great London abbey—not much more than that; and this has no Dickens or Livingston or titled dead with whom we may be said to have been acquainted. But for all that and all that, there is glory and gloom enough here, in the presence of the dead of whom there is no record outside of these walls—in the memories that cluster about this district and centre here—according to the chronicles of the sages in the dawning of this national history, as now accessible to human perusal and scrutiny.

In the splendid abbey at Westminster you must ordinarily share your privileges for inspection and meditation with many men and women (if you can call that meditation, which you have in the way of thoughtful retrospect and serious contemplation about now and a to-come, in the midst of a promiscuous crowd or circle of stranger visitors); and probably you will suffer there from direct intrusion on your own wise or your own morbid reflections such as you do or can indulge in. Here I have this sacred edifice all to myself. The minister sends the key by a man who describes himself as "he who blows the organ." No questions are asked, no companions gathered to make a paying party for the talkative old verger; no time set in which the visit must be made and an exit taken. For a time unlimited—say for an afternoon—I am the householder here. It is well. I will repeat my service over different stations that will be mentioned and return to my seat in the nobleman's pew and resume my writing. True; the comparison and contrast—the difference—is wide, between the Abbey of the Thames and an ancient church of the monks of Sweden, remaining in a country place; but for all that and all that, the veins of thought and reflection that are opened here, are much the same and often identical in nature of retrospect. The floor is paved with brick—large red brick—and so hard that, although it is the veritable pavement of five centuries ago, the blocks are not worn down more than two inches on an average. Here and there are many huge slabs, 6x4 feet, at the very least, on which are inscribed the names of holy men of old, who were buried beneath these stones during the thirteenth, fourteenth and fifteenth centuries. One in particular has attracted my attention. I cannot, without some aid from the present pastor (which I may solicit by and by,) exactly make out the inscription; but I know from the decipherable letters engraved, and from the rude and yet not inartistic outlines of a man and woman on the granite, that *hic jacet* a God-fearing, flock-guarding pastor of the fifteenth century, with his wife, Johannah, by his side. He obeyed the master's injunction and fed the sheep; and she was a helpmeet, and kept open house for the poor and needy. And she and he were worthy of burial close beside the altar; and let every one mark the end of these righteous persons, that it was peace; and tread reverently when you walk near this precious dust; for precious in the sight of the Lord are the ashes of His saints.

The reredos stands eight or ten feet from the rear wall, and is of carved and gilded wood. There are a cross and life-size statues of two Apostles; and a prayer-book rests on the large velvet-covered, fringe-decorated cushion. The book is dated 1771, and the letters in it look as though the ink was not yet fairly dry. It would seem as if the publishers of the few religious books that were issued a century ago printed " for all time," as it is said the Egyptians built and Willam Shakspeare wrote.

In the pulpit, which projects from one of the pillars that is nearly midway between the altar and organ loft, there is an old bible that is of day and date—as was the phrase of the man who let me in—1701. There is not a leaf missing, nor one page torn or mutilated, Certainly most of us have seen bibles printed in America of much older date; but the state of preservation here, as well as the excellence of the workmanship, would challenge the respectful consideration of my friends of the book trade who are fatigued by their enforced familiarity with such antiquities.

By the way, I was in an antiquarian bookstore in Stockholm, where I tried to make a small stationery purchase. The youthful clerk could not satisfactorily interpret my recent Swedish, until I finally contrived to inform him that I was an American from San Francisco, where we had an antiquarian bookstore, with the proprietor of which I was slightly acquainted. This I finally made clear to his *icke forsta* comprehension: and thereafter everything I uttered was plain to his understanding—so he protested. I believe the young man dissembled, out of pure civility or out of an increased or new-born sentiment of politeness that came in honor of a foreigner who lived in a city that was of sufficient importance to have an antiquarian bookstore in it! I was tempted to ask him if he knew or had heard of N. Choynski; but I was afraid that he would somehow imply that he did, and deepen his already manifest guilt in the line of courteous equivocation.

I estimate that this sacred edifice at Monktorp will hold 2,000 people, and last Sunday it was packed—so says the organ blower. There was not standing room after 10:45. Eight hundred persons took communion.

The organ is a magnificent instrument; larger than any we have in San Francisco. It was built by the late Herr A. P. Hallden, and has been appraised since his death at about 5,000 crowns, or about $1,300. It would be worth fully $15,000 in the United States.

The pews of the church are raised above the pavement and are floored with plank.

By the side of the pulpit, convenient to the hand of the preacher, are four half-hour sandglasses. How suggestive of the two hours of sermon-speech that we once listened to, as a boy, in a church in Western Massachusetts.

"Do they still keep up that practice of elaborate discoursing in Sweden?"

"Nay," says the organ blower, when so inquired of at the churchyard gate, "only about an hour and a half." This uttered as though the reduction in time was enormous and greatly to be deplored.

The view from the belfry of this church extends fully fifteen miles on every side—a greater distance, in fact, on the East. With a glance you can thence descry the tower of the cathedral at Westeras.

This parish embraces half a Swedish mile on one side of the Kyrka—to the West, and about three fifths of a mile on the other points of the compass, with 4,000 names of living members on the baptismal register. Every child is looked after with scrupulous care. At Christmas time and Easter and Midsummer Sundays the church will not hold the people who come here to worship. It should be remembered that the established church in Sweden is *Episcopal* Lutheran, and not Evangelical or Congregational Lutheran.

In this connection our readers may be reminded that a Swedish mile is 6 64-100 English miles. The quarters are marked on the side of the road by iron plates, about three feet high by one foot in width, which are firmly set in a stone curb, which is built up four or five feet from he ground. The measurement is from the principal cities or towns of the district. The mile-stones are stamped with the name of the sovereign who caused them to be erected; with crown and date.

You will notice here old foot boards, marked with names or initials, set at varying distances along the side of the public highways. These mark the sections of the road which are to be taken care of during the summer by the farmers residing within the given boundaries; who are thus notified to "turnpike" in the Spring and gravel cover in the Fall. And by the same token, it is ordered that this year certain denoted portions of the road are to be kept open during the Winter by certain individuals.

Just outside of the churchyard we see a snow-plough, twenty-three English feet in length, regularly broadening from the apex to the fifteen feet of prescribed track width. Those living alongside or near the public road must keep a path open for travel through the snowy season on peril of a heavy fine, which is inavaribly imposed and exacted where there is failure to comply with the law.

"How deep does the snow fall in this vicinity?" we inquire.

The reply is: "Well, this is the grave of Herr Hallden, who built the organ you admired so much. He was buried here in February, 1881. We had to dig a trench from the top of these trees (pointing to a branch at least ten feet high) before we reached the surface of the ground in which we made his grave."

We went on to say: "Then the quarter-mile plates are covered up in Winter?"

"Nay: they must be uncovered, or it must be shown where they are when the road is broken."

The walls of this church are five feet thick. There is no provision for heating in Winter, and the cold is, of course, often intense. The women bring their foot-stoves with them, if they have such comforts or luxuries; and the next neighbors—those living nearest to the church—heat bricks for the poor old women who have not or cannot bring live coals on which to rest their feet.

"What does the minister get per year—that is, what does his receipts amount to in money valuation?" we inquired.

"About 6,000 kroners," is the estimate of our vagn driver.

"What is the pay of the organist?"

"Well, Herr Hallden got about 3,000 kroners a year; but he was worth as much as the minister, and more, too. He was every man's friend that needed a friend, which is more than can be said of the minister."

These people will drag in a great deal of side-bar information and comment; and here I find much of it—in my notebook.

"What wages do those women get that are working in the field yonder raking hay?"

"Seventy-five ore a day, if they work full time."

"What is full time?"

"From 5 o'clock in the morning until 8 at night."

"But they have an intermission for meals?" we suggest.

"Two hours in all—half an hour for breakfast, an hour for dinner and half an hour for evening lunch."

"These women with yoked pails are going to milk?" we say.

"Yes; only women folks milk. No men milk. It is against the law."

"Against the law for a man to milk a cow?"

"Yes, all the cows would go with full bags to-night if there were no women to milk them."

"But the men *could* milk as well as the women?"

"Nay, the women must do the milking!" (Spoken with an almost provoking emphasis of contempt for any other idea; spoken as if I proposed to change the custom of ages and put another yoke on the already overburdened male population of this district in Sweden)

"Do you see that space in there, surrounded by a circle of stones?" inquired one of our companions, as we rode along on the wooded knoll that separates the parishes of Monktorp and Kolbeck.

"Yes."

"Well, there was the last execution for capital offense that has taken place in this vicinity. I remember it. A woman was beheaded there for poisoning her lover's father, who would not allow a son to marry a servant. That low spot right opposite is the spot where the execution block was set up."

The driver uttered a long whurr, which is the signal here for horses to "whoa," at the instant when he was tapped on the shoulder with an umbrella that was in the hands of this witness to the execution. "There is where the block was; and the soldiers stood around here, just outside of this line of stones. There were hundreds of people crowding up to see the bloody sight, but not one-half of them had the satisfaction of seeing anything but the headsman and the axe and the bloody stains on the block and ground. Only those close to the circle of soldiers could witness the beheading. The body was taken away as soon as the decapitation was performed. But for years afterward people would come here in scores—particularly on Sunday—to view the place."

We rode on perhaps a half of an English mile, when we came to a cluster of cottages; two or three on each side of the road. We go into one, to make a specimen observation of the homes of the laboring classes in this section. There is a loom here, as there is in nearly every one of the houses in such little communities. There was a very old lady in the corner nearest the hearth—which is raised, as in all cottages, like a blacksmith's forge. A copper kettle is set over a few sticks of wood; and we presently ascertain that it has a dozen small potatoes in it, boiling for a family of four. Another elderly lady sat on a bench or lounge near a window which was on the side of the room opposite to the fire-place. Both of these dames were engaged in knitting; although the one first seen had before her a reel, from which she began to unwind yarn soon after we entered.

We were bade to enter as soon as we looked at the open door; the dames rising and courtesying as we entered. How pleasant it is to see this old-fashioned method of female salutation. "Will we be seated?" And the younger of the two old ladies goes to the chimney corner and takes down the copper coffee kettle. We know what is to be proffered: the invariable coffee invitation in these hospitable homes of the poor. It is easy to get in conversation with these people; and they are unmistakably pleased at our visit. When we tell them that we are from America, they start and stare—evidently more gratified by our visit than before. And when we say "California," "San Francisco," they exclaim: "O! that's so?" and after a long breath, "That's so, O!" We inquired, How old is the eldest of this aged couple? "Eighty-six last November." She is very much stooped, but she is still able to walk about quickly; and her eyes are as bright and her cheeks are as red as those of a girl of 16. She knits without glasses. We make remarks about her not looking as old as she admits she is. She replies: "Oh, yes; I was 86 on the 20th of last November. But I am bent down with hard work." This is said in a cheerful tone of voice; a simple statement, doubtless, of the fact. The younger of the two is 71, and, positively, she does not look to be over 50 years of age. There are no gray hairs in her head, and very few in those of her mother-in-law; such proving to be the relation between the two. One of our companions, who had been in this neighborhood before, begins to inquire about this and that person who formerly resided in the parish. There is no hesitation in the replies. These women know or knew them all; and for a radius of ten miles—as we are told on good authority—their domestic information is ready and complete.

The husband of the oldest has been dead these fifteen years. Her son, aged 68, is in the fields, earning a kroner and a half a day by working from 5 in the morning until 8 at night. The two women together can earn at home, with their knitting and weaving, about eighty ore, or twenty cents, a day. There is a daughter of 47 years at work in the fields also. She earns seventy-five ore a day by laboring the same hours that have been already recorded.

We ask: Do they own the house in which they live? "Nay; it belongs to the estate." The estate is in charge of a superintendent, to whom so much service must be rendered for the land, and so much labor done for a stipulated amount of mackerel and rye and potatoes. But this family is not bound to the great farm and its management, as are most families who live under similar renting.

How much is the rent of this cottage—two rooms down stairs and two rooms up stairs? "Thirty-five kroners a year. A patch of two acres and a half for potatoes goes with the house, on the same rental."

We inquire: "Are there any children belonging to this household?" "O, yes." The widowed daughter of 47 has five children. One child is 25. He is a soldier. One is 20 years of age. She is a girl in service near the castle. She is a good cook, and gets one hundred kroners a year. This is dwelt upon with great pride. She wants to go to America; and we must see her and tell her all about that country; what line she had best sail by, and where she had best land;

what wages she will get in America, etc. And then the thought of parting with this daughter brings tears to the eyes of both these women. They go on to tell of the loss of a daughter's husband at sea, in a way that makes us weep with them. There is a boy in a blacksmith's shop at Westeras; he is 16. And the two younger children are working for neighbors, raking hay—all at work. This is not considered a home of poverty, by any means. For poor people we will have to look elsewhere.

We go into the next house. Two aged women sit here also. The members of our party look at each other with an inquiry on the countenance of each, "This is the allotment of old ladies for every peasant's home?" But presently we discover that this is a poorhouse, in fact and name. It is not a county or parish poorhouse; but it is a house set apart by the estate for the shelter of the widows of those men who with their wives have worked on the farm for a year or more, and thereby "acquired a residence" and a habitation. The proprietor is not bound to provide food, but on demand he must give shelter. He can put as many poor persons who have acquired such claim upon him in this house "as can be provided with bed room in it." But there must be "no unreasonable crowding." Sometimes both man and wife are harbored here, when stricken with age and infirmities. Such was the case in this instance. One woman had a husband lying sick up stairs. We went into the loft above, by a flight of stairs on the outside. In a low garret room, without a fireplace or possibility of heating except such as the chimney bricks would give, lay the aged laborer. He reached 79 years of age the preceding month. It is evident that he has not many days to live. He is rheumatic; he can barely move on his bed. "How long has he worked on this farm?" we inquired. "Twenty-eight years." His bed consists of a tick filled with hay, on which a ragged comforter is spread. A thin blanket, which is patched with pieces of cotton and calico—so light that it does not seem as if there could be any warmth in it, and so dirty that it suggests that it was recently taken from the dusty road —is all the covering he has except his shirt and pants

—the latter made of a coarse Kentucky jean quality of stuff.

We return to the room below and inquire as to how these three are provided for. It is mostly a matter of free, neighborly contribution. They get more from the neighbors as voluntary contributions than from the management of the estate of the district. They complain, or rather, they state, when directly asked about their condition, that they are not as well off as the widows of those who have worked on the great estate at the castle. There, at the castle estate, the widows have a regular portion of wood and food; enough to comfortably keep body and soul together at least. Here they are often hungered, and feel pinched pains for the want of food almost every week in the year. Both earn what they can with knitting. They have no loom. During the Summer months one carries the mail a little distance in a hand-wagon, and gets a kroner a week for daily walking six of our miles.

Do not the rich people in the neighborhood visit them occasionally?

"Never." When they ride by, they turn their heads in the other direction. Only the poor come in to see them and help them.

Are there no authorities to whom they could make a successful application for further assistance? Could they not go to the county poorhouse?

No; they are fastened on this estate. If they had sufficient means to buy bread they would be "well off." They get ten ore a week from the district. This is their story, nearly verbatim. They do not know who we are, but they answer without reserve and with no expectation, apparently, that their statement will bring the slightest relief from us. When we give them a kroner piece they get up and shake our hands violently and courtesy, and turn around and courtesy again and again, until we imagine that they are or soon will be very dizzy. They wish to know, "What is this that has come down upon us out of the clouds?" We never could have dreamed that there was so much generosity and benevolence incarnated in a quarter of a dollar. We leave them in the midst of their ejaculations of thankfulness and amazement—in some amazement ourselves.

There is a soldier's home a quarter of an English mile distant. We tell the driver to take us there. Each district must provide a soldier for the regular army—that is, each district must furnish him with a house and a patch of land and contribute so much to the support of his family. Each district must set apart for him two tunland or two acres of land to grow grain upon; and pasture land for one cow must be provided. And then there has to be provision made generally on an adjacent piece of property, for the superanuated or pensioned soldier. There is a contest being made in the Legislature or Rixdag on this very point; the party of the country insisting that this tax upon the people in the country shall be removed. This fact we ascertained in Stockholm, while looking over a list of bills at the State House.

On our way from the hamlet to the trooper's cottage, we notice in the groves we pass huge ant-hills, four and five feet high—habitations such as we did not before suppose existed outside of Africa. They resemble hay-cocks, at a distance; and on close inspection appear to be of a saw-dust nature in composition.

We soon arrived at the door of the house that is provided for the soldier who is in active service. It is comfortable within and without, and there is, up to the bounds of comfort, evidently no lack. The wife is a tidy, and even a handsome woman, and she seems to consider herself in fortunate circumstances. Her husband has just returned from the camp and is at work in the meadow close by, and him we congratulate on his happy and well-furnished home.

We pass on to another dwelling, a few rods distant, in which resides the discharged predecessor of this lucky trooper. This house is much more humble in appearance, and the same may be said of all the surroundings. With the wife of this ex-soldier one of our party was well acquainted some years ago, and she expects to have a hearty greeting with her. On entering the one room that is set apart for family use, we find the old soldier at work patching a child's shoe, while on the narrow bed that stands against the wall, alongside of the fireplace, is his wife. Prostrate, paralyzed, barely able to articulate distinctly a single word. She recognizes our companion; although they had not met for eleven years, and although, as we learn, she often was not able to recognize her own kindred. The spectacle was painful in the extreme.

We ask, "How long were you a soldier in the service of Sweden?" "'Twenty-five years." "Were you honorably discharged?" "O yes," he replied. "What is your pension?" "'This house and an acre of ground, as you see [it was pasture land, as it seemed to us] and fifteen kroner a year in silver." A soldier of twenty-five years service pensioned with $3.75, payable at the expiration of each twelve months.

He was asked: "Why don't you send your wife to a hospital where she can be taken care of under the best medical skill?" He answered, "I sent her to the Westeras Hospital, and kept her there as long as I had money to spare or could earn for that purpose, over and above what was necessary for my child and grandchild's absolute wants."

One of our party said: "But we were told in Stockholm that the great hospitals of the State—some of which we visited—were always open to the members of the families of ex-soldiers." He said quietly: "It is not so; when my money was exhausted they sent word to me to take my wife home. Of course I could make a great deal more if I was able to go out and work as a shoemaker or a tailor. I tried to have them keep her for what I could earn or save, over and above what was necessary for my own support and the support of the two children that are still dependent on me. But they would not. I cannot stir away from the house so long as she remains here, and I would not think of doing so."

The woman was entirely helpless and her husband was her only nurse. There was a delicate boy of 13—their own child born when his mother was 48 years of age, and there was a grandchild that had been left on their hands for support.

Our companion, who had expected a very pleasant meeting here, and who was proportionately shocked by this scene of misery, said that this woman was once the most active person in the vicinity; noted for her industry at home and for her speedy dispatch on errands of mercy and charity, whenever she heard of any one in distress to whose relief she could with propriety contribute. Her husband gave audible expression to his surprise at her recognition of her friend.

The poor invalid managed to stammer out in broken words and long detached syllables: " I felt who it was. The angels from heaven have brought her here that I might see her face once more before I died." "I know that you are ready to die," said our companion. "Oh, yes," she said with a smile; "I long to go and be at rest with my Saviour. It is better for me—and for him," turning her eyes with a look of great affection toward her husband—" and for our little ones, that I should go quickly. Now that I have seen you, I am the more willing and anxious to go. I have been thinking for several days past that my heavenly Father was holding me back for some special purpose. I think now, it was for the pleasure of seeing you once more and telling you that I always loved your mother and yourself above all other persons except my own relatives."

Afterward when we spoke about this dying woman in the presence of a lady in the family of a teacher at Kolbeck—not more than an hour after we left the soldier's cottage or hut—she remarked, "Yes, there is a deathbed of a truly Christian woman." Whereupon one of our party said: "But why is this Christian woman left to die in that miserable hovel, when Sweden has so many public hospitals for incurables and homes for the sick of almost every name and description?" The reply was: "O, each district must take care of its own people, and each parish or district is supposed to do the best that can be done under the circumstances." This was not said in a heartless tone of voice; but I am sure that I have interpreted what was said correctly. And now that I write it out for this letter, the speech seems to me more cold blooded than I regarded it when I heard it spoken. It was a reply made in a matter-of-course way, and as a perfectly conclusive and satisfactory explanation of this condition of affairs.

I made further inquiries, and found that this veteran soldier, John Brunberg, was not only an honorably discharged cavalryman, but that he had served according to the record, a quarter of a century in His Majesty's army; and furthermore, that he was a worthy man in every sense of the term;

sober, industrious and economical. Such was the testimony of three persons with whom I conversed about him during our visits elsewhere, at three different places. And I thought of the homes I knew, in which once dwelt the pensioners of our Revolutionary war and the war of 1812; bountifully supplied by our Government. And one of our party broke a long silence during our drive from the school house—(in which I am sure we were all thinking of the same subject)—by an exclamation: "Well, thank God! I was born in or have become a citizen of the Republic of the United States. Our veteran soldiers who have been anywise disabled in service, and their wives and widows, have some care that is worthy of the name, at least." And twenty-five consecutive years of service in the prime of life is a "disabling term;" of itself. And we severally proceeded to recount particulars of our visits to English hospitals and asylums for the aged or disabled soldier and sailor and their dependent families. And we felt a much stronger interest than ever before in our own California Veterans' Home.

With all her vaunted public institutions of benevolence, Sweden is behind the two other greatest nations of the earth, in her compensation and oversight, with respect to the old and worn-out servants who have spent the best portion of their lives in her armies; and yet in this very line Stockholm has examples for the world to imitate. She is at the same time lacking and yet in the van.

Is the noted and deplored deficiency in the care for her veterans due more to thoughtlessness than any thing else? We venture to say to his Majesty and the Riksdag: "'Turn your attention of inquiry and reform in this direction."

IX.

IN THE KOLBECK PARISH.

There is the rock, the stone, the "boulder" we would call it, to be seen of all men and women, however incredulously disposed. It lies near the East bank of the Kolbecksa-fed stream, about a quarter of a mile North of this place. When Christianity was first literally planted here, by the erection of a church, the pagan giants who inhabited the mountains above Skansan became incensed at the sound of the holy bells, which the Pope had blessed and sent up to Kolbeck to be mounted and rung. So they determined that they would demolish the steeple and the temple at one fell blow. They picked up one of their pebbles, with which they were accustomed to play base-ball during the Summer twilight, and fastened an iron chain to it by a bolt pushed through a hole drilled in the centre. This chain was originally fifty feet long, and of itself weighed a ton—nearly as heavy as the granite sling-shot itself. With this weapon duly prepared, Gordeswandtorgamism, who had been selected by lot to do the throwing, whirled the boulder around his head five or six times, while the priestess of the clan uttered a prayer and an imprecation over a kettle full of boiling pitch, and then cast it straight toward the hated building. Not for lack of strength, but because of too great caution lest he overshoot his mark—which he had never missed before, according to the annals written and preserved by the chronicler of the tribe of Skansantongorialying—he failed to hit the target; coming short in his ten mile aim a trifle of 1,500 or 2,000 feet.

The rock protrudes a little above the water, and a red log has been laid upon it to warn mariners at a distance. About a score of links of the chain also remain to aid in keeping this one ancient item of history out of the domain of interdicted legend and superstition.

It was part of the inflexible law of the Clan of Giants

spoken of, never to permit a second attempt to do that which any one of their number, after due preparation, had made an unsuccessful effort to accomplish. Hence it was that no new sling was rigged, and hence, doubtless, it was that the tower, if not the whole church at Kolbeck, was spared, and that the sacred summons peals forth on every appointed service day—from the time when the chime was first hung in the belfry until this very hour.

Very few foreign born people will believe this story, because it is true—a complaint against chronic and inconsistent incredulity reaching back to the days of Diogenes;—whereby hangs a point of punctuation. But every patriotic Swede in this region is said to have implicit confidence in the chronicler.

The roads in this district are excellent. Within every 500 yards of distance you will notice piles of gravel by the side of the roadbed, put there by the farmers, as leisure permitted, for use in filling up the highway at broken places when the rainy season shall have arrived. This gravel is taken from knolls, the removal of which will ultimately provide more land for cultivation or open shorter paths for travel. There are evidences of general and judicious management or supervision in all such matters in this vicinity.

The crows in this neighborhood (and I am told that it is the same throughout Sweden) rarely fly in flocks, or in larger companies than four at the most. Usually you see them—I should rather say you meet them, for they are very tame—in pairs. They are not entirely black, as with us, but with the exception of their coal-dark head and wings, their feathers are of a dun or mulberry color. They are a handsome bird, and they will strut close up to you and chatter at you in a very familiar manner.

The magpie is a still handsomer fellow,—a pretty blue and white; and I have seen several that were domesticated like chickens. They have a decided and sometimes, at first, rather alarming liking for the strangers who venture to walk about their premises.

The nightingale is here; I have seen him, but I have not heard him, as I hoped and expected to, in conformity with the Spanish picture. Only an occasional note or bar; apparently as an echo to the lark. There is a dispute here among the peasantry as to the time when the nightingale will sing in full strain and spirit. Some say that he stops with the cuckoo, just before or after midsummer; while others declare that they have heard him at his best as late as the 20th of August.

But the lark is here and in complete voice and ambition. As I write one is circling above me pouring out a flood of melody from his little throat, and I can catch the more distant notes of his brother, who is concealed somewhere in the low-hanging clouds that curtain the sky to the west.

Sparrows abound, of every species; and one kind is of a partly white and partly slate-colored body, with black head and black tail and wing-tips, that suggest a great grandchild relationship to the Swedish crow. They often come to the windows and door-sills when it is raining, and eye the people within and chirp at them with a sense of personal security from harm and with a degree of saucy freedom that at first surprises and always delights you. Swallows are also here, innumerable and impudent. I have many times inquired whether there was any bird-shooting in this district. Many of the little feathered songsters are so tame that it seems natural to suppose that the law forbids the killing of them. Not so. It is said that the officers at the castle frequently take their fowling pieces with them on their way to and from the riding-house, and on a slight detour they bring down sparrows enough for a mess.

Great quantities of fish are caught in the Malaren; but I have not seen a single specimen in this neighborhood, although I have been most of the time during the past ten days close to some inlet from the lake. But I have talked with fishermen, who say that they annually pay a thousand of our pounds of the best fish for the privilege of drawing nets along a mile of the lake shore. A. P. Anderson of Dovon says that the poor hereabouts cannot afford to have fresh fish at any season of the year, except they are in the business of catching or unless they take the risk of "borrowing." The principal fish market in this district is at the city of Westeras, and to that place and Stockholm go large shipments from this end of the lake every day in the year.

One ox harnessed to a low cart is pulling past the porch in which I sit. I call out to the driver, a boy of about fourteen years, and ask him what he has for sale. He is going to Stromsholm with a load of vegetables. He has one small sack of new potatoes, and three large sacks of rutabaga turnips. He expects to get a kroner and a half for his potatoes —a kroner for two gallons, as they sell potatoes here—and six kroners for his turnips. I should judge that they would be worth nearly that sum in San Francisco to-day. We ask him how much he gets a day for his services. "Fifty ore"— about thirteen cents. And he works how long? From 4 in the morning until 8 at night.

The turnips are of the coarse variety. We say that we suppose they are cooked by boiling? And we proceed to try to inform a landlady about Colonel Sellers. We assure her that it is quite within the Swedish vein—with respect to which she at first expresses doubt—to enjoy the humor of the "Gilded Age," as is shown from the fact of its translation into the language of this kingdom. These turnips are boiled; but they are not prepared by those who buy them for "eat wholesale" —such is the phrase. O, no. The poor could not afford that. These rutabagas are cooked for soup. One of these, about two and a half inches in diameter, is allotted to about three quarts of water. Colonel Sellers' essay on the value of the turnip as a sufficient staple for family diet would be no-joke among the masses of womankind and mankind in this section of the kingdom of Sweden.

Of the many tales of peasant life drawn out by the best endeavor that we could make for such a purpose, at our cottage visitations—obtained sometimes by repeated visits and the manifestation of such kindly interest as was calculated to remove suspicion of a merely passing or any sinister or morbid curiosity—I will take the case of Carl Erickson for a specimen and epitomizing statement.

Carl and family live in one of the houses of a great estate, whose borders lie in Kolbeck and in at least two other adjoining parishes. The cottage is about 28 feet long by 14 feet wide. It is of one story and divided into two rooms. The room occupied by the family is about 15 by 14 feet. Out of this space comes the chimney and the blacksmith-forge-like fireplace which is at least four feet square. In the alcove or recess—partially partitioned off—occupying a space of about 6 by 4 feet, is a loom. There is one bed, 2 1-2 wide by 6 feet long; one wooden settee or bench, on which another bed can be laid; one table, 4 by 2 feet; and one chest of three drawers, occupying 1 1-2 by 4 feet. There are two wooden-bottom chairs, and two or three stools and a cradle. The other portion of the house has a separate entrance, and is used as a storeroom, a pantry for milk, etc. There are two underground cellars, about two rods distant from the house, in which potatoes and other vegetables may be kept during Winter, safe from the frost; and one rod beyond these is a barn, capable of holding a cow and calf and a pig and a dozen or score of chickens, and hay enough to feed the animals during the severest portion of the snowy season. On about a quarter-acre of the land allowed this man—for that is all he can possibly utilize out of the ground in his reservation—he has planted potatoes, as he always has done since he became a householder here. He has the privilege of gathering wood for fuel from the groves and forests of the estate—no more than is necessary; and he is required to be as economical as he can be in its use. He must obtain his supply of firewood at times when his services are not required on the estate-work; which means practically that he must do this out of regular working hours. He has pasturage for a cow, and he may glean hay enough—or his wife may—to keep the cow during the Winter. A half barrel of the poorest quality of mackerel is also a part of his "privilege."

Now, I think you will be apt to say that Carl has probably a good average opportunity, for this section, to support his family and enjoy life. That is my judgement, at all events; and I am here on the spot to see and to compare. You only need to know his money-wages and the number of his household, in addition to what I have already stated, in order to have a full basis for reading the subjoined conversations.

Carl is a man of 43 years, with a wife and four children. The eldest child is 16, the next is 14; having lost three bairns by death, his youngest are aged respectively 5 years and 2 years. This sober, industrious man has resided on his estate since boyhood; and here he has married and struggled to support his family as best he could. He receives 115 kroners a year for his labor; that is about $30. He has his house barn, cellar, a quarter-of-an-acre potato patch, the privilege of gathering fuel and gleaning hay sufficient for his necessities, a quarter barrel of brine-preserved fish, and 115 kroners a year in money.

Carl makes no complaint; he answered our questions in a way that indicated no grinding sense of poverty or want. He rises at four in the summer and works until 8 o'clock at night, with half an hour for breakfast and an hour for dinner. His breakfast, as well as his dinner, is sent to him at the stables or on the field. In the Winter he must put in twelve hours work per day; and he may be, and often is, required to do extra work, over and above this recorded time for labor, on the call of his foreman.

Carl's wife, a little woman of about her husband's age, who looks as if she was worn to the bone with hard work and suffering, can and does make the real revelation. "Clara" is her name. These people know and call each other by their Christian names, throughout the parish. We opened the conversation at the second or third interview.

"You have a good husband, Clara?"

She replied: "As good as ever a woman was blessed with."

"I suppose you have always considered yourself in as comfortable circumstances as a majority of families on the estate?"

She replies: "As well off as many; as well off, probably, as the most of the families that have an equal number of children."

"Do you and your children have plenty to eat?"

"Oh, we are very thankful for what we have."

This evasive answer to this question was repeated several times, as we came to put it in different forms during the successive visits. It was at first the conclusion of the conversation on this subject.

Omitting much necessary preparatory and oft-repeated

questions and answers, which were leading to a better acquaintance, and to a confidence sufficient for a free and full statement and confession, we come to the detailed facts of suffering.

"Have you ever known what it was to actually feel pain from hunger?"

She answered: "Oh, yes; many times."

"Have your children ever cried for bread which they really needed?"

"Oh, yes; many times. But I have done the best I could to apportion out what we had to give them and keep absolute starvation from the house."

"This is the season of the year when you are best supplied?

"Yes."

"Haven't you an abundance to eat just now?"

"I myself always portion out the food with care."

"You don't answer the question, Clara; you reply evasively. I am not making these inquiries of you for an unworthy motive. I am not going to inform the superintendent of the estate of what you tell me, and at the same time I do not wish you to say anything to which he could justly take any exception. I do not wish to torture you; though my pressing these questions may seem to indicate something like that. I am seeking to know the actual condition of this peasantry class, of which you yourself think that your family is a fair sample."

She answered again: "Well, I will tell you that I have to apportion our meals carefully. The father has to be provided for first, as he must work, and his strength must not fail. I have to see to that. If it was left to him, or if he understood the matter altogether, he would not take what was necessary that he should have to keep him up. Little enough he gets at the best: but he must be served first. Then the youngest children come next; then the two oldest. Then, if there is anything left, it is my portion."

"But if there is nothing left, Clara?" we say to her.

The woman burst into tears, and throwing her apron over her head cried out, "O, God be praised! I have had the strength to go without anything, and not let my husband or children see me weep. At many such times He has often, in answer to my prayers, given me such support that I have not felt dizzy, as I confess I sometimes have done after having gone twenty-four hours without a morsel of food."

"But," we persist, "have you got plenty now—right at this present time? To be candid with you, Clara, you look as though you had not had enough to eat this season. We may not judge you correctly about that; but we have thought so."

She answered, "Well, if you have to portion out a cow's milk for three meals and six persons, when it is not really more than enough for half that number of persons for two meals, you must stint, of course."

"I understand; you are on short allowance all the while; you have not had what you reasonably require for food to-day."

She said again, "We are all very thankful for what we have had."

"Clara, I feel almost ashamed to urge you to tell me anything more, or to speak with greater explicitness about your way of living; but it is very generally supposed in the nation where I come from, that since there has been so great an emigration from Sweden to America as has taken place during the past few years, there is no actual want among your laboring people; except such as is brought about by dissipation or wasteful improvidence. Now I want to know if that is really so or not. I see these broad acres which should yield an abundant supply of food for all the people living here, and I would naturally think that the report to which I have just referred was true,—unless I had positive testimony to the contrary. And, besides, as you are a very intelligent woman, I wish to mention to you the fact that some professional book writers who have visited this country during the last ten years have represented in their books, which have had large circulation in the United States and in England, that there was no lack of food in any sober, hard-working man's house in Sweden. And this district has been spoken of in this very connection; and; if I am not very much mistaken, this very estate has been mentioned as the place of residence of a peasantry that were happy and contented, because, among other reasons, they had good wages and an abundance of good food."

"I have been happy in the love of my husband and children," replied Clara, "and I hope I have been, or will be, forgiven if I have unjustly murmured at any time; but now that I understand your motives and object better, I am free to say that those persons who had written as you tell me have not told the truth. They probably did not mean to tell falsehoods, but they certainly did not tell the truth."

"Now you see, Clara, the necessity or propriety of my asking you the questions which I have repeated so many times. If the truth is not worth knowing at all with respect to this matter, it can be only, or best, obtained and spread abroad in the way I purpose following. I myself have believed these rose-colored sketches of modern Swedish life among the working classes until I came among them. I thought that most of the misery of this kind of which we have been speaking, that existed in Europe, was to be found in Ireland at the present time, and I expected to write about such matters from there alone."

"I cannot say that we have been on the verge of starvation," said Clara; "but I have many, many times thought that we would be soon. Last Winter was the hardest season I have ever known. I thought that the emigration would be a benefit to our people who remained here, as I have heard it said that it would be. But the wages of my husband have not been raised, and prices have not come down for articles that we must buy at the store. Last Winter we had a present of some American potatoes from a friend—a few gallons. And just before our supply was exhausted I went into the cellar and counted those that had been given to us by our friend for seed. He didn't know that we needed any potatoes for any other purpose. Then I knelt down and prayed to God that we should have strength to resist the temptation to eat these potatoes. But it came so hard upon us that we had to eat them; little by little they had to go! And I often wondered during the Winter if I should ever know the time when I could eat all the potatoes I wanted. Wasn't that a ridiculous idea?"

This is precisely what Clara said. We asked: "What did you have for breakfast this morning?"

"For breakfast we have had a little barley meal, boiled so as to make porridge, and the youngest children have had a little milk with their portion."

"What did your husband have?"

"I sent his breakfast to him."

"What did he have this morning?"

"I sent him some of the porridge and two pancakes."

"Clara, did you have anything at all to eat for breakfast this morning?"

She hesitated, but we were relentless, and the question was repeated. "Did you yourself have anything to eat this morning, Clara?"

"I did not," she replied.

"Do your children or does your husband know that you had nothing to eat this morning, for breakfast?"

"They do not."

"What did you have for dinner?"

"My husband had a loaf of bread [a loaf of Swedish bread weighs about a quarter of a pound of an English pound] and a small piece of mackerel and a little mush."

"What did the children have?"

"They had half a loaf of bread, a little mackerel and a bowl of mush and milk."

Clara's bowls hold about half a pint.

"What did you have?"

"I am going to eat my dinner presently."

We said: "It is now 2 o'clock in this day, on the 14th of July, in the midst of the harvest season, when food is supposed to be cheapest and in greatest variety, and most accessible, and you have not broken your fast yet?"

She replied: "I am going to eat a half loaf of bread soaked in some juice from the mackerel."

The mackerel had been boiled, and she was going to dip her bread in the water in which it had been prepared for the father and the children.

"Clara, from what you know of this neighborhood, do you mean to say that the majority of the working people in this district are as poorly provided with the necessaries of life as you are and have been of late?"

She replied: "I think we are better off than some, which should make us thankful for what we have. Of course I don't know how all my neighbors live, but I believe that the majority of them are not any better off than we are or have been during the past ten years. Maybe I am wrong, though."

"Could you give me the name of any neighbor that you know positively is or has been within the last few years as poorly provided with food as you have been—who has suffered as much?"

The reply was: "I am satisfied that there are many such, but of course I don't absolutely know from personal observation."

"But from what any member of a household has told you?"

She said: "From that and from other sources of information."

We asked: "Name another such a sufferer."

She replied: "I will not do it."

"Why not?"

She said: "Go and ask them, as you have asked me. Maybe they will tell you. O, I could name them; but don't ask me to do that."

We said we did not intend to use her name if we made further inquiries, and we appreciated her sensitiveness in declining to point out as requested; but we would like to get two or three more witnesses, and as our time for examination was limited we thought she might aid us in finding additional evidence at once.

"Well," she replied, "not now; at some other time,—perhaps."

We asked, "When did you have fresh meat last?"

"We have not had a mouthful of fresh meat since last Fall."

Here Clara's husband came up and confirmed this last statement. For eight months not one of the household had tasted fresh meat.

"Our cow was dry for sixteen weeks this year," said Clara, "which has contributed to make it very hard for us to get along. We had a cow two years ago that was not dry more than two or three weeks at a time. But she would not allow any one to come near her or to remain in the lot where she was, except myself, so we had to sell her."

"How did you manage about seed potatoes when your stock was eaten up, this last Spring?"

"It was February when the last of the American potatoes were eaten up. Carl borrowed some money, which we owe yet, to pay for the poorest kind of potatoes, which we used for planting this season. We would have had a great deal better crop, I suppose, if we could have saved the American potatoes for seed."

We asked, "Have many persons gone to America from this section?"

"A dozen or more. All that could get away, I think," said Clara, with a laugh that was almost cheerful. And then came a quickly following, irrepressible sigh.

"Would you like to go to America?" we asked.

"Oh, yes; but we can never get enough money together to do that."

"But your husband might go and in a few years bring you out after him."

Clara gave a quick look at her husband as I spoke, and her face became very white and thin:—it was pale and pinched enough ordinarily, heaven knows.

"Don't be alarmed, Clara! I am not going to take your husband away from you. But I have just learned that an emigration agency has been established at Gothenburg, and I will leave you the card from that agency that has been sent to me. Perhaps you may manage at some time in the future to raise money enough to pay your husband's passage, not only to America, but to the best part of America—the United States."

"There is nothing about farm work or horses that Carl does not thoroughly understand," said the devoted wife; and a gleam of pride mingled with her other indications of countenance as she looked steadily at her husband.

"Your children are at work. I forgot to ask about that?"

"Yes; the boy earns forty ore a day for driving." That is about ten cents.

"And the girl?"

"Sometimes she earns the same, by raking hay, during the Summer season. She has just been confirmed, and will probably go out to regular service next year."

X.

THE STROMSHOLM VARDSHUS FAMILY AND NEIGHBORS.

Every window of every sitting-room and bedroom in every house in this country, so far as we have been able to note, is filled with flowers. From the highest to the lowest, from the oldest to the youngest, there seems to be a passionate admiration and love for the blossoming plants. Looking right across the inn yard—from the Stromsholm Vardshus—to the front of Froken Stackelberg's rooms, I can count three pots in one window, four in another and six in another. The Froken has three different varieties of geranium. She has verbenas in two of the windows, and an oleander that bears beautiful pink flowers very much like a rose in texture and perfume. A heliotrope is near the doorway, and its delicate aroma is so penetrating that I became conscious of our proximity to it before we had passed through the hall that leads to her parlor. It scented the whole building, as you may say. Madame Hoglin, widow of the late Postmaster at Stromsholm, who resides on the north border of the Castle park, has a St. Joseph's lily that would be a prize for any of our California conservatories. She has also a bleeding geranium that has exquisitely tender veins and hue. These adornments from and of nature's choicest ornamental plants you might expect in the homes of the noble or the rich, but they are everywhere in Sweden. I only instance these two places because one is before me and the other has been recently visited by us.

Why, yes: it should have been mentioned that Carl Erickson's poverty-stricken cottage gives no evidence of distress through a lack of the usual possession and display of flowers of exceeding beauty. And from the sailor in the forehatch of the canal-boat on the Gotha to the Barons waiting in the outer chamber of Oscar II., there is the nosegay or the rose in the botton-hole or hat-band: testifying to the universality of this taste and affection for the garland or blossom—in man as well as woman—the former exhibiting this interest and pleasure without strut or pretense, and the latter enjoying the sight of their plants with a simple but unmistakable enthusiasm of delight. So, indeed, it should be in the land of Linnæus.

This section of country, from the mouth of the Stromsholm Canal to the paper mills, a distance of seven or eight miles, strikingly resembles Sonoma Valley in many particulars. Here there is greater breadth at one place; but save in respect to this swelling out to a circle midway between the Malaren and the line of Kolbeck, and in spite of that, the likeness is so remarkable that I cannot forbear alluding to it; and I tell these good people of it;—adding the statement that our Sonoma meadows are never covered with snow and are green a larger portion of the year. " Ja sa !!" Precisely.

Froken Stackelberg is especially interested in such comparisons and in any enlightening information in regard to the "glorious climate," remarkable fruit crop, fast horses and high railroad fares that characterize the Golden State. It is strange that she should manifest such a strong concern about all our affairs; a curiosity that cannot be feigned, because it is searching on lines that show her thoughtful consideration in the premises. An omniverous reader, a systematic and acute examiner is Froken Stackelberg. And she is more worthy of description than any landscape on the face of the earth. She is a curiosity and a marvel in herself.

Here is the daughter of a Finnish nobleman, 79 years of age, living in one small suite of rooms at one end of a royal tenantry building belonging to the castle property, having charge of the porcelain, linen and silver of a royal residence—what is left here of such articles—and radiating an influence that is most precious for the community and kingdom. "Noble" she certainly is, by birthright, as the titles ran in this country 75 years ago. She can trace them with great genealogical precision. Her mother was of noble descent, still further ennobled by her first and second marriages. Once she owned 2000 acres of land of the finest quality—nobility of soil proprietorship, if you please!—with a mansion that approached the size and dignity of a chateau. Her family lands and houses, and a high-walled and iron-gate-guarded grave, we have seen and can give evidence upon; all being of ancient estate which was in Froken Stackelberg's mother's possession in 1799. Bad management, not to speak of dissipation on the part of her father, resulted ultimately in financial ruin to his widow and child;—poverty coming upon them shortly after his death in the service of the Swedish navy. Noble she is: with the portraits of three field marshals hanging behind her, as she sits on the sofa from which, as from a throne, she bids you welcome in the Swedish, French or Italian dialect.

But "noble" Froken Stackelburg certainly is, in an "American sense," as she was kind enough to phrase it in our presence a few hours ago. For with the little patrimony left, and out of the small stipend that is granted her by the Government, she does a vast amount of judicious charitable work; and for that, and for her valuable counsel and advice to all worthy, inquiring friends, she is renowned; she is beloved wherever there is personal knowledge of her daily deeds of charity and her sentiments with respect to the true standard of royal humanity.

"If there ever was a noble lady by right of blood," said Froken Stackelberg to us, as we sat beside her bountiful board, "my mother was of high degree: but in her day of prosperity and pride, as well as when she came to experience the reverses of fortune, she always instructed me in the truth that there was only *rank* in the names of earthly nobles, and that all *that* ended with the grave; only intrinsic merit of character will amount to anything in our favor beyond that. This will doubtless seem to you an unnecessary concession," she continued, "if not a plain, simple statement of fact, and that only, Monsieur; and perhaps I had forgotten that I was addressing an American. But in Sweden, where there has been so much abject homage to a titled class whose representatives have not always been deserving of any man's respect, the instruction to me was valuable and was needed. Of course, I have long ago found out its truth in my own observation, and from the teachings of God and my own conscience. But I think it well, sometimes, that such declarations should be made by one of my inheritance."

And Froken Stackelberg was charmed with the verse which reads and rings :

> "Howe er it be, it seems to me
> 'Tis only noble to be good ;
> True hearts are more than coronets,
> And simple faith than Norman blood."

If you get an invitation do not fail to go and take tea with Froken Stackelberg, when you come to Stromsholm. As the Froken proclaims herself "partial to, and delighted with, people who speak English"—to use her own oft-repeated phrase—and as I make due report of her announcement, it is to be expected that at least those Californians who shall hereafter travel this way and stop at the Stromsholm Vardshus will avail themselves of the advantages and pleasures of such a call.

The Statcarter or Dagman tenement houses and the large dwelling in which the gardeners and watchmen and housekeepers of the castle or chateau reside—a community of residents often seen—and the inns in this part of Sweden, very closely resemble each other, and may be described, so far as their exterior is concerned at least, by the same sentences. It is a two-story building with eight feet height for the ground-floor story and six feet for the upper story. The roof sweeps down from the apex, which is twenty-five or thirty feet high, with such a bow-fashion curve, and turns up at the eaves with such a graceful line, that a little one in our party described it appropriately as making a flourish like the shaded part of a copy-book "S." The length of the building is usually about 200 or 250 feet, and the width about twenty-five feet. There will be separate entrances for each fifty feet, and from the halls that dip half way into the structure, doors will lead on either side, close to the front wall, to a stairway landing and—as in the case of inns and the houses of the well-to-do—past that to the (first) sitting or dining-room, and then (second) to the parlor. At the end of the hall will be the kitchen of the inn or of the tenant best able to have a large cooking apartment. In such case the kitchen extends the width of the hall and runs to one side as far as the width of the stairway landing, or perhaps the sitting-room space. In other cases the kitchen occupies only the part in the rear of the dining or sitting-room and the stairway landing. Where there is a second story the stairs invariably wind around half a circle so that you come at your entrance hall at the stair-landing, (on the first or second,) directly before a window looking into the yard in front of the house. In the inns there are precisely the same partitions above as below; but in the tenantry's houses there is, of course, more sub-division; usually obtained by running a narrow passageway through the centre of the building. Rooms are sometimes, but rarely, partitioned off in the attic. There the servants sleep in the Summer or during the warmest season of the year. The ceiling is not boarded or plastered. The floor of the first or second story and of the attic, laid upon timbers that are at least six by eight inches, and not more than three feet apart, is, together with the beams, painted white or whitewashed, and the walls are papered. The whitewash in this country is so prepared that it does not mark clothes that may come in contact with it.

The better class of houses are painted inside and out every two years, and the amount of scrubbing that is done on the floors and windows and sills and every portion of woodwork is (I was going to say) distressing. Early or late in the inns in this district you will almost constantly see or hear the scrubbing-brush in motion with such emphasis that you know it is the planks that are being washed. On particular days, as on Saturday and Wednesday at this tavern, there is the nearest approach to an uproar that I have heard about the establishment; all on account of a small army of maids at work with brooms, brushes and pails filled with suds. There is no corner left without special attention, and that directly from the hand of the servant. There are no mops in Sweden. Such implements for distant approaches to dirt with a washing-cloth or rag would not suffice here; and observing the absence of our familiar household weapon of warfare against the dust and stains of our American habitations, I made inquiry as to the remaining untraversed districts of this country, and am able to set down the very important wholesale statement as above. As with respect to Ireland and the snakes, so here may it be written: "SWEDEN AND MOPS. There are no mops in Sweden."

But the noise in cleansing that is daily heard is not distracting—not in this inn, this vardshus, where there is every possible care taken not to disturb the guest when he is within —save in the way of inviting him to his meals and the like. You are asked in the morning at the hour when it will be discovered somehow — I don't know how—that you are awake, if you will have your coffee; and the mid-day meal (dinner) will be announced in the same pleasant way. But when you leave your chambers, at any time from 5 to 9 in the morning, your departure will be noticed and such advantage taken of it that the work of the servant is completed before you return, although you may be absent not more than a quarter of an hour. The sweeping, dusting, first bed-making and the arrangement of wearing apparel (the mattresses are piled together in the morning and spread for your rest in the evening) is all "done in a jiffy," and yet neatly and thoroughly done, by the girl appointed to attend upon you.

Not only upstair service but all cooking is done by women, and mostly performed by women that in age and action come under the denomination of "girls." The chambermaids are as spry as kittens though by their countenances you might judge some of them to be 30 years of age and over. And the young women of Sweden like this kind of work.

Here is "our girl," Anna Jawzan, who is as lively as a bird on the hop and merry as a cricket. She need not work out; the landlady has told us so repeatedly. But she loves to work, and especially delights in this class of labor. Last hiring-day her mistress advised her to go home, because her parents could well afford to support her and desired that she should return, but although she loved them dearly —and partly on this very account—she begged the privilege of remaining. Anna says she loves to work and to earn money with which to buy presents for her folks; and as they have no need of her at home, she thinks it is right and best that she should serve where she can be useful and earn wages. She has a friend who has gone to Marysville, California; and this friend will be married to a gentleman who was charmed by a photograph of the maiden he is to wed.

Anna is greatly pleased with the compliment that is paid her by the intimation that she has only to send her photograph to the United States or allow it to be placed on exhibition in San Francisco to bring to her address a flood of offers of heart and hand. She evidently likes to revive this subject for conversation. The compliment is deserved. But all the while Anna says she is content and very happy where she is. She gets 60 kroner (or about $17) a year, and her board and lodging;—for work during at least sixteen hours, in the day with the privilege of eating her meals at odds and ends of "made" leisure time. The members of our party are unitedly of the opinion that she does not put full faith in our statement that she could get as much per month in California for her services—if she obtained a situation where she worked as faithfully as here—as she now received as annual payment in full.

In the matter of cooking I am sure that most Americans will feel that they are approaching home when they change from England to Sweden. It is not well, perhaps, to talk very much upon this subject, lest one be suspected of epicurianism or of a chronic disposition to complain. But the risk of that private criticism in the mind of the reader must be borne by the conscientious writer. It is one of the things to be noted, for the sake of information and with a view of joining hands with experienced and with future travelers on a crusade of public sentiment against the atrocious cooking that is the cause of so much relative misery nowadays, endured by patrons of the restaurants of London. As already recorded the cook in Sweden is a woman ; and may God bless her, wherever she is. She is not as artistic, perhaps, as our friend of French extraction, but within the limits of her school she is a minister to health and happiness. She does not revel in grease ; and her white bread and her cakes do not present to you crust-covered balls or parallelograms of sour paste or demoralized dough.

But of all cooks with whom I have made a middag and sexsor acquaintance, and for whom the female members of our party have formed a personal friendship Anna (favorite name here) of the Stromsholm Vardshus is the most highly esteemed. Sweet little bit of a body that she is How she can fly around that range, and prepare and lay down and turn over and season and serve up the meats and vegetables for the dish and platter !

Do not mention it please, but here is another case of anxious desire to emigrate to America ; and that would be a wise head over the household of abundant provision, that should send out a ticket with an engagement contract-paper for re-imbursing service, to Anna, queen of the kitchen at the Nyckterhet Vardshus, near the Castle of Eleonora at Stromsholm, Sweden

And this inn, taken altogether? It is a home. There is peace and comfort that come from large airy rooms, good beds, the best of simple food, excellently cooked, neatness, order, alert attendants, and, with all and in all and above all, the sense of a welcome that is unaffected, unpretending, unobtrusive, heartily sincere. Glad to see you. Glad for a very reasonable sum to entertain you, and give you her own attention in a hospitable hostess way—is the landlady of this stopping place for the pilgrim, this rest for the weary. Last year she was housekeeper, and now she has a ten-year lease as proprietress of the establishment, and there will be many additions every year to the number of those who shall join in praising the administration of the handsome Hostess Marie Anderson; whose likeness is hereunto appended:—

LANDLADY OF VARDSHUS.

XI.

STROMSHOLM TO VESTANFORS.

THE Stromsholm Canal, which was constructed in 1777-95, and straightened and enlarged in 1842-60, starts from Lake Malaren, at a point about one mile distant from Stromshold Castle. With the intervening locks and river passages the distance by the boat from the first lock to Smedjebacken is about sixty of our miles. In this distance an ascent is made of 327 feet. This is twenty-seven feet higher than the highest point above the level of the sea reached by the Gota Canal. This elevation is reached at Lake Vefungen, about fifteen miles from Smedjebacken. To make this trip from Stockholm, you go on board one of the boats that ply on the canal at 8 o'clock at night, and leaving the Capital city at 11 P. M. and traversing Lake Malaren arrive at the mouth of Stromsholm canal at 5 in the morning. At the first lock, or at the bridge on the road that leads from the castle to the house of the Superintendent of the royal estate of Stromsholm, passengers get on or disembark.

At the first lock, distant from the Vardshus half a mile, we stepped on board at the hour named, and began the journey. We had no exalted expectations in connection with this day's travel, so far as the pleasure of beholding charming scenery is to be considered, for neither guide books nor the descriptions of the passage which we chanced to hear or which we could elicit from others, indicated anything unusually fine in landscapes or the views of water and sky to be seen along the route. So there was a surprise in store for us, as the panorama unfolded was in many points equal to that given on the Gota inter-lake sections, while the hight and water plunge of the double locks was in some respects peculiar and new to us, and is and must ever be gratifying to witness. You never tire of looking at a steam engine, and especially at a locomotive in motion, or at a ship under full sail. There are sights that im-

prove upon repetition—grow upon you like a great edifice;—
and the same may be and must be said of such spectacles as
are presented at Skansen and at other places where the flood is
let in upon your boat from second story traps.

Five o'clock is an early hour for rising at any season of
the year; but when the sun does not set until eight, and the
twilight holds bright until eleven, you are apt to cultivate
a habit of late retiring, which makes it impossible for you to
sleep before midnight. So it seems extremely cruel on the
part of the servant girl when you are first conscious of the
fact that she has pulled off your bed clothing and is shaking
you and commanding you in a most imperative voice to get
up and dress, and take your coffee and your departure.

The morning is inclined to be chilly, although it is the 21st
day of July, "the dew is on the rye," and there is a light
mist coming up from the marshy ground by the side of the
canal, in the upper portion of this great valley. The lock is
only a quarter of a mile distant from the inn by the across-
lots path, and we are there just in time. Here we step on
the *Pius*—the smallest steamboat on our travel calendar
page as yet—as it rises in the long narrow cistern to a level
convenient for the reception of passengers. Very slowly
through this portion of the water road, for the distance of
half a mile, our small vessel (of 38 tons measurement) pushes
its way until we reach the junction with the Kolbackso, when
the "go ahead" lever is swung to the last notch by the
Captain himself.

As we are familiar with every point in this end of the plain,
our attention is devoted with more than usual keenness and
exclusive care to the officers, men, maids and passengers that
are to be our companions during the next eighteen or twenty-
four hours. Captain Frans Emil Talen is a man of about
thirty years of age, with a countenance that showed intelligence and a spirit of humor. It was easily to be seen at a
glance that he did love a joke. And when he heard a child
in our party address some words of English to us, shortly
after we climbed upon the steerman's deck, he left the wheel
to his principal sailor (as he described him) and came up to
us and said in English, "Can this little girl tell me how old

she is ?" It transpired that he had been three years in the English merchant-ship service, and had touched at Charleston, S. C., and had sailed around the Horn and up the Pacific Coast as far as Callao. Acquaintanceship, or rather intimacy, was at once established; and there has been another one (No. 3 !) of those boiled dinner parties which a Yankee will frequently enjoy in these days, in travelling on the Swedish steamers at sea, or on the lakes, rivers or canals of the kingdom. We have been told that we shall not always find courteous officers, but we have yet to meet with an exception to the rule.

The small vessel is every inch economized. Sixty-two feet long and sixteen feet wide, she has no room to spare; and the curiously ingenious manner in which space is made, as it were, affords constant little surprises to the younger members of our company. Even we, of older date, often are reminded of and inclined to repeat the ejaculation of the queer old clerk of the great criminal lawyer that is portrayed in "Great Expectations":—" Halloa ! here is a breadbox !" " Halloa ! here is an ale-bottle case !" "Halloa ! here is the Captain's office !" Doors open in sharp corners and disclose shelving for linen; seat-bottoms turn out to be lids, beneath which there is a great stowage of preserved fruit and pickled edibles of many sorts; and when you imagine that you have gotten inside of a four by six feet dining-room that has no possible interior, lo, and behold ! panel after panel is pushed aside, as occasion requires, and a series of cupboards exhibited, to an amount and in a way that suggests the conjurer's tricks of multiplied platters and inexhaustible pitchers. Since the era of canal boating such devices have been unquestionably the frequent subject of human invention, but this specimen of area-saving for useful purposes is entitled to mention for its cunning and its completeness. We were continually arriving at and departing from the ultimate inquiry as to where else on or about this vessel any other barleycorn of space could be utilized.

The cabins are under the forecastle; and while they are not as spacious or comfortable as a room of similar name on the Mississippi or Fall River boats, they, too, provoke wonder at the skill of the planner and the success of his cubbyhole draughtmanship. The big "sights" of nature and of art, questions of state and the appearance and speech of the distinguished men of the different nations, do not alone form proper subjects for observation and remark on the part of the traveller, my friends; but even these little matters become at times full of interest, and seem to a wandering note-taker from California well worthy of a touch of mention, for the instruction of his readers. Yankee whittling knack is here, also; and my brethren of Connecticut and Massachusetts and Vermont must look out for their honors at the next great international exhibition, where Stromsholm and Gotha canal boats, as well as a racehorse Malaren-lake pleasure steamer (an improvement on the one exhibited at Philadelphia), will surely be on the platform as competitors, for award. The carpenter schools now attached to almost every "primary" and public academy in this kingdom may have something to do already with this production of Wolcott-desk vessels, for public transportation on the inland waters of Sweden.

The sound of the American mower is heard in the land as we plow into the Kolbackso Channel. I know, my dear Captain, the brand of the Stockholm Foundry is on the frame and on the sheath and on the blade, but "that ere consarn" was got up in the United States of America. And if our folks do steal books in the absence of an international copyright law—which, I grant you, ought to be passed—your folks take (I wouldn't say steal) our brothers' inventions, in spite of the patents obtained for them in your own offices. I have seen this sort of thing before. True, the patent in this particular case may have expired; but you had this article in operation, without compensation or credit, long before the right of the inventor ceased under the Statute of Limitations. And why don't you give him or us better credit for the razor now, when you assert or admit your conscience has no check or burden on account of pecuniary considerations or apprehensions?

As has been noted, this canal was remodeled in the years from 1842 to 1860, and the name of King Carl XV, on iron plates, stares you in the face at every lock. When the work of reparation and enlargement was going on, many convicts were employed at different portions of the line. On our left, in the upper portion of this Stromsholm Valley, there were barracks provided for the accommodation of several hundred men in penal servitude, who had to labor on this neck of the enterprise. It is said that the officers appointed to superintend and direct the work of these men were often very cruel in their treatment of the prisoners, and tales are told of brutality that are of a shocking character. The place where these barracks stood can now be determined only by the memory of

SKANSEN LOCKS.

the older inhabitants of the district, or a very careful examination for foundation abutments of the buildings. As we pass this end of the valley we see the spot often pointed out to us by our van driver, Lagerquist, where the convicts were housed at night during the period of their labor here; and we recollect the fact that he and others testified to us that after dark it was often difficult and sometimes impossible to get a nervous horse past this point except by jumping out of the conveyance and leading him—keeping company with him side by side until the line of the temporary and demolished buildings was left behind. When we expressed incredulity—and especially if we hinted at anything like commiseration for persons afflicted by superstitious imaginations—we were invited and urged to make the passage ourselves at night, with the reins in our hands and without a precise knowledge of the beginning of the haunted ground.

And right here we put it down as a valuable piece of advice to a traveler in this part of the globe: Don't you utter or intimate doubt as to the truth of any fairy or hobgoblin stories that you may be regaled with on your winding ways. In the first place, don't do it, because you may anger your guide and friend, which, of course, you will not wish to do; and, secondly, don't do it, for the reason that thereby you may prevent his telling you many an entertaining tale as you pass along to points beyond.

At Vesterqarn, where there is a large flour mill, you ascend a double lock—the first we had seen in Sweden and among the largest that have been constructed. You are pushed into a granite parallelogram, as a Euclid youth on board described it, and there you are closed in upon for wide hydraulic hoisting. Distant from you 100 feet and more the big flood faucets are opened simultaneously and the yellow but translucent liquid—a 3x2 feet of solid stream on either side—having the appearance of being pressed and yet fringed at the four corners with foam—dashed out with thundering roar. The deep, narrow chasm holds the sound and bears to you the noise of the rush and the fall of the water before there are any echoes; and presently many reverberations are come down upon you in artillery intonations from the upper air. A score of rainbows play on each wall; a brilliant kaleidescope is vouchsafed on this schedule at this season of the year by the aid of his gracious majesty, the morning sun. The guidebook advice is here, as well as elsewhere, to walk around the locks. My peremptory command is to those who like to heed me: Stay on board.

It is not simply the old Erie Canal elevation that you will enjoy at Skansen, where you reach the second of the double-lock locations. For reasons above indicated, stay onboard.

And because, also, of the beauty of the vision you will have when you get up to the level of the gate, this direction is given. Even our worthy and mild-spoken companion, Baedecker, says of this place that it is "the most beautiful point of the picturesque scenery on one of the most interesting canals in Sweden." You fairly rise out of the gloom of the cave through artificial waterfall fireworks (if such a phrase is permissible—which, I know it is not), on to the level of the closely-shaded avenue of trees which border the way for a space of half a mile beyond.

An elevation of 60 feet is made by the last of these double gates, and at Trangfors you are about 140 feet above the Malaren Lake.

A little way beyond Skansen you enter on a small lake (pond, we would call it), in the midst of which is situated the Island of Despair. The whole area of the water is not more than two miles long and a quarter of a mile in width; and nearly in the centre of this sheet is the oblong-shaped acre of land on which the tragedy that gave the title to the place was enacted. With all names and dates, one of our party entertains, or, I should say, horrifies the company on the steersman's deck by telling the story,—as the little vessel glides up to and past the spot.

It was in the year 1858, when the work of rebuilding the canal had been nearly completed, that one of the lieutenants of the force of officers in charge of the laborers, made love to Nedar's daughter (Nedar was a wealthy farmer, living in the neighborhood of Skansen), and won her heart; and "she sweet creature, doted, aye, doted in idolatry upon this military and bewitching man." The parents were bitterly opposed to the suit. They had great influence with the youth's commander, and obtained the orders of the commanding Major or Colonel for the imprisonment of the unwished-for lover, during the time that their fair child attended a ball, that was given on a certain night in jubilee over the completion of a set of granite ways. The daughter apparently acquiesced in the decree of her father, which was well known throughout the camp, to the effect that she should never see the trespassing lieutenant again. On the day before the ball, she was seen to

go into her parents' bedroom and open some of the drawers
in their bureau. But this was not thought a singular action on
her part, as she had often done the same thing before. But
after the tragedy it was known that on this visit to the family
chest she had taken out her father's razor. After the dancing she was missed from the pavillion, and then search was
made for her and her discarded lover, who had also disappeared from his quarters. As neither could be found at once,
there was a general hunt instituted for the pair; the natural
suspicion being that a runaway match had been agreed upon
between the two. No trace was discovered of the fugitives
until the following morning, when they themselves disclosed
their place of hiding by coming to the border of this little
island and singing. As the venerable father, accompanied by
a pose of officers, approached in a boat, his beautiful girl was
heard to exclaim, "What you are to do, do quickly!"
Whereupon her lover cut her throat with the razor she had
taken from her home, and then severed his own jugular vein.

Several witnesses of the dreadful deed are still living on the
shores of this lake, and it is said that they delight in telling
this story, with all its horrible details. So said our narrator,
after having given the account himself with great fullness and
with a boasted precision in pointing out places, etc. This
awful but true tale might somehow be woven into a novel that
is yet to be written, entitled "The Mystery of the Castle of
Stromsholm." The unanimous verdict on our steamer's deck
was to the effect that a fellow who could be guilty of this act
of throat-cutting deserved to have been separately hanged several times over—before the hour appointed for the murder
and suicide.

The ride from Skansen to Ramnas unrolls a panorama only
less beautiful than the similar passage from Motala to Berg,
on the Gotha Canal. The charming little lakes of the Nedre
Nadden and Ofre are reached through a double lock, which
excites all the interest that was experienced in the jaws of the
giants below. At least it may be said that one does not
quickly tire of such majestic handiwork of man.

At Seglinsberg there is a large iron manufactory, close to
the curbing of the gate; and I jumped from the boat to the

sidewalk as we rose to the upper level, and entered the portion of the great house in which the forges were located. A molten stream of iron lava was pouring out of one of the furnaces, or rather, was being blown out, with a hissing noise and a dazzling light; and in company with two or three other passengers I enjoyed the spectacle for several minutes. Then, judging that it was about time to return to the steamer, we walked toward the wharf that was still above. On our way we were met by the Captain and a gentleman by the name of Andersen, introduced as the bookkeeper of the establishment. "Come on with us," said the Captain. "We have been in the works," we replied. "O I am not going to take you into that building," was the response; "come with us and we will show you another part of this manufacturing concern."

We followed up the hill by the side of the building we had visited a distance of about one hundred rods. There on the summit of the ridge, in the midst of a yard 500 feet square, was the covered stone foundation of a house that stood on this spot, and was destroyed by fire nine years ago; and beyond, on the west, we beheld a park, whose avenues, rows of trees, flower beds and bypaths we could trace at a glance— for the grounds from the square on which the building sat was terraced down twenty or thirty feet. In the centre aisle were two large pedestals of granite, on which busts of Linnaeus and Swedenborg had once appeared,—which are now barren of adornment. This scene was so wholly unexpected that no member of our party had a word of inquiry to make, for several minutes after the plateau and garden were shown to us. It was remarked at last, "Well, this does overcome us with a special wonder." Then as a matter of course, there was the simultaneous inquiry as to how came this so. Why was it thus? When will this house be rebuilt? (The charred timbers that composed a part of the covering told of a fire, and some of the stepping-stones had been evidently cracked by heat). The noble building that at once stood here and this adjoining pleasure ground were formerly the property of a wealthy gentleman, who spent nearly all his Summer time and some of winter weeks at this place. He sold the premises to a company after the house was destroyed, and now these grounds were used as a Public Garden. A band of music plays evenings and on Sunday afternoons during the warm weather; ball-platforms which we did not see being provided in an adjoining plot.

No one would dream of his proximity to such a cultivated spot, from the condition and appearance of the village right at and immediately about the sooty landings of Selingsberg. Our Captain and his comrade, the bookkeeper, were evidently accustomed to the trick of leading innocent passengers to this hilltop and enjoying their amazement at the sudden change in the countenance of the country. As much in the temper of fun as in a spirit of courtesy, they acted as guides on this occasion; and they managed to leave many questions unanswered until they were repeated for the tenth time—more or less—with an evident sense of delight at the puzzle that was in their possession and the natural and morbid anxiety on the part of the tardily tongue-loosend company that surrounded them. It was as much of a surprise scene as though you came upon Woodward's Gardens as they now are, after an eighth-of-a-mile walk over the Market-street sandhills that once were.

To show the sentiment, I will record that when we had returned to the boat and resumed our journey, many dwelt for some time in their conversations upon the beauty of the grounds we had been shown, while one sat in rather a sullen mood—this exceptional individual now and then admitting the justice of the eulogiums passed, but at the same time expressing a wish that he might "get even" with the Captain.

"I told you I would show you something you wouldn't be looking for," remarked the Captain, breaking in on the general talk among the passengers, with a manifest appreciation of all that was being said and felt.

"Yes," said a testy, wheezy old gentleman in knee breeches and red-bordered, Delcarlain long coat; "yes, but you led us to suppose that we were going to see something extraordinary in the way of a manufactory; you know you did;" and the irrascible muttered something which I judged must have been the equivalent for "You young scoundrel!"

"Why, *you* ought to have known all about that place; you have been up and down here a dozen times before."

"I didn't know anything about it, and you know I didn't; and when you come to Bolanger I will show you a canal boat running on dry land."

"Now I know what you will give me, beforehand."

"But you will forget it before I give it to you, and you don't know what it is; and what is more, you ain't going to know until I get you where you see it."

Here was an enigma sufficiently outlined to provoke inquiry from all present; and the questions which followed and were pressed upon the ancient, and which he did not answer—not so much as by a hint beyond his orignal statement to the Captain—thoroughly satisfied the worst malcontent of the passage.

This Park must go into the Mysteries of Stromsholm Castle.

After steaming up the Virsbosjo a few miles—as delightful a ride as was ever provided on similar low lines of distant mountain and narrow river and lake-waters alternately set in land and meadow belts and fringings—we swing around the point of a little peninsula and come alongside a wharf at a place described as of some importance and called, according to the sign over the railroad station door, Engelsberg. A short piece of the Stockolm and Storvick Railroad is in sight, and there is a handsome station-house, with a little wharf and platform on the same level with the rails.

This is Engelsberg, so far as appears to the traveler by the Stromsholm Canal, in this year of the world. Here there is unloaded a dozen barrels of petroleum, having an American stamp on them, and as many sacks of rye flour. Here come on board half a dozen gentlemen of large waists, who take a cheerful drink of brandy with the Captain. From hence we make a sudden departure, carrying off one of the men of huge-grown proportions referred to, who is subsequently landed at a point a half mile above Engelsberg by means of a fisherman's boat that is called for by the importunate whistle of the *Pius*.

I saw the merry twinkle in the Captain's eyes when he took the wheel and sung out "framat"—that same flash that was detected when we first greeted him at lock number one, Stromsholm Meadows. And I noticed through the glass the unmistakable lines of appreciative wrath, so to speak, in the face of the fat individual aforesaid; when he tumbled out of the boat into the mud, and tossed a kroner to the boy that paddled his canoe to the worst place there was, anywhere within a quarter of a mile on either side for a boat, to to effect a landing. There is going to be retaliation here, also, without any warning in public. I should like to ride with this Captain for a week; but one would need to be on his guard, lest he himself serve as a victim of misplaced confidence.

Lake Ammanninger is next entered; and here there is an hour's sail that is also of fairyland enchantment. Our sunset pictures here were among the feasts of eyesight, and will remain among the most entrancing recollections of life.

At 9 o'clock we reached Vestanfors, where Bessemer steel is manufactured. It is well known that Swedish iron surpasses in excellence of quality that produced anywhere else. It ought to be known in our country, also, that we would have a very large direct trade with Sweden if our vessels could have reliable return cargoes; as, for instance, bars and implements of iron and steel. Take off the duties on these commodities, and California canned fruits will have an immense market demand and draft direct from this country. A little reduction in prices here for our preserved meats would result in a great sale for our beef and pork that are prepared in sealed cases and everywhere acknowledged to be the best packages of their kind in the world. And our wheat marketing, or direct grain exporting, would be vastly increased—and that immediatley and with rapidly enlarging calls—if the tariff that is on Federal statue books was judiciously revised and reformed.

We visited the great forges at Vestanfors, at which every kind of bar and sheet and roll of iron and steel is manufactured out of the finest ores that can be sorted in this hard, ore-ribbed country. We looked, also, into the little shops where provisions are sold, and found articles which our people most conveniently, profusely and cheaply produce, in the lines already spoken of for sale at a figure that almost prohibited purchases on the part of the middle classes and the pretty-well-to-do mechanic and artisan, to say nothing of the peasantry. And I renewed and intensified my allegiance to the doctrine of a tariff for revenue. Let protection as the first consideration come under that fundamental principle; subject to the estimates that are made first of all, on a liberal calculation, for the expenses of the Federal Goverment. Under such doctrine in law made manifest, the ocean commerce of our country would double in a few years, and American ship building would be revived as a common industry. Citizens living and laboring in California would have great reason to rejoice, because of the vastly enchanced prosperity of all men diligent in mechanical or manufacturing or horticultural or factory or farm labor, or in any of the numerous businesses or pursuits connected with the exporting and importation of goods.

—o—

XII

AT SMEDJBACKEN.

Rising through the three locks into Lake Vefungen, at Semla, we are soon between banks that form a part of the "classic soil of Dalarne." The twilight deepens so that we cannot see much of the scenery that borders Sodra Barken and Norra lakes, so far as detail of view is to be mentioned; but the out-lines against the horizen, now equally luminous at all points in the circle, have a great deal of suggestive beauty. The close-by and the distant black tracery immediately under the heavens, and our first long watching here of the dimly, gently, shining constellations—it seems to us as though we must mention these, if only to hint as to the lovely and inspiring sights which the compass of this volume may not always permit us to attempt to extendingly describe.

When such "darkness" as they possess here at this season of the year—late in July—had fairly settled down on the face of nature we retired to our pocket cabins, but were speedily aroused from sleep by the voice of the Captain speaking to the steersman from the miniature forecastle over our heads, with that fat, unctuous and yet musical drawl and emphasis which he and his brother officer on the *Venus* always put upon the first syllable of the last word of the phrase of caution singing out: Mycket lidet sak̄ta (very little slower); and we then knew that we were close to the wharf at Smedjbacken. Presently that little steamer turns its prow around so that the flames from the great Smedjbacken furnaces that have their mouths at the very head of the harbor, cast a blaze of light into our cabin windows. We look out and see the firemen in their long canvas sacks, with their wire eye-shades protruding half a foot over their foreheads—hydras and gorgons!—and watch the rollers, grasping the big chunks of metal from the door of the last furnace in the range, and by successive racings, passing them under the revolving grooves that gradually reduce them and lengthen them until the thirty feet of thin slats or inch rods are allowed to shoot through the smallest pinchers on their own account;—left contemptuously, as it were, while a jump and running is made by the second set of workmen for the next gob of white-heated and viciously spitting iron! The roar of the blaze, the thumping of the ponderous jaws of the shaping shafts, the apparently desperate leaping around of the furnace men—now rushing at, now fleeing away from, the molten logs at the gates of the ovens or the lessening but out-stretching javelins of light:—here was another midnight spectacle of thrilling and abiding interest. But even while we rest our chins on our bull's-eye windows and gaze at this scene of industry among the Vulcans, tired nature asserts her sway, and we doze and unconsciously drop back upon our bunks in our cabin on the *Pius* by the side of the long low wharf in the town of Smedjbacken.

One cent and a half a mile for a first-class passage, including stateroom, on this trip on this steamer. One cent and a half per mile for passage on the railroads above this line, as far as Falun.

With a little lock, the steamer could ascend to Ludivika, twenty miles North of this place, and without much intervening canal construction, a clear through route for a vessel could be made to Mora. There is not merely a chain, but a network of lakes in this part of Sweden; and the Captain says that it is well known that with no greater difficulties to overcome than were encountered on the Gotha they could all be connected for the purposes of continuous navigation. Next year the company that now owns the *Pius* will put on a swifter boat, by which the passage can be made from Stockholm to Smedjbacken in seventeen hours; which would make about eleven hours from Stromsholm. Travelers will then have no ground of complaint on the score of accommodations on this route—until they get to Smedjbacken.

The boat arriving here early in the morning, as indicated, Smedjbacken can be "seen" in the forenoon; and I advise that the afternoon train hence to Ludivika be taken. At the last-named place there is a good hotel, admirably situated facing the lake; and, as Bædecker writes, it is not expensive. The inn at this place is kept by a widow lady, whose husband died a few years ago, leaving the estate in debt 4,000 kroners. The pecuniary situation of the concern is told to every guest, in so many words, and the size of the reckoning would imply something of the kind, if not a direct syllable was uttered on the subject. The European tricks for raising hotel bills to an extortionate figure have all been imported into Smedjbacken.

Where shall we drive? There are no mountains, valleys or plains of particular interest in the neighborhood. The honest hostler tells us that we can walk to the ridge beyond the church and get a good view of the lake—the best in the country for a Swedish mile around.

The town of Smedjbacken sits on the slope of a gently rising hill, and from the principal street near the the church you look to the Southeast upon Lake Norra, three hundred yards distant, and across a mile width of waters to the low lying forests on the farther shore; and over them to the mountains of moderate hight which at a distance of ten and fifteen miles —as the ridges varyingly run—form the extreme Southeastern background of this pleasing view. A more salubrious or prettier situation for a village it would be a difficult to imagine. The church is planted at the most eligible spot on the plateau that is convenient to the business portion of the settlement, a real fact of statement and not a mere fact of singularity like the remarkable running of the great rivers past large cities in the interior of America!

The churchyard slopes very gradually down toward the lake and approaches within a few hundred feet of the waters. As we pass by in the morning we notice a newly-made grave, and on our returning and inquiring we learn that a recently-deceased young lady of the village is to be buried in the afternoon. The sides of the grave were lined with evergreens and the bottom was already strewn thickly with flowers.

The hotel-van driver took us to the rope walk, which he said was the most important manufactory,—after the iron furnaces. Four boys and three men were at work; the elders spinning, three boys turning wheels and one sorting flax. The boys, who are very adroit in their labor average a kroner (or about 26 cents) a day, for twelve hours work; the men receive twice that sum. The rope was for halters, fishing nets and packing thread, and has a very wide reputation for its excellence. Raspberries are just coming into the market, and the ropewalk men clubbed together and bought four quarts for fifty ore, or 13 cents.

We asked the driver how long he had been in his place, etc. He had been foreman of the stables and coachman for six years and over. His wages were 500 kroner a year, out of which he must pay all his expenses. He said that he could not save anything after he had provided for his family and supplied himself with the fine clothing which he must have in his position. He did not speak in a complaining or murmuring tone at all, but after the manner of the country—frankly in reply to our questions. He wished that he could save enough to go to the United States, but he had nothing "laid up" at the end of the year. Simply this. But he does not like the nobles. On this topic he was strong and even vehement in his expressions. The country he said was cursed with the nobility; such were his sentiments. And among other matters that he mentioned in this connection we noted his statement that the poor in the parish said that the rich and titled could eat all the eels that are caught in the streams. "Those creatures are as much snakes as if they had rattles on them," said our guide and rein-holder; "they act precisely the same as hoopers when you put them in a pot. We have tried them, and we all say that the nobles and big bellies can have all of that kind that there is in the market. That is one luxury that they are welcome to at any rate."

We drove to a large manufactory where every sort of agricultural implement is made—a great shop and turning mill that is called "The American Iron Works." The men were going to dinner at 1 o'clock, and we inspected the machinery at our leisure. We could not learn that any American was on the premises, in the superintendency or foremanship of the place, but we thought that there were abundant evidences of coyping after our foundries and engine-fitting works in New York and San Francisco.

The hour for the funeral was set at five o'clock. We reached the churchyard at half-past four. The grave was already surrounded by a large gathering of women and girls of the village and vicinity; all engaged in conversation respecting the character of the deceased and the circumstances of her untimely death. We soon learned the name of the dead; often uttered with tender and tremulous intonation—Minna Carlson. She was just past her twentieth birthday. She was the handsomest girl in the neighborhood; for a long time the belle the of parish. Her father, who died not many years ago, was a wealthy merchant. She died of a broken heart: deserted by the suitor who had gained her affections and then taken his unannounced departure for unknown lands. Such was the story that we gleaned from the whispering speech of the companions and acquaintances that surrounded her fir-lined and garlanded grave.

It was not until half past five that the great bell began to ring—not toll—signifying the approach of the pall-bearers with the body that was to be laid in this yard this night. After ten minutes of ringing the head of the little procession was seen coming around the corner of the street, at the South and West of the church inclosure. There was no hearse. The coffin was borne by six young men, who held it between them upon broad, black linen straps, which passed over their shoulders. There were no female mourners in the procession; the only relative present at the sepulchre being her brother, the officiating clergyman. He was a young man of not more than 30. He walked to the grave leaning upon the arm of a middle-aged man, who clasped his afflicted friend across the back and held him up, literally at times, during the religious ceremonies. The body being lowered into the receptacle prepared for it, the brother cast a bouquet upon the lid, and many others then and afterwards walked up and dropped their wreathes and bunches of roses and violets where his costlier offering was laid. Then there was the singing of a hymn,—wretchedly sung by the choir master or organist of the parish. Then the young priest raised his voice—after several ineffectual efforts to do so—and read the prayers that are set down for such an occasion. Then he cast the earth upon the coffin: "Earth to earth, ashes to ashes, dust to dust." Then another hymn was sung; and then came a funeral discourse by the brother, uttered amid many interruptions from his own irrepressible sobbing and cries of sorrow from the weeping multitude that crowded around the place of interment. The young man took for his scripture the inquiry as to How it was with the child; the reply that the child was asleep, and the following declaration that it was well with the sleeper. For half an hour the preacher, with earnest eloquence, expounded the doctrine of the text. In his closing passages, where he bade farewell to the sister—"O, how beloved in her own household and by all without the family circle who came to know her well,"—there were no dry eyes in the throng, while the sound of low wailing told of many women and men in close communion of suffering and sympathy with the chief of mourners at this fair one's tomb.

"Farewell, O, my sister! a bride now within the gates of Paradise. Thou knowest how my soul goes out to thee; thou must be conscious—I am sure by reasoning from the memory which our Heavenly Father will leave to you of the blessed past that was in this life—that we are weeping over thy dear remains. You knew that I would be here; you feel, without a sense of pain, but in the bright expectation that comes quick to you of our meeting hereafter, that I am beside your lowly grave. And can'st thou see this troupe of loving friends? And dost thou know that thy precious form reposes upon the fairest flowers of the vale, brought by their hands? O, God! if by nature or infirmity she loved too much within this cold world's orbit, we trust and believe that much will be forgiven. And strengthen me and all of us from this hour, that, as she followed or strove to walk in the footsteps of her Saviour, despite all weakness or infirmities of her nature, we may steadily push forward in the path of devotion and duty. Farewell, O, sister! For nearly a score of years we have been conscious of our companionship in a household of unselfish affection. What sweet memories are ours together, and ours alone, only we and our Saviour know. But we will yet testify of a friendship that passeth human speech to describe, when both shall stand in the presence of our Maker and our Judge. Farewell, O, sister! And yet not farewell. It is the bitter night of our parting; but the day of a never-ending reunion is at hand."

At the moment of uttering his last sentence the brother fell back into the arms that were open to receive him, and the huge, deep-toned bell began again its solemn chorus; and as its mournful, now-muffled cadences were sounding in our ears, the coffin was covered with the sand and the sods of the cemetery; and he, stricken down at last to unconsciousness despite all his manly resolution, was carried by the pall-bearers to his mother's home.

XIII.

DELECARLIA.—SMEDJBACKEN TO LEKSAND.

A BRANCH road comes down from Ludvika to Smedjbacken, a distance of about twenty miles, and from the last named place you can take your railway departure at 5:30 A. M., by stepping on board the train that halts beside the platform at the rear of the one hotel of which Smedjbacken boasts. For a little over one cent a mile we ride to the pleasant village and watering-place of which we have already spoken. At present you must walk a half mile from the branch railway depot at Ludvika to the station on the main line that runs thence to Borlange.

About an hour and a half is occupied in traversing the distance between Lake Vessman and our jumping-off place on the trip through the province of Delecarlia. The railway runs through an interesting section of country and encounters but few formidable obstacles to the engineer. There is, however one tunnel, a quarter of a mile long, about which there was at first much bragging, on the part of a few of our many fellow passengers, who evidently had not been far from their native home, either by travelling or reading. Soon however we were told about the Alps and the Hoosac mountains and the Los Angeles and San Francisco Ranges ("Ja so") and *their* tunnels; so informed by Froken Wanberg and other very intelligent members of the company with whom we here first made an agreeable acquaintance. For some time our nationality was not suspected, but so soon as it transpired, our brighter Swedish chance companions were determined that we should see that *they* at least were not ignorant of the great railroad engineering achievements of the world. The road was bordered most of the way by pine groves of recent and slender growth, while close beside the track the magenta and other wild flowers blossomed in great profusion. We passed several of the largest mines in the kingdom; and in many an opening in the woods the long pumping arms, distant in parallels from each other ten or twelve feet, were seen slowly and irregularly swinging on their tent-stretched pivot rods.

As the train moves down into and at one edge of the vast valley, in the midst of which Borlange is situated, there is presented a magnificent view of plain and far-off amphitheatre mountain sides. The two great churches that are embraced in this landscape form very interesting objects upon which to rest the eye and fix the line of different pictures that you desire to retain in your memory. At Borlange we take what is called a "diligence" and ride three miles to Basta, on the Dalaf; said diligence being a vehicle very much after the style of our smaller emigrant wagons. These conveyances —there are two of them—hold nine persons,—four on each of the side seats and one with the driver; but the measurement is for persons that are under rather than above the average dimensions. One corpulent gentleman threatened to squeeze the complement unmercifully, but on his appearance two young men who had taken seats agreed to walk (as the majority of the passengers did) between the station and the boat-landing; and we had the jolly fat man as the lively joker and story-teller of this short parenthetical ride.

At Borlange we were introduced to a wealthy and widely known Delecarlian who resides near Leksand; whose daughter recently married a German nobleman. At the wedding of his child he had five Governors present, and for six days he kept open house in celebration of the nuptials. He wore the costume of his District, and he desired to have us know —and he impressed it upon us by several repetitions—that his daughter wore the dress of her village when she stood at the altar. A fine looking man was he, and we could well believe the statement that came from every quarter to the effect that his daughter was a beautiful child. [There is a sweet Swedish phrase for this eulogy.]

At Basta, which is a "village" of three houses situated ten rods apart, the little five-ton steamer is waiting for us—a boat about the size of, and with the exception of the cabin in the after part, resembling the boats of the Thames. Passengers have time to run up on the Predikstol, not twenty rods distant from the landing, and enjoy the view to be had there—a landscape that takes in twenty or thirty miles of meadow and forest.

We were two and one-half hours ascending the river Gagness Kyrka; but it is only meager justice to this part of the trip to say that the ride is so pleasant that you regret that the distance is not twice as great as it is. The banks are generally high but the pictures of the river avenues are fine. A few miles above our starting point we pass under a temporary scaffolding constructed alongside of half completed bridge works of the best character—designed as foundations for railway arches.

At Gagness Kyrka we have a diligence ride of a mile to Grasta, where we take passage on the handsome steamer Gustaf Wasa (of 30 tons burden, with amid-ship located and handsomely furnished dining-room, and cabin, etc.): ascending on this boat the Dalaf and Insjo to Leksand. At the landing at Grasta we see a half-dozen of the Delecarlian women attired in the dress we had admired so much at Stockholm —each one with a little babe on her lap and a stocking in process of completion in her hand.

The hour's ride on the Gustaf Wasa to the foot of a South-east bay of Lake Siljan, is between banks that much resemble those that stand on either side of the river from Basta to Gagness; only that the stream is somewhat wider and deeper, you could scarcely mark any distinction at all. But there is "variety" in the passage, derived from the internal domestic fact that the Gustaf Wasa is "navigated" by a drunken, noisy master who, as it subsequently appeared, has acquired a reputation for insolent abuse towards the patrons of his company—a reputation that extends from Mora to Stockholm. The woman who had charge of the saloon told one of our fellow-passengers that she had been praying for a month that some one would report the Captain to headquarters. But she said that usually travelers declared, that as they had to ride with him frequently they were not going to make an enemy of him; and as for the tourists, they soon discovered what kind of a creature he was and treated him with contempt,— replying when urged to complain, that it was the duty of those who were his regular customers to testify about his outrageous conduct, before the company's agents at Mora or Leksand, and that they

LEKSAND CHURCH.

would not go out of their way or stop to do that kind of public service. Every one admits that the dirty fellow should have been reported, and reported long ago. If Gustaf Wasa were alive and should come across such a Captain on board of a vessel bearing his name, he might be expected, according to Northern "orientalisms," to take the wretch by the nape of the neck and fling him over into the Baltic Sea.

The landing at Leksand is much like the steamboat wharf that once was at the foot of Omaha Bluff, before the building of the bridge across the Missouri at that point. You ascend fifty or sixty feet, by a circuitous path, to the level of the one long village street that runs close to the line of the Ostervick bank. The visitor by this ascent reaches about the middle of the village, as measured from the Kyrka on the Northeast to the end of the row of buildings that constitute the stores and residences of the Leksanders proper.

Close to this point, is the house of our entertainer, Andreas Gustaf Wickstrom ; and we have reason to feel grateful to friends at Smedjbacken, who gave us his address. In a spirit of gratitude and in obedience to the golden rule, we mention his name and advise others to follow our example, and prefer his accommodations to those of the landlord at the large hotel.

We have observed all along this trip from Stromsholm that the crops look unusually well (for we join to our own notice of their excellent present promise the statements of comparison made by our fellow-voyagers, who are familiar with the country, from place to place). We have been surprised to see such splendid rye, often five and even six feet in length, with kernals apparently filling to fatness on every straw. But many ominous shrugs of the shoulders and occasional exclamations of fear on the part of those with whom we converse on the subject— inhabitants of this District—tell of the possibility of a wet season that may possibly beat down and diminish the quantity and impair greatly the quality of the grain. Here they say that they are never sure of their crop until they have it in the bread. Already there is whispering about the potatoes showing signs of rot ; and O ! if they should !

As already sufficiently stated, perhaps, Lecksand is situated on a bluff, with respect to the lake, at the Siljan edge of a meadow plain. At the Northeast end, close to the water line, is a great church, with a turnip-shaped central tower. At the Southern extremity, or foot of the street, is a large white house—contrasting with all other dwellings by its color and size—in which we are often and explicitly told, Don Pedro of Brazil did lodge when he condescended to visit this District.

From the Wickstrom Mansion, not far from the line of the steamer landing, to the gate of the churchyard, a distance of a quarter of a mile, is an avenue lined with birch trees, set about fifteen feet apart, and of the growth of one of our mature maples. Between this line of trees, on the left hand as you go toward the church, is a green field. On the other hand houses and building-site lots alternate.

On Saturday afternoon, shortly after our arrival, we started to walk from Master Wickstrom's to the Kyrka. Down this pleasant road, at about mid-distance, we met an old lady, with a cane in one hand and a basket in the other, very slowly making her way toward the centre of the village. She did the best she could to courtesy to us, and we stopped and inquired her name and age. She said that she was ninety-two years of age, and was dependent on the town or parish for her support. Then she asked our names and nativity, which we gave her. We then dropped a small piece of money into her basket, whereupon she trembled violently and let her cane fall and picked up the coin. We were passing away from her when we were stopped by her exclaiming: "O! what is this? Silver! Strange people giving silver to an old woman like me! Silver! May the Lord be in your heart?" And as she took the stick, which a little child raised for her and put in her hand, she repeated her grateful wish; and as we moved on, and during our walk for a distance of twenty steps beyond the spot where she stood, we heard her saying to herself, now in a low tone and again in a high-pitched voice, "O, this is wonderful! This is something that cannot be studied out!"

The church will seat two thousand people, and is the first edifice of the kind that we have seen outside of Stockholm that has a central tower instead of a steeple at the front; in this respect being like nearly all the Established Church buildings of worship in the Swedish Capital. The surrounding churchyard embraces fifteen or twenty acres, and is used, of course, as a place of interment by the parish. When we spoke of the comparatively few number of gravestones or monuments, in conversation with a man whom we chanced to meet in the inclosure, he remarked : "Well, we don't scatter our dead as you do. A family whose members love each other in this life want to be buried together and rise together."

Here was information, explanation, justification (if need be) and sharp shot at our lack of affection for one another, as manifested in our cemetery arrangements (it may be), and theology withal,—all in one condensed and compact dose. We must have a care how we question these Delecarlians, lest by our inflection we seem to imply some or any sort of criticism on their habits, fashions or methods of treating or disposing of their dead !

A Summer Sunday morning at Leksand Kyrka is a far-famed date and location for a spectacle worth beholding. A thousand farmers and farmers' wives, sons and daughters are in attendance, dressed for the most part in their picturesque costumes—coming in small companies—five, eight, and even a dozen in a party. They begin to gather in the churchyard at half-past 9 o'clock, and from that hour on to service-time there was also an entertaining and enlivening scene of processions of boats coming down the lake, bearing families and neighbors from adjacent settlements or bees. Before Siljansnäs had a church of its own, it is said that more than half the congregation came from across the lake on a Sunday or feast-day morning.

The men and women sit on opposite sides of the church, which rule resulted in bringing about five hundred of the dalkuller, or young women, into one division of the building;—right under my eyes as I sat in the big pillar corner of the men's side of the gallery, immediately below the organ loft. This position I reached, I may mention, by the rather undignified process of climbing over the partitions—two of them—between the entrance platform of the ladies' gallery and the premises allotted to the male sex;—having unwittingly ascended on the wrong side of the Southern end of the church. Two boys, about sixteen years of age, before whom I finally took my seat, were very much amused at my expense.

As I have not anywhere seen a full or accurate description of the peculiar dress or costume of these people—and as much as possible I seek to avoid dwelling upon those matters spoken of in the guide-books or the published books of travel—I will give as complete an "inventory" as I can. As to the girls and matrons first, of course.

The Leksand women wear a low-cut shoe, manufactured out of very heavy calfskin or cowhide; some have a birchbark layer in the soles. They are fastened by lacing with leather strings. The heel, which is about an inch long, is set under the middle of the instep, or nearly so; tapering from the width of the sole, which is three or even four inches wide, to a bottom an inch in diameter. Sometimes the entire bottom is shod with iron—a rim around the front like a horseshoe, and a full metal cover or plate for the heel. In Summer, however, many of the younger ladies, especially those that go South for employment during the warm season, discard the iron border and penny heel-tap, for the reason of comparative lightness; adopting a shoe that is made exclusively of skin. This—let it be noted—is confessedly on account of the appearance of the article.

The stockings are knit of coarse, strong woolen yarn, the hard texture of which is declared to be unendurable by some of the Swedish peasants who live in a lower latitude. The wool is dyed a flamingo red, before it is spun, in some instances; though the coloring is usually delayed until after the spinning has been completed. It might as well be stated here that in the matter of bright colors, such as are selected for the garments of this peasantry, the Delecarlians have no superiors as dyers. Brilliant and abiding red and yellow they produce to the pitch of perfection. The stockings are very thick, as well as coarse and tough, and above the lacing of the shoe they have a flush and often baggy appearance—not very noticeable, perhaps, except upon close or frequent observation. When the stocking is not pulled or stretched as tight as it can or ought to be, it will not look neat about the edge of the leather; but this defect is rarely permitted to be seen.

The skirt is made of closely-woven material, entirely black, with little gathering or puckering at the waist, and reaches the ankle. The apron is made of woolen cloth, lighter in texture than the skirt, and covers the entire front of the skirt, except that it does not fall to the bottom by three or four inches. It is colored an intense canary yellow.

The waist is generally made of fine home-spun linen, differing according to the taste of the maker or wearer in thickness; sometimes as thin as muslin, and often as heavy as tablespreads or napkins. The body is about as full as a gentleman's shirt, fitting close to the neck. The sleeves are large, but not flowing; being gathered on the wrist by a band that fits neatly, and that is adorned with the finest style of needle-work that the owner can produce by her own skill or purchase from others. It is supposed to be a point of good faith that the fancy embroidery on this part of the costume shall be specimens of the best accomplishment of the wearer herself—her own handiwork. The bosom, collar and wristbands are worthy of minute examination, for there the Delecarlian families display consummate art. They are proverbially and justly proud of their superiority as mistresses of the needle.

Over this white garment goes a skeleton waist, made of red woolen cloth, with cotton lining. It is about four inches wide at the girth, at the bottom of which is a roll an inch in diameter, over which the skirt is fastened. Of the same materials are shoulder-straps, of ordinary suspender size in front, which meet close up under the neck on the back; there being from that point to the junction a double width, down to the top of the crimson band. At first sight it looks as though the white and red garments were one, but in point of fact the latter is a sort of open jacket. This outer woolen waist or "vest" is fastened around the body by lacing; there being four ornamental eyelets for the tape or strings of braided ribbons that cross and checker and bind immediately in front. This jacket is also variously and handsomely ornamented with stripes of worsted seams.

The cap is the article that distinguishes the married from the unmarried; the difference being that the matrons wear a close head-cover that is entirely white. There is no difference in the pattern. The hair is done up in flat braids or plaitings, and so laid upon the head that there shall be no noticeable protrusion or nob at any point. The cap is skull-close on the forehead and down the temple and around to the back of the neck. There is the same round puff on the crown, pitching back at an angle of forty-five degrees, that our own grandmothers exhibited a quarter of a century ago. Indeed, save in the character of the material and the adornment, a description of the form of the one would nearly nearly answer for the other. The ground-work of the maiden's cap is usually of a creamy white; and the rich and often beautiful figures, wrought in needlework or painted in dyes, are displayed on the flat surfaces and streak up on the saucer-cover from behind.

The dress of the Leksand District yoeman consists of a long coat—heavy, very short-waisted, made of dark woolen stuff; having a red cord edge, and fastened with hooks and eyes. Their vest is of similar but lighter fabric. They wear knee-breeches of buckskin or corduroy or (sometimes) strong satinet. Their stockings are knit of white yarn, although to the uninformed observer they appear to be made of felt. They are carded on the outside after they are knit, which gives them a hairy-looking exterior. Over this stocking the knee-breeches are buckled; and from a band on the end of the breeches red and black tassels are suspended by long strings—the end of the tassels sometimes reaching down as far as the top of the ankles. For foot covering, these mighty men of Delecarlia have a shoe made of cowhide uppers with soles fully an inch thick and composed in great part of birch bark. They wear a broad-brimmed black felt hat.

The men of Mora are similarly attired, except that they wear roundabouts or jackets, and huge leather aprons which cover their person in front and on either side from the neck to the shins.

The dress of the females in the Mora District differs from that of the Leksand natives with respect to the skirt and apron and the covering for the head. Instead of a cap they usually wear a handkerchief at a three-cornered tie. Their skirt and apron are of black woolen goods, precisely like that of their Leksand neighbors in quality; but instead of the yellow apron there is a bordering of two stripes running around the bottom of that article, of dark-red or yellow color. Sometimes this adornment is also placed near the end of the skirt.

Having digressed so much to describe the costumes of

these people, I return to my post—pillar, I might say—in the gallery of the kyrka at Leksand.

The priest is dressed in a long frock coat, and wears behind him a long plaited, trailing strip of black cloth, as wide as the space between his shoulders, fastened in front by a buckle on the neck-circling ribbon or band. The gorgeous garments which we had seen in the ante-room are only worn on special occasions, duly prescribed in the calendar. Here the same man officiated at the altar and in the pulpit. He preached from the text, "Make to yourselves friends of the mammon of unrighteousness." The matter of the discourse was most excellent. The delivery might have been worse, but in what respect we cannot exactly say. It was a monotonous whine from beginning to end. It may be said that he did not deliver his sermon at all: he sniveled it out. The same composition uttered by a good elocutionist would have been very effective. We wished, for the sake of the audience, including ourselves, and for the sake of the cause, that the young man who stood and spoke at the grave of his sister at Smedjbacken, a few hours before, had had that manuscript on this occasion, and in this place, for a pulpit ministration.

We are satisfied that we do not write from any personal prejudice or unfair judgment; for the two lads that sat behind us, and who had made merry at our awkward predicament and manner of escape therefrom, and who had joined in the singing heartily, went to sleep, with their two heads laid at roof angle against each other, directly after the preacher began to talk or to cry! and another individual, a man of middle age, who had looked at me with a severe and reproving aspect—as I thought—because my attention was not riveted on the prayer and hymn-book, also fell asleep, and once or twice nearly toppled over the railing in front of him, on which he had lain his head. I had been conscience-struck by that man's accusing glance I had, perhaps, misjudged that man. I drag him in here now, and compel him to be a witness to the estimate which I make of the character of the pulpit work of the assistant rector of St. Peter's and St. Paul's Kyrka at Leksand.

The organ had a most unpromising exterior; but, though

it was apparently very unskillfully built, it gave no uncertain sound and was melodious in all its pipes. Each line of each hymn was sung with a most marked isolation, and where the sentiment did not separately stand according to this division, I could not resist a sense of the ludicrous in the performance. After the church services were over, we met the man who answered our cemetery inquiry, and asked him why they didn't sing their verses as they buried their dead. He didn't understand what we meant, and it might have been difficult or unsafe to explain.

I should mention that for the final ceremonies in the church, for the morning service, the organist and the singers who were in the organ loft sang with an accompaniment in our modern style a hymn of consoling import, to the tune of Old Dundee. How refreshing and grandly it rolled out amid those ancient and elephantine arches!

—o—

XIV.

LEKSAND TO MORA.

Mora is at the head of Lake Siljan; or rather at the head of a small bay with which the great lake proper terminates at its Northern extremity. Formerly vessels passed around the Southern or Southeastern end of the town and landed at the bank of the main feeding stream; but a channel has been cut through the shallows that divide the bay or harbor from the lake. The steamer Gustaf Wasa now goes to a wharf that extends out about a hundred feet from the line of the street that runs parallel with the water, immediately in front of the most thickly settled part of the village. About two hundred yards from the wharf is a church, which stands on a slight elevation, and from its doorways an extended view can be had to the North and to the Northeast.

There are a number of Bys (pronounced bees,) which is the name of hamlets or small clusters of farmhouses, on each side of the town—if you chose to take Mora by that title—and on a solitary walk of observation among them I started early on the morning after our arrival there. Along the street that led back from the harbor directly to the East, or nearly so, I took my winding way. It is a circuitous, narrow passage, between low log houses, very few of which were

MORA.

painted red or any other color. As you increase your distance into Delecarlia on this route, you see fewer buildings that are painted, until you come to villages that are like Mora—where the plain hue of the timber is rarely changed by the brush. And after the familiarity you have had with the bright glaring scarlet of the houses below the line of this District, these more Northern towns, and the dwellings around them, have a shabby appearance.

Through this by I was passing, with a curious peering into

lakes and courtyards, when I met face to face and alone, another solitary walker. He was a full-grown specimen of the Mora peasant, with an apron of such dimensions as to fairly push out beyond the sides of his jacket. Hanging in his belt, in front, was a sailor's knife, in an ornamented sheath. He had a surly aspect, and stared at me at first with that aforementioned, "What are you doing here?" kind of a look, that, under the circumstances was not altogether pleasant to encounter. However, he was apparently mollified on near approach. If he *was* really scowling when he caught sight of me—or whatever the fact in that respect may have been—while the mist still had an obscuring effect on his outlines, I was rejoiced to notice that he smiled, and presently he snatched his hat from his head and saluted, "God dag--dag." As I returned his greeting in my best style, I felt that some one inside of me was saying or singing the adapted rhyme of the first edition of "Mother Goose," with which I became acquainted:

> Early on one Wednesday morning,
>   When foggy was the weather,
> I met an old man all clothed in leather.
> He began to laugh, and I began to grin;
>   How do you do? and how do you do?
> And how do you do, again?

Here I was joined by a companion, who came up to where we were standing and at once took part in the conversation. For the sake of separation we will take the reporter's divisions, whether the sentence is in fact interrogatory or not:

Question—How is the weather for your harvests? Answer—It cannot be told yet. Our rot day was rainy, but it does not always turn out as it once did—a rainy month following. There is time enough yet to ruin the greater portion of the rye.

Q.—To absolutely ruin it? A.—Well, to make it very watery and light, besides the damage in breaking down.

Q.—When I was below I heard it said that you could not raise rye up here, but I see that the finest looking grain is in this section. A.—O, when we have a good season our rye is as excellent as there is in the world.

Q.—You have not taken your trimmings down from your midsummer poles? A.—Nay; we let them stay until they drop off, before August.

Q.—Are there many of your neighbors thinking of going to America this year? A.—Are you from America?

Q.—Yay; from San Francisco, California. A.—You don't say so! [with a sharp, long stare and a brushing back of the apron behind the coat or jacket]; that is a terrible distance— all the way to America!

Q.—But is it as far from New York to California as from Liverpool to New York [determined to dwell on this evidently weak point of his wonder]. A.—Shoo! you don't say so. My boy has thought of going, but it is too far! [This worthy peasant *looked* away a few thousand miles as he slowly repeated this exclamation.] Is it really a good country?

Q.—In what respect do you ask? A.—Are the people moral? Have they schools?

Q.—We have more churches and schools than you have in Sweden, so far as that goes. A.—Buildings don't make Christians?

Q.—I was going to say something like that myself. They don't necessarily make people or a majority of the people moral,—of course not. A.—But California is a very bad place.

Q.—I am sorry that we have that sort of a reputation; if we do have it in this vicinity? [This was adopting a favorite Swedish fashion of doubling the same sentence:—regrets and inquiry in the same breath.] A.—O, you kill good China people on the streets.

Q.—Who told you that? A.—I know it. I read it myself.

Q.—Do you believe all you read? A.—My paper always speaks the truth; that I know.

Q.—Its character and your faith are remarkable; but if your paper stated that we are in the habit of killing innocent Chinamen as a matter of common occurrence on the streets in California, your paper stated what was not the truth. A.—It was a translation from some of your own papers. My paper states that every immigrant must have ninety kroners [about $25] when he lands in Castle Garden, New York, in order to get to a place where he can find employment.

Q.—As a general statement, that is entirely untrue. I was in Castle Garden myself a few days before I sailed from America, and I know that Swedish servants of all classes were then in demand. I talked with the matron in charge of the female department on this very subject. Forty-nine thousand Swedes emigrated to the United States last year. A great many Swedes—say as many as 10,000—are going to the territory of Montana this year; and to reach that place there is a high rate—higher than there ought to be—for car fare. From New York to Montana is over two thousand miles. A.—Is that so? [repeated many times; breathing hard through a puckered mouth, between exclamations; and brushing back that enormous apron with a vigorous dashing around of the hands every time the sentence was finished.]

Q.—I have just received a letter stating that the writer, who is a wealthy lady living in Philadelphia, will pay the passage of a good Swedish servant; wishing me to leave her address with the proper officer or person in Stockholm or Gothenburg for this purpose. [I knew this would be surprising intelligence to this man, simple as the statement may seem to my American reader.] A.—Why so?

Q.—Such is the fact. Swedish servants have a high reputation in America. And I think the same may be said of Swedish farmers and mechanics. I am not here as an emigrant agent, and can have no possible motive to induce emigration by exagerated accounts of the advantag s my country presents to the laboring man. A.—Come to my house; I want to hear you folks talk in the presence of my wife and children.

We went back to the upper part of the village of Mora—as near as I can designate it—to a settlement separated from the main cluster by a field one hundred and fifty rods wide. At a gesture of invitation or command, we glanced, with our new-found friend through a cottage window into a house of mourning—where an infant was lying in its grave clothes. We entered a dwelling of two rooms—a house situated in a yard surrounded by houses set at various angles; one among a dozen, I think. The wife was cooking at the fireplace at the blacksmith-forge stand, as we best can describe it. She was aided by a daughter of seventeen years—[this fact of age afterward appeared]—who had the cap of the district, but otherwise was

COTTAGE SCENE IN DELECARLIA.

dressed very much as our own people of similar age and occupation. Two children, aged respectively eight and ten, sat on the bed, that had been pushed into its day dimensions and covered with a calico spread.

The Moran—Here are Americans, from San Francisco, California.

The Chorus—O, welcome, welcome! sit one of you down on the chair.

Now, *the* chair was a Boston rocking-chair—a chair after our forefathers' pattern, and somewhat higher than we were accustomed to in our early days,—only differing in the one respect mentioned. My companion took the proffered seat. We observed, meanwhile, that the food that was being prepared was made out of rye and water, with a little milk and salt contribution. The contents of the pot on that fire were being stirred with a little birch-twig broom, and the daughter took the mother's place in this duty as we sat down.

Stranger—I have often heard it said that you had no rocking-chairs in Sweden. I have read that statement in one of our newspapers. Now you see how *you* are misrepresented by our press.

Moran—Not so. Rocking-chairs are a modern introduction. I remember when we didn't know of any such thing.

Stranger—But you have always had cradles?

Moran—There is one in which I was put to sleep myself when I was a baby. [He is now 54 years old.] This man says that America is a good country, and that California is very good, too. I want you to hear him talk.

Stranger—I am ashamed to attempt to speak very much before such an audience. [By the by, two neighbors—middle-aged women—had come in and taken positions near the door, evidently as summoned spectators and listeners.] I will leave my companion here to talk to you.

We did our best to present the United States of America in as bright a light as we could, having due regard to the responsibility of our speech under such circumstances. We had the most attentive, the most considerate, the most eager audience that we ever possessed. We told of the scenes we had witnessed in Castle Garden, New York; told what we had learned respecting the steamer lines to America; gave the general geographical outlines of our nation, and, of course mentioned the fact that California was the paradise of the world. As we got no hint to stop from our auditors, we cut our speech short off and rose to go, when the daughter furnished us with coffee.

I am conscious of having too long delayed a special, if not an extended reference to this truly national beverage of Sweden. There are points with respect to it that I have not seen menitoned anywhere, that deserve notice. In the first place, let us agree that it is a most singular fact that the best cup of coffee in the world is prepared in Scandinavia. The far North takes the tropical berry and converts it into the most delicious non-intoxicant table drink that civilization has yet produced. Its use is so frequent and liberal here as to be rightly termed a beverage. And in speaking of its superior excellence I do not—of course I do not—rely on my own limited personal knowledge; but many men and women from among those most competent to judge, who have traveled through the Oriental countries, have joined in this verdict or award, in conversations where I have recently been a participant or listener.

And, parenthetically, I would like to mention that next to the diabolical decoction that is furnished forth in London in many so-called first-class restaurants under the name of tea—to which I think I have made a slight reference hereinbefore—next, as perhaps properly it should be, on the score of atrocity, is the mixture denominated coffee.

Tell it not in Stockholm, and publish it not in the villages of Delecarlia; but the truth is that the coffee as well as the tea set out in London, from the tables of the Grand Hotel to the arbors that border on Kew Garden, is oftentimes merely—well, enigmatical. [That enigmatical is a good word, in this connection, I solemnly submit to former and future travelers; and it saves violence of expression.] Well, to put this comparison to one side and come to the question of How it is thus?

I have catechised on this subject, as in duty bound; not only in the regions below, but in the very spot where I am sitting at this writing. I have not been neglectful of my privileges and obligations in this respect. I have told the man's houschold about it, and laid the matter with my most persuasive speech—would it were more seductive on such a mission—before the old man's daughter.

A Swedish coffee-house in San Francisco, [and why not in New York?] with Delecarlian maids in costume for waiters, would prove a success. That is, a real, genuine, no-mistake Scandinavian Java service restaurant. And, of course, the same might be said of other large American cities—inclusive of our national capital. And, by the way, why was there not a Swedish cafe cottage at the Centennial Exhibition, as well as a Swedish schoolhouse?

But why this actual superiority in the quality of the preparation? Why this luscious and, at the same time, not nerve-shattering fluid out of the same berry that is the presumed basis for a drink that goes by the same name in other and warmer climates? There is the usual explanation on the ground of adulteration, of course; but that is not sufficient. That will not answer where the berry is taken from the bag and roasted and crushed in the same kitchen, so that there can be no mistake as to the purity. I have replies from a number of intelligent Swedish ladies of blood royal, and from some peasant women at whose firesides we sat; each and all to the same effect and comprehending like reasons. Some of the reasons—and I need not detail them all—may excite a smile; but I believe that each one should be considered with respect.

A cause of this effect and defect here spoken of, is given in behalf of the copper kettle in which these people almost invariably boil their pulverized berry. Then I have brought in another cause and suggestion in the last adjective: go backward for explanations and reasons. It is fresh roasted and fresh from the hand-mill. And with respect to the roasting, there is a precise art. The beautiful berry is rebellious on rough or cruel or inartistic treatment while in the oven; it must there and then be looked after and treated with delicate and distinguished consideration; it must be heated and browned to a crispy turn—not burned. O, how some of this Swedish nobility do rise from their cushions and protest against the manner in which this great gift to humanity is ill-used by the slovenly, ignorant creatures of everywhere else; who in private service or big manufacturing establishments do abuse and murder this queen product of the tropics! With what commendable faithfulness and jealousy the red-capped maiden that we spy through the window of an adjoining cottage is even now shaking the little roaster over the coals. Can, pan and pot are kept as closely sealed as possible, and the aroma is husbanded to the uttermost.

Then some stress is laid on the excellence of the water that is to be used in the preparation; and a Swedish lady who has lived abroad many years told of her failure to get anything like satisfactory results in the United States until she had procured a filter jar and changed the high-priced liquid that went by the name of water in the Atlantic city where she resided into something approaching the Adam's ale of her native land. I was particularly charmed with this lady, I would like to mention, because she answered an impudent fellow who was introduced to the company we were in at one time, when he declared that he had tasted as good coffee in Great Britain as ever was brewed in Scandinavia, with a remarkable smile—nothing more. She just folded her arms and smiled most significantly, in a manner both contemptuous and commiserating, yet entirely lady-like withal. Blessings on her head.

Regular hours for coffee are immediately after you rise in the morning, and between 2 and 5 P. M. But hospitality is liable to show itself at any time of the day when you chance to call, in the proffer of this delicious cup.

You may challenge the judgment and comparison herein published, with suspicion that experience and trials have been limited elsewhere or confined to the humbler class of inns or catering establishments; but you will accept this statement in its sweep and import-force—the statement that you will find no better prepared coffee anywhere on the lines in this country which we have traveled; some better than others, but none that is not good and worthy of the title of excellent.

And now here, in this lowly habitation, in this little By of the Mora parish, there is served up to our welcome and entertainment, not a muddy solution of sassafras, chickory and licorice—such as we have tried to drink at a six-course dinner, as a guest, in all obligations of hospitality bound, in one of the great dining-rooms in London, where everything else set forth for the taste was very nice;—nor yet the fair to middling and undoubtedly pure article that we get at our San Francisco lunch-houses: but a nectar for the gods!

Query—What did these people do before the discovery of coffee and potatoes as articles for drink and meat preparation? Ans.—They did as the Romans did—had for before-discovered substitutes barley water and onions.

MORA-KULLA.

Returning to our examination:

Question—How is it that your daughter is not in the South, as many of your young women are? In employment for the summer months with the people of Stockholm and vicinity? Answer—We have two daughters at service in the Southern counties. We could not spare Minnie this season. Mamma is getting old—too old to do all the housework;

though, of course, she don't have as much to do as she did before the most of the children were grown up. You should have seen us when we had five babies, and the oldest only five years of age.

Q. Yes, I should liked to have called on you then. Mamma must have been busy about those days? A. It was spring, spring, spring, with mamma then. ["Spring" means run; but run don't give the exact emphasis. Spring is the word."]

We did not doubt the last statement, and said so; and bidding our entertainers a temporary farewell—adieu! adieu! we hastened to meet the members of our company who had appointed to visit the Mora church at the hour that was now being struck on the tower bell. Mr. B. V. Nordstedt of Falun appeared at the cafe with the keys of the sacred edifice; three on the string, and either one as big as a San Francisco policeman's club. Iron is cheap in Sweden.

Before entering we should itemize the tower. It is two hundred feet high. It is a square brick structure for the distance of one hundred and twenty-five feet. Under the clock there is a sign reading: "Guida till ara hafver kung carl xi ar 1673, latit byggia detta toru."

The clock is the handiwork of the Delecarlians of this neighborhood, who manufactured and presented it to the authorities a few years ago. As clock manufacturers the Delecarlians are the rivals of the Connecticut Yankees; or have been such until recently. I believe it was rather of an affliction, when it was stated at the cottage to which I have just referred, that the landlady at our inn had a New Haven timepiece. But it is claimed that the home-made clocks are more durable than ours; which was denied by us, of course. The Delecarlians put only one pointer—an hour hand—on their tower clocks.

The church is cruciform in character, as are most buildings of this kind in this country. It will seat over 2,000.. Our friend, Nordstedt, used the equivalent to our phrase "comfortably seat," etc., in speaking about this church's accommodations. But I knew better, and I had the " courage of my convictions" adequate to sustain me in very politely but distinctly saying as much.

Above the altar is a painting of the crucifixion. On one side of this painting is a large gilded cross; on the other side is an anchor, leaned upon by effigies. At one side of the chancel is a very ancient picture of the baptism of Christ by John. Immediately over the altar, and under the painting, is a medallion representation of The Last Supper. On the altar is a cross and four candlesticks. Portraits, (supposed to be) of former kings and queens—a dozen of them, I think—are on the walls on the inside of the choir end of the building. In the closets in the sacristy there are a score of highly ornamented robes and crowns. In England or the United States the interior of this edifice, like that of most of those we have entered in this country, would at once impress the visitor with the belief that he was within the walls of a Roman Catholic church. Not until he observed the absence from the altar of the receptacle for the communion bread, and remarked—as he probably would very soon—the sexton or verger walking around with his hat on, would he suspect otherwise—under like appearances in any other land.

The altar cloth was made in 1794. There are seats around the chancel for the comministrars. Denis Borg was a warden, appointed in 1880. So reads the record on the wall.

A list of the pastors in this church is painted on the panels of the first of the five galleries that face the altar. The other panels, sixty-one in number, contain cabinet paintings, supposed to be illustrative of Scripture. Some are horribly grotesque. For instance, one represents Christ as a little child standing on a table or pedestal, with the blood spurting out of the centre of his breast. A couple of miserable-looking creatures, somewhat after the similitude of men, are catching this blood in a large bowl. There were other representations that were, if anything, more shocking than this, which I would not venture to describe here.

Matthias Laurentia was pastor of this church in 1372; and the grave-digger, whom we afterward met and conversed with in the yard, said that he was a very good pastor for his day. When I inquired how he knew, he bluntly smiled at me and said : "Yes, of course it must be so, or his name would not be on the roll." I afterwards had the question put to him by a friend from Borlange, and the reply was the same.

Immediately in front of the altar is a stone slab dated 1759. On it, among much engraving, were these words : "Magister Peter Wollenius. Here lie the tired bones."

The pews are raised above the stone floor, as noted in the Leksand and other ancient churches. The pulpit is of the wine-cup pattern that is seen in every church in Sweden ; with sounding-board and hour-glasses, and furnished with a Bible dated 1708 and a prayer-book published in 1845. There are six panels on the pulpit, with very much gilded representations of passages in the life of Chrtst. Christ Talking With Nicodemus at Night and Christ Talking to the Samaritan Woman at the Well, are uniformly seen in such panels, where there is any medallion work at all. In this instance Nicodemus and the Samaritan woman were hideous enough to satisfy the malevolence of any enemy of their respective tribes. There are seven gilded cherubs under the pulpit, and some of them appeared to me to have an irreverent giggle on their countenances.

There are four entrances to the church ; three of double doors, ten feet in width. Last Sunday the building was densely packed, and it was estimated that three thousand persons were in attendance and that nearly one thousand took communion. This is a church-going nation.

There is a great deal of whittling on the railing of the pews in the galleries, showing again the natural, and probably the actual genealogical affinity of the Delecarlians and the Connecticut boys. Ed. Erickson has done a large amount of work of this kind, in two or three of the galleries ; and his capitalized signature or his skeleton mark—as E-D ER K N—is seen so frequently in close proximity to the name of Anna Larson— who I am sure never did any jack-knife work here at all—that we suspect that Ed. has been over on the side reserved for the girls, and carved both names as a hint of his affection.

The pillars are octagonal, and five feet in diameter. There are two great iron stoves, recently set up ; and the stovepipe that emerges from the ridge of the roof is constructed in the shape of a cross.

XV.

AT MORA AND UTMELAND.

The great object of interest in this section is the scene of Gustavas Vasa's concealment and escape, which is situated about a mile and a half from the Mora Church. To that point, under the guidance of the son of our landlady, our company started at noon of this day. Our pilot—a lad of eighteen— K. A. Sedjfors by name—purposes going to California in the Fall, and you can imagine the interest he took in showing us all the courtesies in his power.

Near the post office we met half a dozen costumed girls from another district. They wore the cross-barred skirt and the sugar-loaf hat which are taken as a pattern for most of the dolls that are sent abroad to represent the Delecarlian dress. By many this is considered the handsomest style in vogue; and this, as a common judgment, would seem to be established by the fact that the pictures most frequently represent this fashion.

Distant from the church half a mile, on the shore of the lake or harbor, is a By—a collection of twenty houses; and three of the dwelling-houses may be said to surround a well and a hayrick. To this sub-division—at the lower end of this settlement—we paid a special visit, to sample the Delecarlian peasant's home. The account we had given of our own call at a cottage in another locality made our less fortunate friends very zealous for observation and inspection here.

As we approached this cluster of dwelling-houses and cowsheds, we saw a sign of alarm on the part of some of the female inhabitants, who happened at that time to be engaged in shaking down the hay from the drying poles that were arranged adjacent to their Summer sleeping quarters. They fled in-doors to change their apparel, and if the whole truth must be known, to add a little more covering to their lower limbs. They had been at work not only bare-footed but bare-legged ; as is the habit of these people in the warm weather while engaged in such business.

We waited at the door of the last house a few minutes, until there was a signal for us to enter. There was one room below, about ten feet square, and an attic with a loose floor—a ladder reaching to a trap-space—constituted the divisions. On one side of the ground story was a double bunk, while a corner on the opposite side was curtained off for a separate sleeping apartment. In another corner was a chest, out of which several specimen skirts and jackets were taken and sold to some of our party. In the attic four beds were spread ; and the accommodation in this Harvest-home was said to be ample for twelve persons.

The cattle-house, which is about fifteen yards distant, was not quite twice the size of the Summer sleeping-house. It was furnished with a stone grate and a large iron-kettle, in which, during the Winter months, the food of the animals as formerly boiled ; a practice now almost wholly abandoned. This mode of preparing the cut hay and straw and vegetables that were given to the cows and sheep had an additional advantage in tempering the atmosphere in the "cattle-cabin" to the Spring lambs and early calves. On this matter there was a great deal of excessively-repeated speech on the part of the natives of this section and the visitors from lower latitudes in this country. There was a good-natured but very earnest dispute concerning the benefits or disadvantages of this and that method of stabling the animals during the inclement season. There was a very intelligent understanding of the latest teaching of the agricultural schools that abound in Sweden.

In the dwelling-houses connected with this circle of industrial buildings we were shown the wool-spinning wheel and card machine in full operation ; for in each place visited the mother was occupied at one or the other, with a child in a cradle at her side. Here, too, are the fixed corner bedsteads. They are very deceptive in one respect. It would seem to the inexperienced that they were too small by about one-half, for the accommodation of a man of average length. The well-known measurement by the eye of the length of a flour barrel, or the dimensions of a horse's head, would not be so far out of the way on the first guess, as are the estimates on these sleep-cupboards. They are five feet eight inches deep, and a tape-line was carefully applied by every member of our party before incredulity would give way to absolute sight. Our Swedish camrades were equal disbelievers with us from the United States, on this important subject; and the torrents of nouns, participles and adjectives that flew around the comparatively few verbs that were used on this occasion by the natives, was disheartening to a pupil in the primary department; and the hearty smacks laid in and over the "att's sa" choruses, were like a tumble-down of a high pile of clapboards on a Stuart street dock.

As we pushed along toward the monument-like building at Utmeland, we measured the hight of the growing stalks of grain on either hand; and we saw several fields of rye, the majority of whose waving heads were over our own a foot or more, and gave every promise of a splendid yield. It was sorrowful, indeed, to listen to the story of probabilities of an almost entire destruction of this growth of the main staple grain of Sweden. But unless the rainfall slackens, as compared with the showers of the past week, and unless the prophecy of rot-day weather is unfulfilled—which few persons hereabout seems to hopefully expect—the rye crop in this region, now so promising, will prove an entire failure.

We happened to say to our Swedish companions: "Of course you have become familiar with the song of our Bobby Burns,—'Comin' Thro' The Rye?'"

To our amazement they one and all instantly replied: "Nay; what is that?"

"What! you never heard of the lines:

"'If a body meet a body comin thro' the rye,
If a body kiss a body, need a body cry?'"

"Nay."

We draw to one side to reflect and weep in solitude. After a little space we returned to the company: "How is it possible that you have never heard of that song? You singing people? You people that must have a great pride over the triumphs of Jenny Lind and Christine Nilsson? Don't you know that Jenny Lind sang 'Comin' thro' the rye' as her principal encore song when she visited America in 1850 or 1851?"

"No," They were very proud of their renowned female vocalists—they called them 'birds' in a very pleasant way;—but they really never had heard anything of Burns' celebrated song. We said: "Why, the very fact that yours is essentially a country of rye ought to have made it inevitable that such people as you are should be acquainted with this dainty little production from the pen of the Scottish bard. And, whatever may have been the poets original intention in the use of the words, "the rye" had popular acceptance as meaning a field of grain."

And we know that we shall have sympathizers the world over, when we say and declare that this matter distressed us considerably,—alternately puzzling and grieving us. But the case was as it was; the fact is on record, and let the sorrow and shame go abroad, as the ignorance of these representative men and women—and they were representative, undoubtedly—may suggest or provoke judgment! We have done our duty. Every incident of importance in the biographies of the two bright Swedish vocalists was known to the excellent people—as it seemed to us,—save this one precious and essential item.

Let it be dwelt upon an instant longer: to add that there are at least a score of persons in San Francisco who sat in Metropolitan Hall, New York city, when I was there, boyhood-days ago, and listened to that matchless human nightingale pouring forth wondrous melodies; and reappearing at the third encore and bewitching us with her rendition of the simple but exquisite song to which we have referred. Of all that I thought, last Spring, when I saw P. T. Barnum at Bridgeport, looking not much older than when he led Jenny Lind on the platform at the Metropolitan, thirty-three years ago.

Where the hamlet of Utmeland once was, and on the spot which still holds the name, there are but four houses now standing; a farmer's cottage and barn and a monument-like building. In the other cottage the keeper resides.

Approaching the historic spot, we pass to the rear of a fine private residence, situated in the midst of grounds on a slight eminence above the surrounding country, and called Catherinesberg. On the opposite side of the harbor is a high knoll, which is called Kristineberg, the magnificent view from which draws commending notice even from the cautious, critical and phlegmatic Bædecker. These residences are owned by two brothers, who put in an occasional appearance, as their leisure from business or as their tastes incline.

We note the short scythes that the farmers use—about half the size of those that are generally swung in America—and as we walk along a friend from Upsala tells us a story about a youth who went to the United States last year and was immediately employed by a kind-hearted farmer in Genesee country, New York. The boy was accustomed to work during all the daylight hours of September, and in that first month of his hiring he was directed at seven o'clock to go to *sleep*. Now sleep in Swedish means to sharpen; and the lad understood that he was to take the sickles that were used for the reaping of the tangled grain and put an edge on them at the grindstone. So he gathered the blades and went to the woodshed, where the wheel was standing in the frame, and there he stood, for half an hour or more,—waiting. Out from the house comes the husbandman and asks why his boy lingers in that place—why he does not go to sleep. The boy replied that he could not do that until he had his girl. This bothered the farmer until after a protracted interchange of wrecked vernaculars, it was made clear that it was the invariable practice in Sweden to have the grindstone turned by a girl, while sharpening of the scythe for the morrow's work was going on.

We remarked that the atmosphere was loaded with a perfume like that which regaled us to surfeit, not to say suffocation, when we attend church in New England on Summer Sunday afternoons; in the days when we belonged to the choir and sat in the organ gallery. Ah! how pungent this same aroma to our nostrils, in those young days of old.

How came it here, and in such heavy volume! It is the scent of the wild kimmel that grows rank on every side.

We passed a very advanced and partly mown field of barley,—sown a month or more before the adjacent acres were planted, as we were assured, and can well believe. "It is the first to be cut in Dalecarlia," boasts the proprietor, as he pauses in his work to doff his hat and "God-dag-i-dag" separately and with most particular politeness. Why, this must be the field and one of the men that we saw at 3 o'clock this morning when we glanced through the glass all around the horizen, and shouted "All's well" in involuntary response to the horn-blowing watchman of Mora. "Ja, ja, ja," this was the place. "Vist, vist." Another chorus of "Att sa;" with not so much clatter of intonation as when it rose and reverberated in the peasant's cottage, but still making a very decided concussion on the all-incasing air. So here it was that we saw—

"In among the bearded barley,
Reapers, reaping bright and early."

It is within a few feet of the water's edge that the structure called the monument stands. The Goverment reservation is about twenty acres, as near as I could judge. The building is of stone, about fourteen feet high and thirty by twenty-two feet in surface measurement. We passed around the walls and we exchanged guesses as to the hight; the keeper declaring that he could not give any figures as to the size of the structure.

The grounds about the site of the ancient cottage, in the cellar of which the wife of Tomt-Mats Larso concealed Gustavus Wasa from his pursuing enemies, are tastefully kept, appropriately arranged in walks and beds and shaded roads.

The keeper is an old soldier, Carl B. Oberg by name. To begin with and to end with first and last, you may be sure you will be introduced into his little office; which is surrounded with a peculiar and very beautiful species of weeping birch. In that office visitors are shown a tempting array of photographs of scenery in the neighborhood of the monument, and photographic views taken from the grounds as a standing-point for lake and distant mountain obervations.

And here, also are pictures of the Brooklyn Bridge and other wonderful structures, "for sale at lowest prices." First or last, sooner or later, you must buy. Carl Oberg is an adroit salesman; he can nurse the slightest spark of desire to purchase into a fire that cannot be quenched—except by taking cards from his hand and passing kroners into the thus vacated palm. He can do more. He can create a resistless wish to purchase. He would be worth $300 a month to Lord & Taylor or Constable & Co., in New York city, or to Doane & Henshelwood, corner of Kearny and Sutter streets, San Francisco,—so soon as he became sufficiently acquainted with our language to compose twenty or thirty soliciting sentences. His bland, gracious, condescending, insinuating, intoxicating, deliriously-paralyzing urbanity cannot be withstood, and may as well be met with a flag of truce forthwith; thereby saving articles of surrender. The only explanation of the fact that he has escaped denominational personal appropriation as a debt-extinguisher or church charity Fair auctioneer, must be that there are not such, or few such, occasions in Sweden as call for this class of purse emptying seducers.

The handsome oak doors of the building that occupies the the spot on which the cottage stood a few years ago, are thrown open with an impressive wave of the arm, rather than with a plebeian push from the elbow, by the aforesaid Carl B. Oberg, His Majesty's keeper at this historic place. "Be so good as to walk in." One of the young ladies of the party remarked that she would have gone in on that gesture, if it had made her freckled for life. Could more be said on this point?

But the doors are opened and we are in the oblong, close-walled room, and feel the presence of the great Gustavus! There is a hush of solemn silence; the prattle of merriment is no more. Let us not be challenged as wantonly seeking to belittle this august scene.

Over the door we read: "Gustavus Wasa, exiled, walked in Dalecarlia and exhorted its men to struggle for the liberty of their country, and was saved on this place from the spies sent by the tyrant, by the presence of mind of a Dalecarlian woman." And again: "Charles X V., the 18th sucessor of

GUSTAVUS WASA'S CONCEALMENT.

Gustavus Wasa on the Swedish Throne, adorned with his own hand this monument, erected by the gratefulness of the Swedish people to the remembrance of the liberator 300 years after his death."

The sunlight pours down through the flat glass ceiling upon the paved floor, on the side of which is a double-trap lid that we at once know must cover the little arched bin or oven where the great Gustavus was quickly and cunningly hidden by the wife of Larsons, at the very instant that the troops of Christian were dismounting in front of the cottage.

Directly facing us as we enter is a famous painting, by J. Y. Hockert—a canvas ten by twelve feet—which vividly presents the chieftain in the act of descending into the cellar, while the faithful friend holds the empty brewing tub in the attitude of one about to cast it over the trap when it shall have been closed. Through the window she sees the advancing troopers already close to the rear of the dwelling and fear and courageous resolution are at the same time stamped upon her countenance.

The subjoined translation of the inscription over this painting is, perhaps, sufficiently full as a description of the scene that is sought to be depicted: "As a hunted game, on roads and footpaths in forests and grounds, pursued by the friends and servants of his enemies, Gustavus came in the days before Christmas to Mora, seeking for protection at the hands of the honest Tomts-Mates Larsson, in the village Utmeland. The spies of his enemies came soon to catch prey, but the ingenious wife of Mats Larsson occupied with the brewing for the Xmas, told the fugitive to go down into the cellar. Then she put the beer vat over the trap of the door of the cellar: thus saving the future liberator of her native country from being discovered by his enemies, who forced their way into the cottage and searched in every crack and corner,—as they supposed."

The face of Gustavus, as painted here, has an appealing and rather distrustful look, which we mention to our cordial guide. "That is correct," he replied; "that is just as it should be. He was advised to seek this cottage as a safe retreat by an old schoolfellow, who was pastor of Mora

Church. Gustavus was loth to suspect treachery on the part of his playmate, who did, in fact, attempt to betray him. So at first, when he saw the troopers coming, his suspicion naturally rested on Mats Larsson and his wife. His last words to her before she closed the trap were 'Woman, if you can be brought to prove false to me you will not lack for money.' But they could not buy her; they could not buy her! Nay! Nay!" And the knightly old soldier rubbed his hands as he said this, as though he were earnestly congratulating himself and his country and the world, over an event of patriotic faithfulness that took place the day before. He impressed us all in that way.

The picture is worthy of study; and we very much regretted the shortness of our visit for gazing upon it. All the details of cottage furniture—for which historic fidelity is claimed—are well presented: and as the eye comes back from seeing and examining them, there is fresh as ever the thrill of sympathy with that brave and beautiful peasant woman: grasping the vat (which, history tells us, fortunately had been emptied a minute before), casting a glance of terror at the mailed and spear-bearing horsemen who are galloping close to her house—about to utter her parting admonition and assurance as one can well believe: "Go! I will trick them: I will save you!"

The painting by E. Berg, of the same size as that from the brush of Hockert, is placed on the left-hand wall, and it presents a view of the house of Ornas, near Borlange, which we shall soon visit; where Gustavus was also at one time concealed, and from which he was enabled, by the steadfast aid of another woman, to elude his pursurers. Over this canvas is an inscription, of which we give the following interpretation: "Gustavus Wasa, expecting to find minds and arms to save his native country, walked disguised from a village in Delarne. At the end of November, 1530, he came to the estate of Arendt Persson. This traitorous friend of his youth, feigning interest for the fate of his country and sympathy with the plans of Gustavus for its liberation, lodged him in an old house, which is still standing, under the pretext of finding out the thoughts of the neighbors. Perssons started to inform the Steward of the district of the hiding place of the fugitive, on whose head a high price had been set; but Arendt Perssons wife, Barbro Stigsdotter, suspecting the plans of her husband, called her guest and procured him means of escape from the overhanging danger."

As a matter of fact, she let him down from a window, in the Kungs-kammare, by a long towel. He was then taken in a boat and carried to the other side of the Lake Rankhyttan.

The painting by Charles XV, which is of equal proportions with the others, and might obtain the same price at an auction where the bidders were exclusively composed of railroad monopolists, is a daub; but as it is the production of a royal hand, and was the well-meant effort of a very popular King—to whom, perhaps, nothing worse than this can be attributed—a "successor on the throne" (by interpolation, so to speak,) and as it makes a corresponding "adornment."—also, so to speak—we may continue to tolerate it in its place a few years longer. It is entitled, "Salen in Lima." It is a landscape; simply that, and nothing more. The inscription over this painting reads about as follows: "After vain efforts to exalt the Dalecarlians to struggle for liberty, Gustavus walked to the boundries of Norway, to leave his country, which he saw no more prospect of saving. In the meantime other fugitives came with the news about the cruelties of King Christian, both in the Capital and in the country. The Dalecarlians, changing their minds, sent messengers to seek and recall Gustavus, who was found in the village of Salen, in the parish of Lima. He returned with joy and was chosen Captain by the people gathered in Mora, and set out in order to drive away the tyrant and his adherents. The saved country elevated the liberator upon the throne, which he confirmed against enemies without and within. The exiled fugitive was the founder of a new ship of state, and the ancestor of one of the noblest royal families of Europe."

The trapdoor was opened, and one at a time we descended and surveyed the cellar. The steps are made of stone, and have been put in at the side, where the ladder rested on which the great Gustavus himself walked down. We measured the hiding place, as the keeper could not give the dimensions. It is eleven feet long, eight feet wide and five feet high from the bottom to the top of the arch. It is oven-shaped, as before indicated. The walls are brick, and they are stained and black with age. Here are inscribed by their own hands, the

MONUMENT OF GUSTAVUS WASA.

names or initials of every Swedish king since the days of Gustavus, who has visited this place.

In one corner of the "monument"—nearest to the door—there is a small table, on which is a register where visitors' names are recorded. We see here only one American autograph,—that of a Mr. Baker,—of Toledo, Ohio.

By the side of the register is a Bible that bears the date 1541. We opened its lids at random and saw two pages of the Book of Esther. This was considered a coincidence.

Going outside we noticed the coats of arms of each State,

upon the corners of the monumental building. The carving and color are admirable.

As we pass through the grounds, back again to the official residence of the keeper, we meet and are introduced to his wife, an old lady who at once manifested some of the same fascinating qualities possessed by her worthy husband. Her name, like that of Madame Stacklebacken, at Stromsholm, is in all the neighbors mouths, as the name of The Woman of Good Deeds.

And now, as we pass back to the town—laden with photographs, as may well be imagined—our youthful guide points out the direction in which the parish of Lima lies. There he has been; there he was last year. There the people are not obliged to work; nay, not at all. They live on the rent money of their wood lands. They can and do rent them out to companies, who chop on them for a term of fifty years. Then there must be an interval of undisturbed growth for one hundred years, during which the Limans must cultivate habits of of industry, according to the Scripture. After that comes another fifty years lease; and so on. Lucky are the children of the Limans of this generation, for they were born into the beginning of a half century's lease. We asked: "You were there long enough to see how these people lived during their independent period? Do they become enervated—lazy?"

"Nay; they work enough for healthful exercise; that is all they have to do, and that is all they do do."

"How far is it from here to that land of the blest?"

"About seven Swedish miles."

Midday Mountain, twenty English miles distant from Mora, is respectfully called to our attention. We had noticed that it was conspicuously there before, and were just going to ask about it. Well, from the top of that mountain you can see seven churches. It is called Midday mountain because at midday the sun stands right over it! On the very summit there is a crystal spring, where the water bubbles up in copious volume, without any perceptible diminution of quantity, all the year round.

Along the side of that mountain are many Sætors, where the cows are pastured during the Summer. Several dairy proprietors in the vicinity of Mora have their Summer quarters (or their milking women have) in those mountain-grass lands. In those rare instances where a Dalecarlian loses his temper and cannot refrain from speaking with contemptuous indignation to his neighbor, he sometimes tells him to go to Sætor; which I took some pains to explain, was equivalent to a common expression indulged in sometimes under similar circumstances in America, "You go to grass." For this explanation, I received a vote of thanks.

We met a tall leather-apron with a man behind it or in it, as we were nearly opposite the front gate, of the rich man's residence, who dwells in Catherinesberg. He dag-i-dagged to us in loud, peremptory manner; and I declare I thought for one moment that he was going to draw his knife on us. He made a sudden motion of his hand to his side and brought forth something that glittered. It was his snuff-box. Most hospitably he held it out to one and all. Then he himself took out an enormous pinch and seemed to toss it in the air, but we all knew that it was not thrown away. We smelt of the pulverized article, of course, for courtesy's sake, and then we foreigners—inexperienced in this prevailing habit among the elder Dalecarlians—gave the whole neighborhood the benefit of our "atts sas" which they won't forget very soon; nor we, either.

With compassion that mighty man of Mora looked at us. He had heard of the Herr from America that was in town. I guessed that it was his brother that I had been drinking coffee with. He would not speculate upon or vouchsafe me any information on that subject at all.

He said "you" to me and to all of us a sufficent number of times to vindicate his Dalecarlian right and privilege in this direction. (The Dalecarlians are the only people in Southern Sweden who say "you," but they take pride in saying this to foreigners and to their king and Princes Royal, so that they may not forget it.) Having you-ed us at least three times, all around, he passed on. We felt a sense of relief in his absence; but we were assured that he intended to highly honor us by his snuff invitation and his *you* iteration. We were satisfied, and rejected the offer to call him back for the purpose of establishing a better acquaintance.

The spot from which Gustavus is said to have addressed the people of his vicinity once upon a time, which is called Klockgropsbacke, is situated in the yard of a private residence, near to the schoolhouse and not a fifty rods from the church. It is a small turf-covered mound, on which has been planted a flagstaff of perhaps twenty-five feet in height. Adjacent to it is a tea-table arbor—coffee-table arbor, I should have written—for family entertainment. Our friend from Falun, who took the lead on our first visit to this spot, hesitated about going into the yard through the back gate that stood open or the front gate that was shut. He was satisfied as we were at the time, with simply taking notes of the surroundings from the line of the fence, twenty or thirty feet distant. But the neglect to make an actual entrance upon this ground haunted us; as we have since learned it has tormented other folks. But we have cured our sorrow and grieving by marching boldly up to the door of the house of the owner of the premises aforesaid, and Americanizing him (we presume it was he) into an agreement to let us walk around the mound and over it once—provided we quit the neighborhood forever after. We passed as prescribed. We are sorry to say that the engravings that represent this spot as a precipitous hill are false, fraudulent and untrue; and there is no tradition of grading, cutting or filling that lends any moral or material support to the historical allegations of the engraver. It is, I believe—as far as I can recollect at this moment—the only instance of deceptive publications that I have come across since I have been in Sweden; unless I have to drag in here, as an exception to this complimentary statement, the ridiculously false statement about American taxation on Swedish immigrants in which newspapers indulge. But, of course, I was speaking about amusements, historic associations and accessories, and all that sort of thing; and only about that sort of thing.

From Kristinberg there is a magnificent view all roundabout, of harbor and lake and of distant mountain ridges that are so very, very blue—with intervening meadow lands, so very, very green.

To the southwest, and about eight miles away, is the long narrow island of Solleron. This island is said to contain the best land in all this section of country, and to be inhabited by the worst people that live in Dalarne. It constitutes a parish by itself, and has for its minister at the present time a man who once was a blacksmith and became a minister long after he had arrived at maturity. He is said to sympathize with the people in unlawful deeds and purposes. When an officer comes there to arrest persons charged with crime, it is said that he will aid in the concealment and contribute toward deceiving or ill-treating the sheriff.

RATTVIK CHURCH.

A woman who lived there from childhood is now under arrest for killing a girl of her own parentage; a child 8 years old. And since her imprisonment, evidence has been obtained which indicates that she had killed ten of her children before she committed this particular murder for which she is now under-going or awaiting examination. The church there is called Sophia Magdelene, but our guide said that the people who live on the adjacent mainland frequently say that it should be called Judas Iscariot. As one of our company expressed it, with that neat Swedish turn for precision, "It seems to be a little land of evil-doers." It lies beautifully at the head of Lake Siljan. (Lord Byron was wont to say that little island with good land locked harbors breed pirates.)

All along the lake shore we mark the track of the lightning on the telegraph poles; often shattering them to splinters—sometimes leaving just enough wood to pospone the day of substitution till a more convienent season; and so letting us see in the sunshine what can be done in this latitude in a thunderstorm, when nature goes into the telegraph business. Insulating telegraph wires have been run from the Mora telegraph office to the lake.

You can telegraph from Mora to the end of Sweden for a kroner; 20 words for twenty cents. The operator here acted as though he was struck by lightning, when I told him what the charges were for telegraphing messages in some parts of the United States of America.

In the midst of a drenching rainstorm we bade farewell to Mora. Nor had the clouds lifted or ceased to send down floods when we reached the picturesquely situated Valley of Rattvik,—the "Arcadia of Dalarne."

XVI.

FROM MORA TO FALUN.

I spoke of the drenching showers that followed us from the head of Lake Siljen to the "Arcadia of Delecarlia"; and now I have to add that this heavy fall of water continued during our entire journey to Falun. There were brief intervals when the rain would slacken, and from some corners of the heavens the sun would peep through long enough to throw a score of curiously beautiful rainbows at so many angles with each other. But it seemed as if these were breathing spells, during which the elements gathered new strength and supplies for the business of deludging the earth. A row of farmers sat at one end of the cabin on the Gustavus Wasa, and talked in a deeply sympathizing tone and manner of the sorrow of their distant neighbors, under this affliction of excessive moisture. They would pass to one another the oft repeated question "what will the poor people do?" And then there would be a pause for several minutes, which would be of painful eloquence, as indicating the profound grief and silent prayer for the bereaved, that was indwelling and outgoing grom these good hearted visitors and neighbors from an adjoining State.

While we did not fail to join in the sentiment and expressions of regret, we sought in vain to cheer up the native mourners by suggesting that it might not be so bad a year for the crops as was now feared by them ; but when we saw that our efforts of this kind were calculated to make these folks think that we were really unsympathetic, we cut short the well meant speech with as sharp an assurance as we could give of our direct wish for more favorable seasons. But we could not wholly regain the confidence and liking that we had lost in the way herein confessed ; and we shall never more make a similar attempt among the inhabitants of this country.

Oh, how it *did* rain ! At times it was of the character of a cataract. Those passengers who walked from the steamer station to Gagness Kyrka, a distance of one mile, had their umbrellas beaten in, and made their appearance at the Dalef station with every article of clothing thoroughly saturated. To one who has been accustomed to the dry Summer seasons of California, there is a sense of novelty in such an exhibition that cannot be adequately explained. It would seem as though the month must be December, January or February ; it was like the case of pinching one's self to satisfy as to identity. It could not be that this was midsummer? The sudden, complete belief [that we were in a California Winter would come, as vivid as a dream ; and then there would be an actual shock and almost audible protest, when the fact of time and place rushed back upon our consciousness.

We had a nobleman with us, from Mora to Rattvik ; a
"no mistake," genuine baron "of high degree ; " one among
the barons of eminent distinction. So we were told repeatedly
by a number of fellow passengers ; who wanted our opinion
as to his looks, qualifications, and as to how he compared
with other persons of his rank, etc.; and that upon very insufficient observation! When we ventured to say that we did
not like the idea of a titled nobleman, we met with unanimous agreement in the little knot of travellers who with ourselves braved the tempest when it was on its lower flood, by
standing out on the forecastle deck. But if there be nobles,
we hope that Sweden will always have as handsome representatives in that line as Baron Plata (or Plater,) who
paced the Captain's floor on the Wasa, on the day and in the
midst of the storm above mentioned. A splendid appearing
man he certainly is ; over six feet high, and rounded out in
due proportion for a man of forty or thereabouts. Fine forehead, and clear hazel eyes that, with the lines immediately
below them, which separated downwards when he smiled, be-
token a kind and generous disposition. A good specimen of
a nobleman to put on exhibition, when the best arguments
in behalf of the system of blooded aristocracy are required.

We waited for the river or dalef steamer for more than an
hour : being housed in an old dilapidated freight shed ; wherein
several companies and individuals who were making this trip
spread their respective lunches and ate heartily ; while there
was the clatter of much conversation and the mingled rattling
and spattering sound made by copious rain showers on the
roof and on the surface of the stream beside us. The drops of
falling water seemed to be of unusual size, and the noise of the
rain striking the river during the heaviest gush of the showers
was sufficiently strong to prevent our hearing each other's
words unless we spoke at a high pitch of the voice.

A peddler who had accompanied us down from Mora, but
had made no effort to dispose of any of his wares while on the
steamer, and who had answered all questions put to him by a
response of grunts, here unstrapped his enormous bundle and
displayed a *diverschandel* establishment that in point of variety
and amount would have been creditable to the average thread

and needle store of London. And who unloosed this man's tongue? what wrought this miracle of transformation from a deaf mute to the most voluble and even most vociferous hawker? Was this the effect of the torrents without and around us suggested one? Had he been to see the monument of the great Gustavus and temporarily lost his power of speech in the presence of Carl Oberg, the King's keeper—only now, at this distance, regaining the faculty of articulation? However this was or might have been it is certain that something was bought from the tremendous pack by everybody in the station, as a declared memento—if for no other reason—of this remarkable outburst of salesman fluency.

In the last minutes of waiting, a loitering, staggering, drenched and drunken peasant came in, out of the thick rain, and immediately purchased a yard of blue ribbon, to lighten the poor man's load, as he said. After this funny transaction and explanation, the inebriate danced a kind of tangle-foot figure at one end of the shed, and then doubled up and went so fast asleep on the instant that he had to be carried to the boat by the baggage cart drivers.

I must not forget to mention that it was raining all this time with such momentary pauses as have been before admitted; and if I should omit to speak of this fact again, it may as well be understood once for all, that water poured down from the skies so that you could not see anything two hundred yards away during nearly all the voyage from Gagness Kyrka to Batstad.

On this section of our return trip we became acquainted with a gentleman who said that he had resided in Boston two or three years,—thirteen years ago. He had forgotten most of his English speech, which he said was once very extensive. He regretted that on account of his age—now 55—he could not well afford to try a business change back again to America. He said he was a small shop-keeper in Stockholm, and managed to just make the two ends of the year come together without bringing him in debt. He had been to the North as far as Mora; stopping at all the principal points on the way down, for the purpose of promoting or keeping up his little business connections. He put the adjective for insignificance before

every important noun that he used; speaking in a very slow
and deliberate manner, as though afflicted with great scrupulosity about his sentences; almost convinced that he ought
not to say anything, and always regretting what he had said the
minute he got a word or two out of his mouth. He even
called his wife "my little woman," although she was as big as
he was, and only then to be properly described as small by
comparison with some other men's wives who were on board.
He immediately and forcibly suggested Snagsby, of Bleak
House; and his "little woman" looked as though she *might*
take on a fit of jealously on less probable grounds than those
from which Mrs. Snagsby inexorably reasoned. However, he
was a valuable acquaintance;—an intelligent man, and one
thoroughly in sympathy with our republican institutions. Kings
and lords and great standing armies he did not like; and he
ventured, with several little ahems, to tell us in a very low
tone—almost a whisper—that he hoped that the next generation of Swedes would peacefully change the little kingdom of
Sweden and Norway into a little government by the people;
with a President at the head, and a Senate and House of Representatives—similar to the political institutions of the United
States. All this he said—with more stretch of words and
phrases than I have given. Bless the little man. My heart
warmed towards him. I took him further to one side and
told him of my surprise and my stronger sentiments on account
of the fact that our Swedish Consuls did not display the
American flag—not on the fourth of July, even; and that the
consular business of the United States in this kingdom was
often left to Swedish Vice Consuls, or to Consuls that were of
Swedish birth and devoid of sympathy with our republic. He
agreed to co-operate in certain little ways that will have a tendency to expose this outrage, and give us representative men
and actions in this portion of the globe; if the consular system
is to be continued and maintained. Bless the little man.

A Leksand girl on board, at our request exhibited some
winter garments that she was taking down to Stockholm for sale.
The coats were lined with wool; and some of her long jackets
or frocks for women were made of sheepskin tanned with the
wool upon them. These people make sheepskin aprons, of

handsome style, which I think would be copied extensively in our country if the model or pattern was conspicuously put on exhibition. They are very neat, are often tastefully ornamented, and are recommended as "lasting-a-life-time." They have the appearance of cloth.

Our new-found Boston friend was interested in these articles of domestic commerce; also in the Mora wig and switch manufactories. Female agents and saleswomen representing these home industries were on board the boat, on their way to the capital, with specimens of their invoices convenient for showing and sale. They take contracts to make a thin-haired or bald headed lady as good as a young lady of twenty—to all head-top appearances. This: or no pay. Could anything be fairer in bargaining, or more conducive to uniformity of fashion in the royal ball-room? As indicated, this work is done by the fire-sides of the Delecarlian women.

From Batstad to Borlange—the three-mile connecting diligence ride—it was a succession of deep puddles; showing that the watering-pot of old Pluvius had been tipped in this valley at the angle on which it was held during the fore part of the day in upper Dalarne. But the sun had fiercely broken through clouds for a steady afternoon visit; and there was a sense of beneficence in his warm rays that made us think again—as all of us have doubtless thought, in times past—that it was no wonder that the ancients, unenlightened by direct revelation from heaven, or the uninstructed savages of the present generation, had their greatest reverence or their religious worship for the king of day. As one of our Swedish companions—Dr. Victor Hugo Wickstrom, Professor in the University of Lund—remarked: It was natural for any man, under the circumstances, to feel like praying to Old Sol to continue to burn up the clouds for a month, and look down evenly on this surface of the globe until the harvest was over.

It was difficult to get our fellow travellers into any protracted conversation about any other subjects than the weather, and the state of the crops, and the farm prospects of the people and for the people during the coming Autumn and Winter seasons.

Borlange has two villages: The railroad station is "number two:"—This is a great manufacturing place, where from the raw ore the metal is treated and manipulated, and "worked up" to the last point of execution; from the puddle furnace to a scythe factory. Water power has been obtained by tunneling through a mountain; water is abundant and, of course, the power is enormous. A foreman to whom we spoke could give no exact measurement; but he believed that the aggregate of force that could be utilized would amount to 400,000 horse power. The wages of the furnace men are very low; from 80 ore to 2 kroners a day. But the machinists—some of them—get as high as eight and ten kroners a day; which, considering the difference in the cost of living is higher than the wages received by some expert workmen in New York establishments from whom I obtained items for comparison.

Between old manufacturing Borlange and the new railroad station Borlange, is a double line of workmen's cottages, of which the people boast. They contain from two to six families—according to household population, of course. They are of brick: two stories and two stories and a half high; and appear to us at first glance as excellently arranged for the accomodation of this class of laborers. They seemed to be modeled after those we saw at Gottenberg, or built simultaneously from the same pattern. Of course, the idea of copying from distant Swedish fellow-subjects and manufacturers was repudiated at the instant of its being hinted. The "nay, nay" came like a flash, and seemed to almost anticipate the remark of a lady companion: "How sensitive some of these people are, on the line of jealousies among themselves!" And yet, this sentiment is only skin-deep, for when we told them at the workmen's houses in Borlange of the condition of the workmen at Gottenberg, and of the characteristic kindness of their masters, our listeners were unmistakably gratified and proud.

And now the great Gustavus Wasa reappears; and indeed we never tire of hearing about him or visiting the places his presence and perils have made memorable. Ornas is situated at the Southwest end of Lake Runn. Here is the house from which he escaped, when pursued by his enemies; being let down from a window by Barbro Stigsdotter. He was not in a basket, after the manner of St. Paul; but he clung to the end of a long towel. The room he occupied is shown, and the bed in which he slept is duly certified as the identical resting-place of the fugitive just prior to this successful flight. One of our Swedish companions stated that which we have never read in any history of this affair. She said that Barbro's treacherous husband, Arendt Persson, who sought to betray Gusvtaus, was so enraged at the conduct of his wife that he would never live with her afterwards; and that he procured a legal separation from her. Of course it is well known that she was pensioned by Gustavus, when he became King of Sweden.

ORNAS.

At the southeast end of this lake is Rankhytton, where Gustavus thrashed corn, having disguised himself and obtained employment in the dress of a Delecarlian peasant. The barn or "king's box" where he worked, is on exhibition also; and we were disappointed in not having the identical flail that he handled, when scolded by his pretended mistress (as a part of the trick of concealment,) for his laziness and inefficiency. After inquiring for it, we were informed that it probably was in existence, and would be sought for at once! And then our local guide gradually reached a suspicion that we were incredulous about the whole exhibition ; for with very severe emphasis, she asked if we had seen the towel with which Gustavus was let down from the window by Barbro?

---o---

XVII

AT FALUN; AND THENCE TO WESTERAS.

FALUN is properly described as a town that has been formed by the growing of a number of separate villages. Historically this is a true description. But we could not see that it was "obviously"—as alleged—so originated and enlarged into one continuous or connected settlement. There was the average homogeneousness in the character of the buildings,etc. Falun is situated between lakes Varpan and Tisken, and the views on the lake as you approach the town are as charming as anything we beheld on the far-famed Malaren itself. A little stream divides the town; but much the larger portion and the best constructed, lies on the East bank; and this section is certainly well built and hansomely located.

The first singularity of the place that strikes a visitor, is the almost uniform building entrance through court yards. There are very few front doors, as we know them; and while this is the prevailing custom and appearance throughout Sweden, it is almost exclusively the fact in Falun. Sidewalks are rare; and those that are to be seen and travelled are for the most part constructed the same as a road-bed: laid with cobble stones of the pointed variety. We are told with a hearty accompanying laugh, very soon after our arrival, that visitors frequently complain of dislocated ankles when they have spent a few hours in marching about town. The cheerful waiting-maid that told us this, was evidently of the opinion that this set forth one of the attractions of the place. And

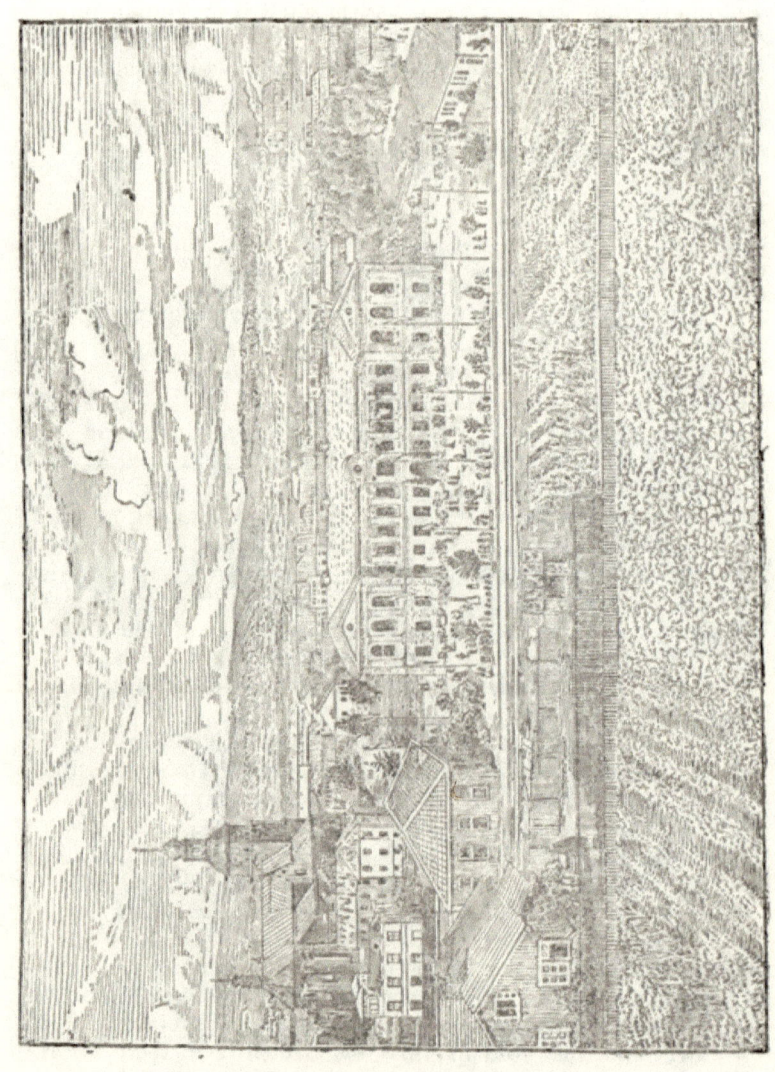

FALUN—VIEW OF MARKET, CATHEDRAL AND COPPER-HILL RANGE.

she asked us how our heels felt, when we returned from our first promenade. She evidently made the inquiry with the expectation that she would have a complaint to add to her stock of items. Day and date she gave, as to this and that limping tourist. But good English walking shoes, and a month's almost daily experience in pedestrian excursions, had fortified us against this test of tendons. Count us not in your hospital catalogue, my merry, merry maid of the Nya Hotellet, at Falun.

To Mr. B. V. Norstedt, formerly and for many years the superintendent here, we desire to express our grateful acknowledgements, for his services as guide over and in and through the copper mines of Falun. For eight hours were we in his company; and fortunate will those be who come after us, if they can procure the attendance of the same instructor. Three years ago, after thirty-five-years employment by the great corporation, he retired, having, as he expressed it, just enough and not to much to take his rest with, for the estimated God-willing balance of his days. One of the lords of this great mine estate informed us that they offered to double Mr. Norstedt's wages (they don't speak of salary here) if he would remain in harness for another ten years. He declined the labor but justly appreciated the proposition.

And from the same source we learned that a little child— a girl of nine or ten—that was with him and his wife when we first met him, was not his own daughter, as we naturally supposed her to be; but a waif that he had taken from the market, as it were, when the effects of a dead man were disposed of at auction. He was present at the sale, and saw the child delivered over to the keeper of a public institution of charity; but the sight so haunted him that he rose from his bed the following midnight and went and took the girl and made her his own. When we heard of this, we knew one of the special reasons for the extreme deference and heartiness with which he was received and welcomed by the workmen, wherever we passsed them on the hills of Falun.

The guide-books speak of the "burnt up" appearance of the whole face of the country to the Southwest of the town or city of Falun—due to the smoke from the roasting kilns. The appearance of the surface could not be more barren; resembling the region round-about Virginia City, Nevada. But the Comstock range did have a sagebrush cover, and still partly preserves or retains it, where actual mining has not been done. These copper hills were once clad with thick groves of pine and fir; and on the summit of the ridges fartherest on the horizon, there is even now a line of stunted resinous timber.

B. V. NORSTEDT.

It is recorded that two bucks became engaged in a battle, about half-way up the hill, immediately to the East of the lower hoisting works; and when the ancients who witnessed the struggle from below went up to separate the "rambankshious animals," they discovered that in their combat they had dug away the dirt from the foot of a tree that covered some glistening stone. Then followed inquiry and examination and ascertaining, and thorough mining work; and lo! the "Treasure of Sweden" was developed!

The ore is still treated in part by roasting; but the greater portion is quietly dissolved by acids which are obtained by cooking some of the rock or earth that lines the leads of copper! Is not this seething the kid in the milk of the mother? Other acids than those required for immediate use have lately been discovered; and two great factories of reducing works have been built here, for the extraction and export market preparation of these valuable liquors.

The town is not afflicted by the vapors of the kilns, so far as we could notice; but upon the hills above the ledges, it is unpleasant to walk through the lines of sulphurous smoke, vitriol of copper, sulphuric acid, and an ochre sediment—the last making a deep penetrating and enduring red paint—are extracted here in enormous quantities.

The preservative properties of the fumes of the old reduction beds is something that has obtained almost world-wide notoriety. All the guide books tell the story of the young man Matts Israelson who for 49 years lay buried in the mines, and who was so well preserved when taken out that he was at once identified by the old woman who, as a girl, had been betrothed to him—49 years before. His remains were preserved 21 years in a glass case, on exhibition; and our guide and friend said that the "spectacle" was not at all ghastly,—like an ordinary corpse,—but was the picture of quiet and blissful sleep.

"Stoten" is the name of an abyss, 1160 feet long, 640 feet wide and 290 deep, caused by the subsiding of the roof of the principal mine in 1687. Underneath this monstrous caving work is now being prosecuted. Visitors are provided with the miners' attire, inclusive of a helmet surmounted by a lighted candle, and a special guide. The descent is by a wooden flight for about a hundred feet; and then business

THE STOTEN ABYSS.

begins on an iron ladder, or series of ladders. At a depth of 700 feet we reach the radsaal, or council chamber. It is a mammoth excavation; but as we were warned by Bædecker, the lighting is insufficient, and the paths are not well selected through the wet and dangerous places. The echoes from gun and pistol firing are lively, lingering and at last sonorously explosive:—reverberation, after reverberation, until there is a cracking, thumping detonation, very much like the sound of a blast as heard at the miners' alcove retreat during the construction of the Sutro tunnel. Then all the responses seem to concentrate their vibrations, and roll along in a peal of thunder. But, my friend, take our word for it:—you will be glad to get back again to the outer rim of this world's creation.

The sound of a muffled bell—it sounded as though it was muffled—attracted our attention and excited our curiosity. What is that for? striking every minute! It means that all the pump works are in order. If any one of the numerous long pumping arms should get "out of kilter", that dreadful bell would cease to be heard; and its silence would give the necessary alarm. This is reversing the rule of notice, in such case usually made and provided; but it is said to work well,—the cessation of sound proving to be a more startling warning than a clang of gongs or crash of trumpets. So it is claimed. There are two large churches at Falun; both of which are worthy a visit. The copper-roofed church—called the copper church—is situated in the midst of a pleasant grove; once, and now accasionally, used for burial purposes. St. Catherine's church has a reredos of carved wood. With central panels that represent (first) the lord's supper, (second) the crucifixion: (third) the resurrection, (fourth) the ascension, and (fifth) the sitting at the right hand of God the Father. The paintings are excellent, and well repaid our study of an hour or more; sitting before the chancel and gazing upon them, while at the same time we enjoyed the private practice and rehearsing of the accomplished organist. This reredos was presented to the church in 1669 by Maria Lemmens and Anthony Trotxict. The sides are adorned with statues of the apostles and of many saints—male and female. It is not plastered over with gilt, as are most of the similar pieces in Sweden. On and about the wine cup pulpit, there is no gilding whatever, save on the sign of the God-head in the ceiling of the sounding board. The panels of the pulpit present the twelve stations of the cross. There is an hour-glass and there is a bible 180 years of age, on the pulpit shelf.

We were shown a priest's robe made in 1785 and still worn, and an altar cloth bearing date 1695.

There was handsome carving on the pews. There was seating capacity for three thousand persons; and with benches in the aisles 4,000 listeners often sat within sound of the preacher's voice. A church going, God-fearing people.

The schools and gymnasiums, prisons and hospitals are of the same pattern, and excellence as similar institutions in Stockholm and Westeras, elsewhere in this volume sufficiently described.

We were to leave Falun by the 7-o'clock morning train; and were up for an early review walk before three. It was light at two. We went into the beautiful park ground that surrounds Catherine Kyrka, and enjoyed the song of the birds, while the morning twilight brightened into sunshine. The swallows were a plague, because with their chirping they broke the harmonious effects from the sweet singers that were in the trees above us,—joining in a melodious chorus. But who could even scold these saucily familiar fellows, that came in flocks about our seats, and soon cultivated an acquaintance with a little girl in our company, to the extent of eating crumbs from her straw hat, when she placed some pieces of bread on the rim.

And again, before the hour of four, we heard the voice of the organ; its claironet pipes sounding most exquisitely at our distance from the gallery. What an industrious master of amusement:—Tom Finch at his instrument again!

Once more we pass around in front of the church, and this time note the bronze doors, bearing date 1670. The left hand door was stamped Batzer Hanson; and on the right hand door was Karmleers Dotter. Those were the givers, who gave 213 years ago.

Once more we go down the hill-side on which the new city—that is, a city of the last two hundred years,—modern in a Gothtenberg sense—is situated; and make the rounds once more on the walks mid-way on the roasting hills. We see workman quitting their cottages, to go to their shift; and in almost every instance there is an affectionate parting at the door. Often the wife and husband kiss each other on the threshold; sometimes she stands and waves a handkerchief or cloth at him until he turns the corner of the street on which they live; often a little head is seen popping out from the upper window, and then a tiny hand appears with the ends of a ribbon or the string of a cap held tightly in the fist and shaken.

Once through an open window on a level with a street we could not avoid seeing the family on their knees, while the father read a few verses from St. Luke and then uttered a prayer. Passing on a little, to the corner of the house, we heard his voice. The supplication was comprehensive: for all men, for all nations, for the king and queen of Sweden and all governors; for all families; for this family especially; for the children that they might have holy habits and grow up in purity of heart; for the mother that she might have strength and wisdom for her sacred vocation; and for the father, that he might be diligent in labor, fervent in spirit, serving the Lord.

Under one of the dump-troughs—which much resembled the arrangements that were made in early Washoe days at the mouth of the Savage and Gould and Curry mines in Virginia City—we saw a very old man industriously at work pounding the large stones or bunches, and sorting the valuable from the dross with great rapidity. We salute: "May we ask how long you have been at work in these mines?" "Yes, yes, nigh 55 years; since I was a lad, mind you." "You worked in the mines at first?" "On top at first; in the mines afterwards; on top again. Second childhood now!" and the old man resumed his work with sledge and laughed loudly over his wit. "May we ask how much you earn a day now?" "Yes, yes. I get two kroner and twenty ore, but part of that is my pension, you see." And he laughed again, more loudly and longer than before; though we could not see, this time, how the laugh came in on any sufficient basis. "55 years! How old might you be?" "Nigh 71. How old are you?" "You return questions like a Yankee." "What is a Yankee?" We explained. He said "Ah, ha." We said we were Americans. He made a whistling noise and exclaimed "O! O!" We added that we were Californians. He dropped his sledge quickly; looked at us sharply; came to us with a slow, uncertain, but not tottering step—a distance of eight or ten feet,—and waving his hand said in a whisper—bowing his head meanwhile—"I have got a nephew out that way somewhere. You may know him. But I am told that it is a great country, and that you cannot be expected to know everybody, any more than we do in Sweden." We took the name: "Talenson;" though he said we could remember it without putting it down, "as it was so much like Falenson." In reply to our questions we were told that the boy went away when a lad of sixteen: sailing in a ship out of Christiana, Norway, for England. Then he reported that he was going on a sea voyage around the Horn to California. Then two letters had come from him, dated at El Dorado (El Dorado county, we inferred from the entire story). Would we inquire for him and ask others to do the same. Of course we promised. The first name was Carl. We told him that the captain of the steamer Pius, on the Stromsholm Kanal, had asked us to do the same for his uncle; whose name, singular enough, bore such a resemblance to his boy's name that his request must put us in mind of the captain's wish, and vice-versa.

"What are the wages of workmen in the mines generally?" "They vary much according to the work," said the old man, resuming his toil, but bidding us stay and talk with him "all the same"—startling us by using the Swedish phrase that corresponds most nearly with the comparatively modern annex to California conversational sentences. "Some workmen get as high as three kroners and a half. Some get no more than one kroner. Most of them get about two kroners, I think; though I don't know so much about it as I did when I worked below."

We told him of our conversation with Mr. Norstedt, in regard to the matter; and he said, "Yes, yes; whatever he says is exact. You cannot study anything out more true than he will tell you. He is a good man, and everybody was sorry when he left the mines." "Are all the mines healthy?" "Yes, yes," uttered with great emphasis. "Why, haven't you heard that the king and royal family come in this neighborhood in cholera times, to avoid the plague? We never have cholera here. You would get fat if you stayed here a year." Then he stepped back and eyed us curiously, and added: "Maybe?" As if he was almost disposed to withdraw his last remark. Of his own motion he went on to say that the workmen were well paid, or considered that they were; and that they were taken care of in their sickness and old age. There was never any trouble on the mine; they were good, firm and steady laborers. Then he pointed down towards the town and asked us if we came up by a certain road or street. As we replied in the affirmative, he went on to say: "Then you passed by the house of a widow lady, whose husband left her a half million kroners And she has given 5,000 kroners for an orphan asylum." Whether founding the institution or adding to its endowment, we could not make out. "You are very handy in telling a good piece of rock from a poor lump?" "Yes, yes. I ought to be; if I was not by this time, what sort of a man would I be?" And here came another fit of hearty laughter. We parted with very affectionate adieus.

Slowly descending the hill we overtook a girl who was walking with difficulty, bearing some burden in a large basket. She turned half way around and courtesied as we closely approached; saying "*God dag-i-dag*," as the people (and the girls especially) in this section of Sweden alone can utter that greeting. My friend, you know nothing of the possibilities of softness that pertain to or dwell in the letter *G*, until you hear it pronounced by a Delecarlian girl. When that Swedish coffee saloon shall have been established in New York, Chicago, or San Francisco, by some wise Scandinavian, with Siljan maids for attendants, I wish to have you patronize it once or twice, at least, until you catch this mallable sound. I don't think it can be exactly, or I should say, rather, adequately described. The nearest I could come with a hint about it would be by the illustration of a 200-pound steam trip-hammer dropping on a base-ball made of lead. Yes! they utter it with great vim, up to the center of the letter—as it were, and there the articulation sinks in delicious tenderness.

The stout word with all is *you* ; which, as before stated, they alone in this country commonly use in addressing strangers and each other. In giving conversations elsewhere I have, of course, set down the *you* as a proper translation ; but it is rarely used outside of Delecarlia, in ordinary communications, by the peasantry, when speaking to elders or employers.

If you will please to turn to the map of Southern and Central Sweden, you will readily follow our route from Falun to Westeras, which we travelled at an expense of a cent and a quarter to one cent and a half per mile.

Returning to Borlange and revisiting some of the houses built for renting to the workmen in the forges, we were less favorably impressed with them than at first. Where the family exceeds four persons—increases beyond man and wife and two children—the upper apartments are very much too small ; as in such case the folks are actually crowded for space. The homes of some of the statkarlars at Stromsholm are preferable in this respect to the provision made here, when the demands in numbers rise above the limit of space for comfort in the rooms assigned.

From Borlange we ticket anew, to Sala ; and again purchase cards for Tilberga. At Krylbo, a junction station, we have to change cars, to reach Sala ; leaving at Krylbo the border line of Delecarlia.

And here we cannot forbear to mention that many writers, including some guide-book authors, deplore the fact that the people of Delecarlia as a rule own the land which they cultivate ; sometimes saying with regretful intimations that there are and can be few rich men in this section on this account. The most independent, the best contented people that we have found in Sweden—taking communities, towns, villages, and districts into consideration—are in Dalarne ; and one great reason for this probably exists in the division and subdivision of land that has been so much and so strangely bemoaned. How true is the

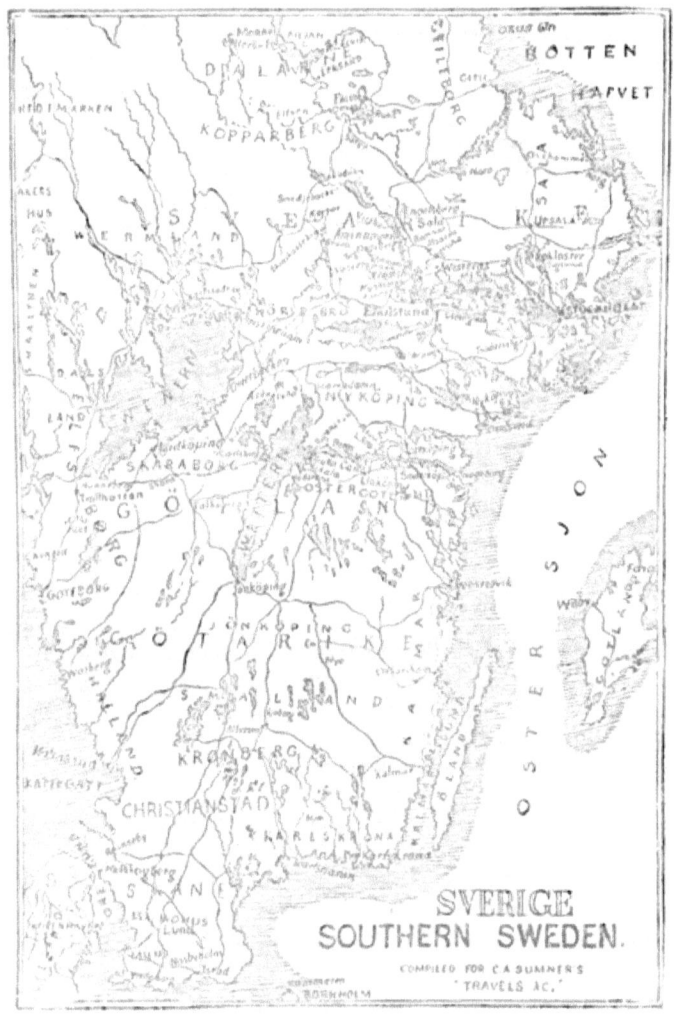

MAP OF SOUTHERN SWEDEN.

saying, engraved in our old Latin copy-books: "The great estates destroyed Rome."

Sala contains the great silver mine of Sweden; at one time yielding $800,000 per year. Now the product is less than two thousand pounds of assayed pure metal. Once, for its riches, it was styled the "Gem of the nation."

At Tilberga, where there is yet another transfer of passengers and baggage destined for the Koping route, we can see in the distance the crown-and-cross topped steeple of Westeras cathedral. It is the most beautiful shaft in the kingdom. And what is more to be said in its favor, it improves upon acquaintance. You never tire of looking at it; as some one once memorably said to me with respect to the steeple of Park Street Church, in Boston.

———o———

XVIII.

A WEEK AT WESTERAS.

As we ride from Sala to Westeras, we hear many preliminary bargains—which is the nearest we can come to the Swedish of it—for service during the coming year. Westeras is the only city in the country that still retains the practice of having a market day for service; and employers and laborers are already on the look-out for their "relations," during the year beginning on the coming 25th of October.

Last Sunday was labor market day here. There were thirteen small steamers at the wharves, which came in gaily dressed, with every flag except the star-spangled banner flying over their decks. Most of those who were brought here in these vessels were in one or the other of the two classes particularly referred to; but there were also scores of peddlers, a Punch and Judy and acrobat show, and a hand organ. The principal streets were crowded at ten o'clock; and the spectacle somewhat resembled that which is presented in several well-known French melodramas and comic operas. Both parties are firmly bound under the law, when the articles shall have been once signed, and severe penalties are attached to the offense of signing more than one contract, and taking advance pay thereon—or "jumping a bounty," as we would say.

I was surprised by the amount of drunkenness that was exhibited on the streets during the afternoon of this Sunday, and the manner in which this condition of inebriety was manifested—almost uniformly—was to us an unusual sight, and therefore somewhat interesting. You will approach a man who is apparently perfectly sober, until just a moment before you have come even with him on your path. Suddenly he will spring out in front of you and begin to caper about in a most fantastic and ridiculous fashion. If we had not had a warning about this kind of demonstration by the twist-waltz that was performed before our eyes in the waiting shed at Gagnes Kyrka, we should have been very much alarmed, undoubtedly, by the first toper that we met on this market day in Westeras. It is said that these subjects of King Brandywine are always harmless if you simply stand still and look at them and say nothing; but that is what has been said about wasps and bumble-bees—and we know that the saying as applied to the latter is not true? So why should it impeach a man's character for the possession of the average amount of courage, if he confesses that being unprovided with any sort of a weapon of defence, he is or was a little nervous in such a presence? But what was more surprising and absolutely uncomfortable, was to be obliged to confront, every now and then, during the afternoon of this day, a drunken soldier, in full uniform and armed and equipped as the law directs. Troopers with tall hats, adorned with a bunch of feathers, and wearing bayonet swords, were frequently seen reeling along through the streets and lanes of the city; and pouring forth oaths and obscene expressions of the most shocking nature. And this in Sweden; and this with officers looking on, and apparently—and really as we afterwards ascertained—not even so much as making a note for correction or reproof. When we spoke of the matter to the worthy Keeper of the castle, Andrew P. Erickson, he answered, "Yay," in his saddest cadence;

only apologizing or excusing, by adding, "There is much allowed that ought not to be, on market day. It would not be permitted at any other time."

And now, before I speak of the city and of the castle or slottet of Westeras, a word direct of its keeper, to whom I am indebted

A. P. ERICKSON, KEEPER OF WESTERAS CASTLE.

for many kindnesses and much information—whose name I have just written. For thirty-three years he has been in His Majesty's employ; and with five years more of continuous service he is entitled to his pension—equal to the pay he is now receiving.

He agrees that soldiers are not treated, at the expiration of their terms of service and in their years of decrepitude, as they should be by the government, which is fairly considerate if not bountiful to the officers in both the military and civil departments. I see that everybody in the city takes off his hat with a very respectful and often deferential bow to Andrew Erickson; and that, on account of no possible motive other than the one I have often heard assigned—heartfelt personal esteem for such an upright and excellent man. I find that he has among those who know him well a title like unto that of Mesdames Stackelberg and Olberg—"The Man of Good Deeds." We asked a porter at the station the day we arrived, if he knew rhe ca tle keeper; and the reply was, "Know him? Who don't? One of the best men that ever lived."

Westeras is now a city of about 7,000 inhabitants, and is what we would call a state capital. It is also the residence of a bishop. Three hundred years ago it contained twice as many inhabitants, and its corporate limits and its line of compactly built houses extended half a mile or more over the hill on the west—where there are now very few dwellings. The site of a large Dominican monastery and of a convent is pointed out to the traveller, on the road to Dingtuna; and the stories of fairy and witch appearances in this neighborhood, with which I have been regaled, would themselves fill a volume. It is said that on All hallow eve—between 3 and 11—gobblings dressed in the garb of monks have often been seen (and testified about) by persons of the highest character for sobriety and veracity. As I have said once before, I think, it is not wise to deny the possibility of these manifestations, in any Swedish company; for with many of my most intelligent acquaintances hereabouts, this is a matter of serious belief. They say that the word superstition has no just application to the acceptance of these accounts as true.

Eleven national diets have been held here, at one of which the succession to the throne was settled on the heirs of Gustavus Wasa.

The present city is very prettily located by the North shore of Lake Malaren, on the side of a gently sloping hill, facing to the Southeast: on the edge of a little meadow valley. It is closely built, and the streets are from fifteen to twenty feet. The Westeras River runs through the centre of the city and is utilized near its mouth by cross-logs eight feet high, which turn the water under a flour mill, whose wheels—and this I must mention—are run so quietly that their noise is drowned by the falling of the surplus water (itself a pleasing sight) over the wide gable-roof-shape dam.

The sidewalks are narrow, as you might suppose; rarely over three feet wide; and they are entirely wanting along several of the handsomest blocks in the city. The streets are very clean, and as might be expected from the location and the fact of tidiness, the health of the inhabitants is officially announced as "remarkably good."

The houses are usually two stories high, with ceilings of seven to eight feet: and the roofs are uniformly painted that bright red which gives such a picturesque appearance to towns, villages and single districts—especially when seen at a distance, and in a view which embraces a large or diversified landscape. The material from which this lively and lasting color is made comes from the "drippings" of the copper mines at Falun.

The market square is situated in the middle of the city, and is about two hundred feet across, both ways—a square in fact as well as name.

On the ridge of the hill to the West, a Prospect Park has been laid out, embracing some two hundred acres; and as it commands from the elevation of thirty feet a view of the entire city and of the meadows and hills to the East for a distance of twelve miles, and also presents a picture of an arm of the Malaren, with no less than eight islands of from one to three miles in circumference within the scope of vision, the charming nature of the scenery can be faintly imagined.

The old Castle, in one room of which I am writing, dates from the 12th century; and was once the property of a "robber knight," also Erickson by name [how unlike my amiable and hospitable friend! who is sitting not far from the table on which I write these words, reading the last number of the Lans tidings-blad;] who is described in ancient chronicles as the "Terror of the district." It was taken by Gustavus in the 16th century, and strongly fortified; five towers being added to it. These additions were destroyed by fire in 1712. It is now and for many years has been the residence of the Governor, and contains a hall in which the local legislature meets on the call of the executive.

INTERIOR OF WESTERAS CATHEDRAL.

The legislative chamber has seats for 62 persons; and is about 50 by 40 feet in floor dimensions. As in other legislative halls in Sweden that I have visited, including those at Stockholm where there is a rack in front of the benches chair, there are no desks provided for members; but the sitting, whether by bench or chairs, is very comfortable.

Immediately over the room in which I am writing is the apartment in which Eric XIV was confined by his brother John—the sometimes insanely savage Eric who was afterwards poisoned at Orbyhus, by the hand of his equally cruel relation. It is a room about 16 by 20 feet, with a ceiling of not more than 6 feet and 6 inches in heigth. Immediately above his place of confinement his wife was imprisoned for sometime; until it was discovered that he could communicate with her by signals from the windows.

About three hundred rods to the West of the Castle, and over the brow of the hill, is Eric's walk ; the little circle, still marked with the stones that were his bounds which he paced for exercise—dragging a heavy ball and chain and guarded by seven relatives of the nobles that he himself had caused to be butchered.

The Castle is four stories high ; and from its present location and from the authentic descriptions of its former surroundings, must have been a strong tower of defense in the days of Josse and his immediate descendants—between the thirteenth and the fifteenth centuries.

Formerly the prisoners of the county were kept here, their quarters being under and above ground. One must wonder at the industry and skill of the Jack Shephards who managed sometimes to escape from here, despite the eight solid feet of masonary or the doubled locked and barred doors that had to be passed through before exit was obtained.

Immediately to the East of the Castle, and between it and the river, is a beautifully laid out park ; under whose trees the people are free to walk or sit and enjoy, in a quiet way, their Summer evenings. But picnic parties are not permitted on the premises, and much it grieves my good friend, the keeper, when he must send word to ladies who come from a distance and who, unacquainted with the rules in this particular, are about to spread their table-cloths on the grass preparatory to the laying out of a luncheon from their mammoth baskets. I have several times been a witness to the manifestations of this distress of spirit. But the Governor is inexorable on this point, and the keeper must "see to it."

To the right of this open ground, and nearer the lake water's edge, is the large garden of the establishment ; comprising, I should say, about thirty acres. Here almost every variety of fruit and berry is grown ; and there is a hot-bed cultivation of the salad plants. Strawberries are here brought to California dimensions ; and as for gooseberries ! I never knew what the bush was capable of doing before, either with respect to size or lusciousness of product. It is claimed that Sweden takes the prize with this growth, in every particular ; but I have arranged for some cuttings for a trial under the fructifying influence of our glorious climate. We shall see about this. But I must first tell you plainly, that here are gooseberries an inch and a half in circumference—I have measured some of them—that fairly melt in the mouth ; having a flavor that is entirely new to the taste of the foreigner, and of an excellent quality.

Westeras is so famous for its cucumbers that many of my readers who are not Swedes have undoubtedly heard of it in that connection before now. In fact, its people go by the Swedish name for the vegetable, as Ohioans are sometimes called Buckeyes. I was disappointed in this article of diet. I had great expectations ; as one very fond of the American specimen. I propose to swap some of our seeds for the gooseberry cuttings.

The Cathedral, aside from its steeple—the highest (310 feet) and the handsomest in Sweden—is an imposing edifice. It is 300 feet long and 150 feet wide. The altar pieces consist of small carved images of personages supposed to have been present at the birth-place and at the crucifixion and at other remarkable scenes in the life of Christ. They are held in cases, but the doors are always swung back—the doors themselves containing half of the sets of figures that are here displayed. At first the whole appearance strikes one as very odd and even grotesque ; but upon close examination, the marvelous art of the chiselers and moulders is discovered, and the feeling changes to one of great if not reverent interest.

Svante Sture and Erick XIV lie buried here ; the latter under a magnificent sarcophagus of green granite.

Over one of the panel monuments to the former bishop of this See, or in the midst of its effigy work, is the figure of a women, in a half recumbent position, and an attitude of throwing something from her. Her face is the face of a maligant devil. This is said to represent a " noble woman " who murdered three of her children, by tossing them one after the another—perhaps on different occasions—into the flames.

When she cast the last of her progeny—an infant of three years—into the fire-place, it is related that she heard a laugh, echoing her fiendish screech of delight. A few days afterwards one of her servants inadvertantly committed an act for which he knew he would be punished so soon as it was discovered. So he resolved to make a clean breast of it, and take his penalty at once. He went to his mistress—who was now a widow—and asked that judgment be passed immediately. She bade him go into the forest, adjacent to her chateau, and cut down the largest tree he could find, and drag it, limbs foremost, to the gate of her residence grounds. The servant went forth as commanded, and while hunting for a *sequoia*, a little man came out of the trunk of an elm of considerable dimensions, and told him that the tree he had just left was the one he should put his ax to if he wanted the biggest on the estate. The chopping was accordingly begun, and when the tree was felled the servant said, " My yoke of oxen can never draw that tree, top foremost. They could not draw it a yard." " I will help you," said the little man; and as he spoke, he put his shoulder under one of the largest limbs and told the servant to do the same under one of the lightest. And together they both pulled the immense giant of the woods to the front gate of my lady's park. When they arrived at this point there was a loud noise made by the foliage and small twigs dashing against the fence—for the little man went through the gate and dragged the tree-top close up against the stone posts. Thereupon the mistress looked out of one of her bed-room windows, and at the same instant the little man gave a kind of a chuckling laugh. The " noble woman " screamed ; for she saw that her time had come. The little man, whom she said she recognized as her former husband—whom she was also suspected of having poisoned—

but who was in point of fact the devil himself, told her plainly that she must dress herself and come down and go with him into the woods. She said she would do so; but requested permission to have her own horses and carriage brought out; and also asked the privilege of being attended by her footman and driver. This was acceded to; but she was told to make haste. Her attendants were also instructed that they must all ride in front and look at the lady, while they were accompanying her on this trip. When they reached the woods, or the part of the road that entered the woods, they forgot their warning. The instant that they looked in the direction where their mistress and the little man sat, the twain disappeared and were seen no more. The servants jumped from the box and ran back to the chateau. No one could be persuaded to approach the woods for many days. Finally, when some one did muster up courage to go and see what had become of the team, they found that the horses had stood still untill they starved to death. And under the carriage were the bones of this fiendish woman. Her remains were taken and buried beneath the church; and the bishop who was alive and reigning at the time of this occurrance caused this effigy to be carved and set up on the walls of the sacred edifice. After his death and agreeable to his wishes, it was assigned its admonitory place above his cenotaph.

The parish in which this woman dwelt was called Pintrop; and the forest in which she is said to have perished still exists unhewn.

I give one version of this remarkable story—and they are all substantially alike;—and I add that it is implicitly believed in—so far as its main features are concerned including the appearance of the devil and *his* doings—by a majority of the very intelligent people of Westeras with whom I have had the honor and pleasure of conversing.

Yesterday I saw the bishop of the diocese. He was about to go on a pastoral visit. He is over eighty years of age; but he preached in the cathedral a few Sundays ago. He very much resembles the late Rev. Dr. W. A. Scott, of San Francisco.

On an eminence to the rear of the castle—at the end of a hill or ridge at the back of the town—is the county hospital, the insane asylum, and the prison of the county. We visited them all; and found much of interest in them. The hospital patients are received and taken care of for forty ore or about ten cents per day. The prison is conducted on the solitary confinement and silent system. Incarceration here is for comparatively light offences, and does not extend beyond two years. Visitors are not permitted to speak in a loud tone of voice when in the corridors. There were thirty-two prisoners in the cells when we paid our visit; all engaged in making match-boxes. The prisoners get four ore out of every forty ore that they can make; and some of the convicts become so expert that they can make twelve and sixteen ore a day by their pastings. The prison is said to be more than self-supporting; and none of the inmates desire to return to it. At no time do the prisoners see each other; their isolation being perfect and uninterrupted. Preaching on Sundays is listened to by all confined here; as the doors of their cells are partly opened and the minister stands in the centre of the corridor hall, at a point where all can distinctly hear his voice.

The day before we left Westeras was the great final market day of the Summer; servants destinations being then made to the third and fourth degree, for the season. The market square and the immediately adjoining streets, and the two blocks of forty to sixty feet width before the court house and on the bank of the river, were packed with little market wagons, stalls, and vegetable baskets as is usually the case on the days of similar appointment, but the peculiarity of this day's offering for sale above every other that we have witnessed in any part of the country, was a display in the pig line; which was very large and attractive. Many hundreds of little squealers entitled to come within the song of the baby melodies, were brought to town and presented to the consideration of the purchasing populace. Of course there was a concert that was mostly chorus, and not unpleasant for a short and enquiring audience. Going about as a spectator, I soon found myself the centre of observation, in the ordinary range of market place vision. "What! An American!" "Yes; and from

California." "He cannot want to buy a pig!" Some of the by-standers laughed with me at this remark; but the person who uttered it meant what he said, in perfect good faith. He was bound to make sure of the possible; for he followed me up and said: "Here, if Herr California wants a pig that is fit for killing, this is the man to buy of. Herr California must know that it will not do to fatten a pig for the market in this country, unless he is to be killed shortly. My pigs are table pigs; and there are very few in the square."

I asked others if the sales were as good as usual; and they all replied in the negative. They said that the farmers had held their stock back late in hope of better prices. They had glutted the market of Westeras, on the pig staple. The little porkers were mostly of the Berkshire breed, and they were all disposed of, notwithstanding the complaint of over-supply, before five o'clock. Most of them were severally bagged and carried off on the back of the buyer.

Home-knit stockings of most excellent quality, and coarse woven dress-goods that seemed to justify the assertion for once that "they will wear a life-time," are on the little single cot-bed size tables of the old ladies, who took their store stations by the river side under the beautiful spreading horse-chesnut trees. Their children, their daughters, took adjacent stands, and offered candies, of Stockholm and of home manufacture—exposed in trays or seductively covered by labels that bore pictures of Jenny Lind, Christine Nilson, Clara Louise Kellogg and Miss Thursby, and unknown beauties. These packages contained "mottoes" of the most moral and even religious type; and there were wound around some one of the pieces a plain and plump invitation to be wed—no equivocation about it. Here are specimens: "Be virtuous and you will be happy," "Industry will have its reward," and "I am ready to marry in November," "What are are you coming to see me so often for?" "I have loved you for a long time." The girls also had for sale large bandanna and cotton handkerchiefs; with strong colors laid in remarkable portraits or scenery. The latter—twenty-five ore or six cent articles—were of that size and of that brilliancy in color of red and yellow, that reminded me forcibly of the calico that was sent to the women of the Washoe and Piute tribes of Indians, by the government of Uncle Sam, through the Walker river reservation agency in 1862. [It was supposed that if anything *could* secure and maintain peace with the Nevada savages, that distribution would do it. And relatively speaking, it did.]

The death of Alex. T. Sundin, of Westeras, a member of the king's Wasa order, is announced in the Westmanlands Lands Tidings—a copy of which lies before me. He left by testament to the public schools and charitable institutions of the city 200,000 rix dollars. He hanged himself, but although he had many brothers and sisters and nieces and nephews surviving, no one of them came forward to challenge the legal accrediting and carrying out of the will, on the ground of lunacy or undue influence over a weak mind. There are two lawyers in Westeras, but they did not incite any one to dispute the validity of the will, and were not called upon to do so in this instance.

In Westeras as in all other places of equal size that I have visited, and in many towns of not over two thousand inhabitants, there are public baths, which are entitled to consideration by our Lick estate trustees. The price is a kroner for a double room, fifty ore for a bath tub alcove. Attendance is precisely the same in both places. The very poor have tickets given them by the corporation authorities. For this sum, in either divison, you have not only an abundant supply of water at any temperature desired, coming through a faucet that at your will or that of your waitress gives a large stream, but you have also as much brushing and rubbing as at Miller's Hotel in New York or at our San Francisco Hamman hot air rotunda, or at Dr. Zeile's establishment. The attendance is by women of middle age exclusively.

The washerwomen of the town have a large house, of the very best construction—130 by 40 feet—and 18 feet high—through which a race-way for water is laid in granite. It is heated thoroughly in winter. This is free to all who will come and wash—and be or make clean.

Before we departed from Westeras, we took a farewell walk through the charming little city park; in the Western side of which, on a mound about fifteen feet high, and on a pedastal of eight feet, is a mammoth bust of the great Gustavus Wasa. On this spot it is said that the illustrious captain addressed the people of Westeras, on one occasion at least ; and I have read somewhere a very eloquent speech attributed to him, as having been uttered at this place. The keeper of the castle

STATUE OF GUSTAVUS WASA.

remarked that "tradition was better than history—more veracious and candid—with reference to what was really said by Gustavus from this eminence. Perhaps he did say all or much that the books put down as words spoken by him on the Westeras mound ; but he also said that which the books do not record. He said that many before him would like to see the axe in him, as he well knew; but they did not care to be seen with their hands on the helve!" From father to son, this plain sentence has come down to the present generation: and on my inquiringly repeating it elsewhere in Sweden, I sometimes found that it was known; and once in Nassjo I heard it referred to with a sentiment of pride at the dauntless courage of the hero. But some Lund Professors said that they had never heard it until I repeated it, and they did not believe that Gustavus ever uttered it.

From Westeras to Upsala the shortest route is direct by rail; but for several reasons which appear of themselves in the course of this sketch, the preferable passage between the points, to those for whom a few hours additional time is not of considerable consequence, is via the city of Stockholm. At ten o'clock P. M., in the month of August—not yet dark enough to require candles—just as the wicks of the lighters of the lamps are being turned up—we left the wharf below the castle; embarked on the sharp and swift little steamer *Aros*, bound for the Riddarholm landing. We are advertised to reach the capital at four and a half o'clock A. M., which means in Sweden half-past three. Oh the sorrow of that parting on the deck of the *Aros* at Westeras!

The accommodation in these diminutive Malaren steamers, as on the canals, provoke wonder and admiration on account of extremely ingenious utilizing of space; and there is the uniform characteristic of neatness. The attendance is good also; and to such an extent is this the fact that I have often heard travellers express the wish that something approximately prompt and intelligent was to be had on the great Atlantic Ocean ferry boats.

XIX.

TO AND IN UPSALA.

By RAIL or steamer you can go on a nearly direct line from Stockholm to Upsala. Advice from every quarter favors going by the lakes and returning on the cars. By steamer called *Upsala No.* 1 we go. The distance is fifty-six miles— fifteen miles more than by the land route; and the fare for first-class passage is less than one cent per mile. The Upsala boats start from the Ridderholm wharf at nine o'clock in the morning, and reach the landing at Upsala about three P. M.

The trip is described—(I should say, perhaps decried)—by some of the guide-books, as monotonous and uninteresting. Even our highly prized Bædecker says something to this effect; although the very same sentence in which this unjust statement is made closes with a qualified or limited recommendation of the passage. Some of the chapters in these books— in the best of them—appear to have been written by commissioners or guides who have become wearied by travelling over the routes they disparage; or the writers have taken their cue from lazy "tourists," who covet the name of travellers—who wish to be able to truthfully say that they have been here and there, thus and so; but who cannot endure without a complaint or a yawn the *ennui* of any mode of conveyance that is not up to the Pulman sleeping car or Fall River steamboat standard of comfort and luxuriousness. Strangers travelling to see and to learn of the country, and who purpose visiting Upsala, will make a mistake if in going or returning they do not take this little journey by water carriage.

The view of the capital city, as the boat recedes from the landing, is always pleasant and inspiriting; and especially so in the bright rays of the Summer morning sun. We soon leave the Maloren; and as it is properly said, the steamer thence "threads its way between the islands and the main land." Large private dwellings, and an immense chateau built by the brother of Charles IX, are passed on our way to the Strait of Staket. This is a strait worthy of the name, in every sense of contractedness: so narrow that you can at several points touch the bank on either side with your cane, and so shallow that you feel the scraping of the soft bottom by the small steamer's keel at almost every revolution of the screw. Beyond this throat we come to an island called Almare-staket, where there are remains of the castle of St. Erick's Borg. Here too is the site of the stronghold in which Archbishop Gustaf Trolle shut himself up, and for a time defied the power and authority of Sten Sture the Younger—an incident of 360 years ago. Many points of interest are noted along the route through Lake Skarfven; and the scenery is delightful.

At Sigtuna, where the steamer stops a few minutes only, there should be set down a mark of reasonable complaint—on behalf of the visitors who constitute the larger portion of the passengers. An hour's time should be given here—half an hour at least—for the sake of affording travellers an opportunity to examine closely the ruins of the old Dominican abbey, whose tottering tower is not ten minutes walk from the steamer landing. Sigtuna is now a village of about 500 inhabitants; beautifully situated on a gently sloping hillside. It was at one time—say a matter of five centuries ago—the largest city in Sweden. There is a long history here of demolition by one set of kings and rebuilding by another, etc.; all calculated to create and foster laudable curiosity which ought to be met and gratified to the extent and in the way indicated, by the steamer company. Why don't the guidebooks say this? Perhaps the author for the section that speaks of this trip has always passed this point as a party of tourists were giving it the "go by," when I made notes for this paragraph. The Captain said that they were playing cards in the cabin.

There are remains of four old churches at Sigtuna; and the tower of one—already spoken of—can be seen for a mile or more down the lake, jagged topped, ivy oer-grown, and surrounded all day by large flocks of birds whose nests are in its upper walls.

On the left is the site of the more ancient town of Forasigtuna ; where is fastened the romantic legend of Hagbard and Signe, and their ill-fated love. Then comes Haturnaholm, and the church of Haturna ; where Dukes Eric and Waldener put their brother King Birger in chains and forced him to divide the empire with them. Eleven years afterwards Birger, pretending to have lost all anger on account of the durance he had been in, sent out cards of invitation to his brothers to come and take a thanksgiving dinner with him at his residence at Ny Koping. The two brothers came ; and Birger told his constables to place them in a dungeon and feed them on air and water. After this atrocious act, let us be glad to remember, Birger received at least so much punishment as could be inflicted by taking away his royal power. Here, at Haturna, his brothers began the quarrel. I have seen the grave of these three brothers, in the Storkyrka, at Stockholm. They were a cruel, pitiless race : those old folkkings.

Crossing the waters of the Skofjarden—a beautiful lake—with many points of interest on either hand, we come to Skokloster, or the " Forest Monastery," as the original name imports. Here is a splendid chateau, where was formerly a monastery belonging to the Dominicans, subsequently occupied by the Cistercian nuns. The present edifice is in the possession of the Brahe family ; and the grounds and the interior of the building may be visited by the payment of two kroners to the overseer of the estate. The structure is 140 feet square ; with a tower at each corner, covered with copper. The main building is four stories high ; the towers rising fifteen or twenty feet higher. The front hall is magnificent; being supported by eight Ionic columns of pure white marble. The decorated ceiling is marvelously beautiful. As has been comprehensively written, the interior is a museum ; there is a library and an armory; the latter containing 1,200 guns and a vast variety of other weapons of warfare, including the broad sword of Ziska, the distinguished Hussite chieftain, and the axe of the executioner at the " Blood bath of Linkoping."

Venitian glasses and gold and silver ware of high value are here displayed in great profusion. Here are also life size portraits of Gustavus Adolphus, Axel Oxenstjerna and Charles X, VI, XII, the latter on horseback. And here is a picture of Ebba Brahe, that justifies all the eulogiums that have been passed on her superlative beauty. She must have been a charmer.

SKOKLOSTER.

The library contains 40,000 volumes; and among the numerous manuscripts visitors may see, on inquiry, the Revelations of S⁺. Brigittae.

The Skokyrka, which is close by the chateau, is also well worth a visit. The figure of the Magdalen is of such excellence that substantially the same expression of wonder was instant and irrepressible from every intelligent person present at the time we stood before it : " How is it possible that this product of a master's hand has been left in this comparatively obscure locality?" The pulpit is a very fine piece of work ; and the paintings on and about the altar are choice in their character and design. Here is the tomb of the "Swedish Sappho,"—a poetess, commonly known in our literature as Charlotte Norden, but whose full baptismal cognomen, as the inscription in this church does testify, was Hedvig Charlotta Nordenflycht. It is said—I say it is said, for I now hear that which I never read about her—that many of her best poems were destroyed by her relatives, because those verses referred more or less distantly to her love disappointment—a sad story of heartless treatment on the part of a successful suitor, ending in her attempted suicide.

Churches, estates, estates and churches, Alsike, Krusenberg, Aker, Dalby, Nas, and Flotsund ; and then the steamer passes into the river Fryisa, which is here about the size of the Croton River at its mouth or the Tuolumne River at Modesto, and as muddy as the Sacramento could be without any injunctions on the hydraulic miners. Far to the North and East extends the plain of Upsala, with the tall, needle-shaped steeple of an outlying parish (Vaksala) in the centre of the horizon.

As we push on and swing around more directly to the North in the narrow channel, the agricultural school of Ultuna comes into view ; situated close by the river's bank. It consists of three buildings upon a fifty-acre farm ; the dwellings and schools being the size of the Protestant Orphan Asylum, at San Francisco. Here, as at the Stromsholm School—which is a very much smaller institution based on the same plan—by a course of instruction running through two and one half years, it is claimed that accomplished agriculturalists are brought or sent forth for foreman's places upon the estates of Sweden. I am told that the students are usually the sons of parents well to do ; and that these charity schools are in no sense for the poor. Some of the most intelligent students with whom I have conversed on this subject have sought to give me very unfavorable impressions as to the effect these "academies of theory" have had upon the culture of the soil of the nation.

Now comes the Lunatic Asylum and the new Hospital; and then we reach the long straight waterway that is handsomely shaded by a park row of trees on the left, and bounded by the southern portion of the city of Upsala on the right. Half a mile of this passage brings us to the wharf of the Stockholm Steamer, in the first university city of Sweden.

The landing of the little steamer is immediately opposite the city garden and café, known as the Stromparterre—a place we visited and to which I shall probably refer hereafter. Coming up the ruddy Fyrisa along the line of the city park, anything like a full view of the little city is prohibited by the shade trees that

UPSALA CASTLE AND CATHEDRAL—GENERAL VIEW.

border the river, and by the houses that are in immediate juxtaposition to the bank on the shore side; and you do not obtain any glance at all at the castle until you have fairly stepped upon shore and passed to the edge of the first bridge that crosses the stream. So that the "commanding vision as you approach" which is often spoken of by the guide books and travellers, is to be dated, as it were, from the railway line, as it comes up from the Southeast on the Upsala plain; from which you do indeed have an excellent picture of the city and its principal edifice long before you have arrived at the corporation limits.

Two characteristics are to be set down at once for this ancient university town—especially at this season of the year. One is the cleanliness—so scrupulous as to remind you of the olden stories of the streets in the cities of the Netherlands; and the other is a quietness that will often make you wonder, as you pass along, whether the buildings on either side hold any inhabitants or no? Arriving here in the mid-afternoon, we met with no hackmen or solicitors of any kind at the dock, and there were but few spectators about; all this in striking contrast to Westeras and Strengnas and Falun, and other towns in Sweden, of city name and of similar size. It is vacation time, sure enough; and we need not have expected to see groups of students here and there—as engravings are apt to give them. But it is on a day preceding a great convocation of teachers and professors, and it is stated that no less than 2,500 strangers—gathered from all parts of Eastern and Southern Sweden—must at this time be sojourning in Upsala. So that we might have reasonably looked for crowded streets.

Upsala is a city of 12,000 inhabitants, exclusive of its temporary residents, the students. Although its corporate limits are not defined by any wall, as of old, yet, like other towns of this kingdom its line of edifices break short off—so to speak—on every hand. Suggesting a preparedness for the construction of a stone ridge of defence, if necessary. Somehow, this idea has struck me on every occasion of a visit of the like nature; and doubtless this manner and custom of building the houses together is due to the original plan of a walled town.

The principal points of interest here are, of course, the Cathedral or Dom, and the Castle, and the University Library—each one as I can now say, well worth a visit and fully repaying of themselves the time and expense of the trip from the Capital.

In our visits to the Church and the Castle and the University buildings, we had for a guide, a lady whom I wish to gratefully mention in this chapter. Mrs. Ebba Sunden, *fodd* Gregersson, wife of a professor—in the professional line herself, with a title to that effect—kindly took us in charge, in compliance with a letter of introduction from Herr J. C. Myerberg, and accompanied us on our visits to castles, colleges and clubrooms.

While you are sure to receive a hospitable welcome in any portion of Sweden—so far as my observation and experience goes—on a proper credential—there is a difference, of course, with respect to the interest that will be manifested in connection with your inquiries and investigations. Now Mrs. Sunden and her husband are great admirers of our Republican Institutions, and appear to have been omniverous readers of modern American literature. This will probably sufficiently indicate how fortunate we were in the companionship of such a lady at such a time.

It begins to rain tempestuously shortly after our arrival. But, notwithstanding this, people gather in the café gardens of Upsala at the usual hour for evening out-door refreshment—between six and seven o'clock—thronging under the canvas or awnings that are provided on the edge of the restaurants. At the upper or eastern end of the city, near the Sala Hotel, and in close proximity to the railroad station, there is a little beer garden and restaurant, with a horse-shoe shaped shed occupied by a band of musicians; and on this night in front of this platform, a stage had been erected for the performance of a gymnast, who, in the midst of a shower, and before an audience necessarily somewhat distant in point of feet and rods, but very respectable in numbers and demonstrative applause, went through his programme with conscientious and heroic fortitude. One of his tricks was novel to us, and perhaps worth mentioning. A pole was erected at one extremity of the platform—its height probably about twenty feet from the line of the floor—and at a distance of six or seven feet above the platform there protruded a series of shelves, one above the other, at an interval of two or three feet. Mounting the pole, and pulling down the first shelf, the acrobat leaned over gradually until his balance was lost, and then descending and striking with his hands upon a table beneath, turned a triple back somersault on the platform. This was repeated—the performer each time mounting one shelf higher—until from the full distance of twenty feet, the descent and revolution was made. From a beginning that was a commonplace exhibition, the exercise grew to be a very thrilling spectacle—as the daring athlete mounted higher and higher.

After witnessing his performance, we strolled down to the Stromparterre; the large city garden already referred to, which is at the northern edge of the city park, and adjacent to the castle grounds. There—the storm having somewhat subsided—we found a gathering of probably 300 persons listening to music from a band of twenty-three musicians, who were stationed at one side of a large and brilliantly illuminated two-story café. Some of the pieces played carried us back, sure enough, to San Francisco; as they were selections from operas made familiar to our people generally by their repitition at our incomparable, popular Opera House, known as the *Tivoli.*

The general topic of conversation was the meeting of the teachers, who were to consider and prescribe the course of instruction that was to be given during the coming year. We paused at no table where this was not the theme of talk; and dignified looking gentlemen who had the air of being teachers and professors themselves, apparently exhibited no more interest in this subject than did the old ladies who had brought their knitting or crochet-work with them, and who substituted discussion about the course of study for the gossip that we would naturally expect to hear under such circumstances in such a place.

Evidently this is a university town in a very striking sense of the term. It is the pride of the people here—this great college of Sweden; and they have a very intelligent understanding with respect to it. We stepped into a number of stores for the purpose of making the chance acquaintance of the proprietor or his clerks, rather than on account of need or desire to purchase; and on a hint that we were strangers, and more especially after stating that we were Americans and Californians, we obtained from one and all a succinct and comprehensive account of the origin of the University, of its progress, of the present number of professors and students, and so forth. All with a degree of particularity and detail beyond anything that we had seen in the guide books, or in the recent volumes of letters of travel which embrace communications upon these points.

The Cathedral or Dom Church is approached from the Southeast by a flight of steps that leads up on to the grand dais on which it stands—approached through a building or series of buildings that border the cathedral yard on two sides. The porter's lodge is on the left as you reach the level of the church foundation. We were fortunate enough to have for our guide,

UPSALA CATHEDRAL.

the porter's wife—the man himself being employed in duties connected with the great meeting, to which we have already referred. Here, curiosity answered unto curiosity, and brought us a harvest of information. The good woman of the lodge wanted to know all about the United States, and especially everything that we could tell her with respect to that paradise land of the earth, known to her—(under a very peculiar and indescribable form of pronunciation)—as "the land of San California." And as if to pay us in advance for all the information we could give, or to make us the more ready to answer her questions, or to volunteer information, I think we had a quadrupled amount of historic and biographical story with respect to the notable points of interest in the great Cathedral. Of course I shall not undertake, in this place or in this communication, to make a report, *verbatim*, of all her recitations. I dare to say that if I did, the printed record would occupy more than any reasonable limits for a "chapter."

Of course the first object to which the attention of the visitor is directed is the coffin of silver in which are the bones of St. Eric. This is on the left hand side of the altar; at the place where the bishop's chair is usually situated in our Episcopal edifices. It is elevated about three or four feet from the floor and is protected from sacrilegious handling by an iron railing and screen. Immediately in the rear of the altar is a chapel, decorated with pictures presenting scenes in the life of the great Gustavus; the figures being of life size, and the execution being of that pronounced and vivid style which characterizes the panorama paintings of the modern French and German artists.

The monument of John III. is a reclining statue, which for clearness of outline is surpassingly fine. It seems as if it was carved out of a large pebble or an immense horn rather than from a block of marble,—the fibre of the stone,—so to speak,—being of such character as to suggest one or the other of the materials I have likened it unto.

I do not know that I ever before saw an effigy or bust, with respect to which, I felt a desire to touch and handle; but I certainly had this morbid disposition here, and I so confessed. And when I mentioned this feeling, I was told that a similar remark had been made by many others, when they first came into this presence.

The altar is beautifully arranged and adorned: all in good taste and much in striking contrast to the ornamentation displayed in other cathedrals and large churches of the kingdom, which I have visited. There was nothing tawdry about it. The pulpit has been the subject of many descriptions and much eulogistic notice, from those who are best able to speak of it in an artistic point of view. It was made after the design of Nicodemus Tessin,—whose name is a household word in Sweden.

Gustavus 1st is represented as lying on his marble monument, between his first and second wife. His third consort,—who survived him some sixty years,—is buried at a distance. I climbed up at one side of this monument,—which is elevated fully eight feet from the floor,—and took a careful view of the reposing monarch and his first spouse. The effigy is said to be a good likeness. If that is so, then the busts which I have seen elsewhere flattered him exceedingly. His second wife was much the handsomest lady; but I was told that his third choice fell upon the greatest beauty in the land. While these facts probably have no historical importance, they were somewhat prominent in the conversation which I necessarily overheard while I stood gazing upon these representations of ancient Swedish royalty.

The grave of Linnæus is near the front door; under a slab that is fully fifty feet distant from the magnificent monument which has been erected in his honor in one of the alcoves of the Cathedral. Mrs. Sunden remarked that Englishmen frequently came to the cathedral and asked to see the grave of Linnæus; and having stood above his remains a few minutes, they went away with the remark that there was nothing else in the building that they cared to see;—adding, if questioned, that they had old cathedrals and old war heroes represented in tablet and effigy, from one end of England to the other, in such abundance as to surfeit and sicken them! But the grave of Linnæus! ah! they wanted to stand by the side of that! The monument of Linnæus is a pyramid of porphyry, with a bronze medallion of the great botanist,—the masterpiece of Seigal.

The porter's wife exhibited to us the precious relics and curiosities in the sacristy, which is on the right of the Eastern entrance. Here are the ecclesiastical vessels of silver and gold, and crowns and surplices and robes, and the clothes of the Stures who were murdered by order of Eric XIV.—as will be hereafter described. Here is also the gift of King Albert of Mecklenberg to Queen Margaret,—"a gift of derision,"— a stone for sharpening her needle; and here is kept her responsive gift—which was a banner made out of some of her Petticoats. In the sacristy are also kept trunks full of valuables belonging to wealthy citizens of Upsala, who are by the Bishop and Chapter permitted to use this place as a deposit for safe lodgment.

The cathedral is capable of seating 5,000 persons; and on all festive days, it is said,—(as always elsewhere)—that there is not room in the building for the people who wish to attend. The organ is nearly the size of the famous Boston instrument.

The memoranda of exterior dimensions are : 370 feet by 141 feet, and a height of 115 feet. The construction of this building was commenced in 1 19, by a French architect, whose contract was written and dated and executed at Paris, in 1287. 140 years passed between the signing of the contract and the date of the final consecration,—for there were several preliminary ceremonies—in 1425. At one time it was surmounted by three towers, two of which were 400 feet in height. But these were consumed by fire at the last of the five successive conflagrations, from which the cathedral has suffered. The two towers now at the Northern end of the church are stunted in their dimensions—their total height being only 180 feet. The same complaint is made with respect to them that is often heard in connection with the towers of Westminster, in London.

Adjacent to this church is the Spring of St. Eric—not more than ten or twelve rods to the right of the building. This Spring is said to have suddenly burst forth at the very place where St. Eric was decapitated. The guide-books say that the water is now used exclusively for a hydropathic establishment, which is situated immediately adjacent to the Spring. But the fact is, the water of the Spring supplies the whole town or city of Upsala. The water has a purity which justifies the praise bestowed upon it. It is of that limpid and sparkling character which country folks in the Western part of New England are familiar with ;—finding it in the natural reservoirs of their mountain towns.

Distant from the cathedral fully half a mile is the eminence on which stands the castle of Upsala. It is situated to the East of the Botanic Garden, through which we passed on our way to the scene of the slaughter of the "ill-fated Sture." This castle was constructed in 1538 by Gustavus Wasa, and additions were made to it by John III. and Gustavus II. It was partly burnt in 1702, and has never been fully restored. It is the residence of the Governor of the Province. From the grounds, immediately in front, there is a fine view of the Upsala Valley, including Gamla or Old Upsala—which is distant about four miles to the North-east—where are the great tumuli, containing the graves of Odin, Thor and Frya. The castle itself is about 60 feet high, between 300 and 400 feet long, and 50 feet wide. It is constructed of brick, and in the rear looks more like one of our modern manufacturing establishments than it does like a castle or an Executive residence.

The place where the Sture were murdered is at the Southwest end of the present castle,—in a ruined fragment of the first building. The room where the horrible butchery was perpetrated, is without a roof, while through the cracks of the floor a mass of shrubbery has pushed its way upward. Through an iron grating we looked in, while Mrs. Sunden re-told the story of the wholesale assassination. The order came suddenly from King Eric,—who is believed by many to have been insane at the time,—(whose own subsequent horrible fate we have already rehearsed),—and the unfortunate victims had no notice whatever of the intention of the guard to slaughter them. When the soldiers entered the dungeon, and commenced the attack with spears and daggers and swords, the "Sture" defended themselves as well as they could with sticks of wood and with the pieces of board which they tore from the wainscot ; crying out in wonder as well as agony, while the butchery was going on ; resisting the assaults valiantly until death put an end to their horrible sufferings.

A new University building is in process of erection—nearly completed—and will soon entirely supersede three of the detached edifices which have been devoted to the objects for which it is constructed.

The Library building (*Carolina Rediviva*) and its contents deserves a notice. The building is about the size of the California State Capital, minus the dome. The Librarian

UPSALA UNIVERSITY LIBRARY BUILDING—CAROLINA REDIVIVA.

began our conversation by speaking of Professor Moses of the California University, from whom he had had many communications. He seemed to have a high admiration for our teacher, both as a scholar and an instructor.

This Library—which contains 200,000 volumes and 7,000 manuscripts—has among its most precious treasures the *Codex Argenteus*; which is a Gothic translation of the four gospels, made by Bishop Ulphilas, between the years 340 and 380. This book is the oldest specimen of the Gothic language, and its typographical value is very great. On this account,—as a representative and a record of the ancient work of writing,

NEW UNIVERSITY BUILDING, UPSALA.

and stamping in printing characters,—it is often called for, and examined by persons of distinction, who take no interest in its religious significance. We had the precious volume in our hands,—that is to say, we had our hands under its silver lids ; a privilege, which we were informed was vouchsafed on rare occasions.

Here also, we were shown several Bibles with chains attached ; which had been placed in the churches in early days, and read by the enlightened few. Here are manuscript writings of the monarchs of Sweden, from 1400 down. On the 9th of February, 1691, Charles XII wrote to his father. We read the letter ; expressive of dutiful affection, and a hope and desire to become a man and monarch worthy of such a sire. When Charles was nine years old he wrote a letter to his grandmother ; in which he hailed her as "The mighty Queen," and "the best of all grandmothers." We were also shown his writings when he was twenty-one years of age ; written when he was in the saddle. Here were also specimens of writings of Gustavus Adolphus ; verses copied by him from the Bible, in a daily journal form. And here was the famous diary of the Vadstena Monastery, written between the years 1384 and 1545. The chirography is as copperplate on many pages.

The library rooms are about 200 feet in length and 14 or 15 feet in height, with a width probably of 40 or 50 feet. The shelves reach nearly up to the ceiling ; and there are four double rows in the body of the halls upon the first and second stories. The upper story is not considered sufficiently strong to bear a burden of books ; and for that and other reasons it is appropriated and set apart as an audience or council chamber. In it there are a large number of statues and busts, arranged on either side of the long chamber, while at the top of the hall is a large platform, on which the "Upsala Students' Choir" play and sing on certain festive occasions.

As we walked from the Library building—which is called the *Carolina Rediviva*—we met one of the students—readily known by his cap and seal. We were shown the rooms where the division of the students that hail from Stockholm meet for social and convivial purposes. The rooms were five in number and were situated near the principal hotel and about two blocks distant from the edge of the park grounds, in which the University buildings are located. The furniture of the rooms is plain but massive. Each division of the kingdom has its separate social society and headquarters; of which the Stockholm rendezvous was, we were informed, a fair specimen.

While walking around the outer ruin of the city, and, when about to cross one of the bridges, of the Fyrisa, at the Northern extremity of Upsala, we were met by a young man of apparently twenty years—a peasant boy, as we judged by his dress and general appearance. When we had approached within a few feet of him he suddenly changed his demeanor from that of a quiet passer-by to that of an active dancer! He jumped up immediately in front of us and began those peculiar tangle-legged movements to which we have already been compelled to refer. There could be no mistaking his condition or its cause; in fact he left us in no doubt on that score, by the language which he used on this occasion. He said, in substance, while actively engaged in his saltatory exercise—or, perhaps, to be more accurate, I should say, he shouted: "You think yourself very fine, no doubt! But what would I be if I had your nice clothes on me! Give me your coat and see what a noble looking fellow I will be." We replied to the effect that his coat seemed to be manly, if not quite as good as that on our own shoulders. To this, the young man replied: "Ah! but look at the difference in the style. You have had your coat cut by a Frenchman. My mother made mine, and she is a good woman. But she don't know what stuff I have got in me to-day. I have got the liveliest stuff in me that I ever had in my life. You think yourself very wise, no doubt. I do not speak to suit you, but I can whip any one of my weight, single handed." There was a concert of assent; there could not be any doubt about that. At this juncture up came a policeman, who began reasoning, or attempting to reason with the rampant youth; who never left off from his dancing—no, not for a moment. Said the gentle custodian of the peace: "Go home, Carl, and behave yourself. You are disgracing your poor old mother. I shall have to take you up and lock you up." Nothing daunted at this, the response was immediate and jovial: "You're a good fellow; I know you well. I knew you before you got all those brass buttons on you. I knew *your* mother and your father, too, before you. Put that coat on me and I can whip all the other policemen in the city."

As we turned away, the young man was still continuing his half defiant and half badgering speech to the expostulating officer of the law.

———o———

XX.

AT STOCKHOLM.

Herr C. J. Meyerberg, the Inspector of Schools at Stockholm is certainly a remarkable man. Remarkable in his scholarship and in his popularity. Or, perhaps, with reference to the last mentioned standpoint, it should be said that it is very strange that the people of a large city like Stockholm have been so uniformly discriminating as to elect him twenty-two times in twenty-two consecutive years. Herr Meyerberg writes and speaks a score of languages, and in his tastes and manner he has the simplicity which is the usual characteristic of eminent scholars and instructors. [He has always refused to allow his photograph to be taken—even declining when we begged for one sitting for our engraver's copy.]

It seems as if we must say of almost every distinguished person with whom we come in contact in Sweden—as well as of the people of the peasantry order—that he or she particularly delights in showing a kindness to an American citizen. I have tried to ascertain whether the English or German or French travellers had a similar impression as to cordial welcome and gladly rendered service with respect to their countrymen, on the part of the men and women of this land who have greeted us. And while I am not positive in every instance, I believe that the preference has been admitted as unmistakably for persons hailing from the United States. And, indeed, why should it not be so? Why not, indeed! We have nearly or quite a million of men and women in our Union who were born in this little kingdom! And we receive from 20,000 to 50,000 Swedish immigrants annually.

Herr Meyerberg resides on the third floor of a huge building; nearly as large as the Morton House, New York, or Bancroft's book house in San Francisco. But the exterior is more like a wholesale store and warehouse on Broadway, New York, than like the front of either building named. And this I mention, to add that this description will answer for most of the older and larger edifices on the main business streets of Stockholm.

We have to wait but a few minutes on the landing after the maid has taken our cards before the professor appears at the door; calling out, "Be so good, be so good," with a hearty emphasis. He says that he must apologize for being in such haste to welcome us that he forgot to change his dressing-gown for a frock coat; and he bids us wait for him in the library while he puts on proper attire. When we tell him that this evidence of quickness to salute us is very agreeable, he laughs and explains: "Well, you must not mind an old bachelor's ways in welcoming his friends. I expect that a married man is taught to be more particular about his dress when he answers a summons for a visitor at his own door."

Over six feet high, strong and lithe of frame, of age about fifty-five, with a countenance always expressive of good nature, but devoid of any grinning habit; a thoroughly frank and affable gentleman,—with "no airs," as we would say. This is a true description, so far as it goes, of Herr Meyerberg, Inspector of Schools in Stockholm these twenty-two years last past. Of course, I write of him now after an acquaintance that extended over several weeks; but we had the correct impression about him the moment we saw him brushing past his servant and bidding us enter his sitting room and library.

"You see," said the professor, "that I have a pretty fair assortment of English books for a Swedish school superintendent;" pointing to a dozen long shelves filled with volumes from American and English publication houses. We noticed Hon. S. S. Cox's latest volume—"From the Arctic to the Bosphorus"—whereupon the Inspector exclaimed: "O yes, I prize him very highly. He is a very humorous man, and as it also appears, a profound and brilliant Statesman. And here is a report from San Francisco," he said, showing us a volume which bore the signature of John Swett. "I see by the picture that you have splendid school buildings; and I judge that your children have as good facilities for acquiring an education as any other boys and girls—outside of Sweden." There was a furtive glance and a sly twinkle in his eyes as he uttered this last clause—as though, among other things, he would like to test our amiability, and yet did not wish to say anything that could be construed as offensive boasting. He saw that we certainly were not irritated by his assumption of superiority for his country's methods of instruction, etc., and so he went on in the same strain: "We *ought* to be ahead of you in school matters in some respects. I think we can decide more quickly, and put in operation with less difficulty. Of course you know that our school house and our steam launch took the first prizes at the Centennial Exhibition?" Yes, we knew this; and we had recently had the pleasure of riding in the little vessel—now called the Filadelfia and running on Lake Malaren—by which the medal was captured in one department of the Centennial. As for the school houses: why, Herr Meyerberg might do us the honor of showing us some of them himself? Of course he would; nothing could afford him more satisfaction; and he would make another change—put on another coat—and go out with us immediately.

It was vacation time; but perhaps there were some advantages in a visit at this season, to partly counterbalance the loss which was evident and unmistakable. We should have been glad to see the boys and girls together in their study and recitation rooms, and in their gymnasiums; but, as Herr Meyerberg observed, it was not very difficult to imagine how they would look and act if the places which they occupied in the school year were filled by them. We could examine the building and the grounds as carefully as we wished. He introduced us to the janitors, and said: "Let these people come and visit here when they like. And if they wish to see anything in particular, no matter if it is for the seventh time, show it to them. They are Americans, and what is better still, they are Californians!" "O! Californians!" the janitors would invariably exclaim—with a glance and a gesture and bow that signified a respectful and cordial welcome. The school edifices in Stockholm are of the best—as good as stone foundations and brick walls can make the exterior. [The view elsewhere given of the Grammar and Commercial School at Norrkoping, is in most respects a truly "specimen edifice." It cost $175,000, in 1868—equivalent to a cost for material and labor with us of not less than $300,000. The Stockholm school-houses cost from $85,000 to $150,000.] Within, the arrangements are uniformly of that excellent pattern which has given Sweden the first name in this respect, the world over. On the gymnasium especial care is bestowed; and plenty of space is devoted to each apparatus, so that there shall be no crowding by way of injudicious proximity of swings and cross bars, etc. Usually in Sweden the gymnasium is in or attached to the school building proper; but sometimes, as at Westeras, the exercise hall is in a separate structure. "It is amazing!" once exclaimed Herr Meyerberg, as we were walking in the Djurgarden, and recurring to his favorite topic, "that your people do not invariably have a room or building for gymnastic exercises for the scholars in your public schools, in every large town in America. I believe that you have the phrase, 'tempting Providence.' Well, it seems to me that you tempt Providence by failing at this day of civilization and enlightenment to have as good facilities for gymnastic training as we give our children, in or adjacent to our school houses in Sweden. What do you mean by being so slow in coming up to our standard, or at least to the German standard, in this matter? O! it is outrageous!" And the Inspector shook his head, as though he was reflecting upon a deficiency for which he was somehow partially personally responsible.

"I wish you would come over and lecture to our folks on the subject," said I; "although I believe the plan of providing those facilities of which you speak is now being considered and acted upon very extensively in the United States." "I *did* lecture to your people on the subject. I gave some of them good talks about it, you may be sure, when I was Commissioner to the Centennial." And hereupon the Inspector began to laugh audibly to himself. We told Herr Meyerberg about our familiar phrase, "A penny for your thoughts." "Well," said he, half checking his chuckle, "I will soon let you know what I was thinking about; but you must let me snicker—I believe that is your word precisely—and a good word to express what the action is. You must let me snicker a little more." And he did giggle—still to himself as it were—for fully half a minute. "You will pardon me; I hope I have not been guilty of bad manners, but really I cannot prevent a rising disposition to laugh when I speak of my speech-making experience in America. I can make my apology best and sufficient—if one is needed or proper—by relating to you something of that experience. I was called upon suddenly, the first time I made an appearance on any stage in company with English speaking gentlemen in the United States, and I felt a degree of embarrassment that I cannot express, when I got up to reply. But after the first few sentences, confidence seemed to come to me as by a sort of inspiration—and I went ahead, with misgivings, at times, it is true, about my grammar and pronunciation, but without much hesitation. I met with most vociferous applause; and when I had finished dozens of persons came up to me and congratulated me; and said, 'You speak as well as a native. Where did you learn your excellent English?' Well, I was very proud of my first effort in this line, which was a success no doubt; but I very soon repented. After that it was nothing but calling for speeches, and speeches, and speeches. Some committee or delegation got me down to Baltimore on one occasion, and they brought me to the platform and began the proceedings with the remark, 'Superintendent Meyerberg, of Stockholm, Sweden, will address the convention this afternoon.' And so I arose and spoke for about an hour and then indicated that I was about to take my seat. But no! They commenced asking me questions; and as soon as I had finished one reply, up would jump another teacher with another question. This thing began about two o'clock in the afternoon, and at about half-past five—after many attempts to sit down and many distinct appeals for a respite—I concentrated my remaining vitality and threw it into a shout. 'No! I won't say another word. I have talked until I am exhausted. If you don't let me go and get something to eat and drink, I shall call a policeman.' And I meant what I said. But do you know, this remark seemed to make them more anxious than ever that I should go on ; and they continued crying to me to go on ; that they would stay there all the evening and listen to me—and many other little flattering suggestions and promises of that character. Well, I told them to please let me go out, and they could wait there until I came back. And they were vastly amused at this most innocent remark of mine. In fact it didn't seem as if I could open my mouth without getting off what they called 'a good thing.' O ! it was frightful—the way they applauded me ! But I finally plumped down quick on the edge of a bench that happened to be vacated just at that moment, and there I sat and looked forcibly-feebly at that audience, and let them keep on trying to get me to 'go on,' until they became convinced that I was not to be forced into any more eloquence. The fact was that I was nearly dead with fatigue. O ! I never saw such a people to sit and listen to speeches. Talk about the Americans loving to talk themselves ? I never saw such *Listeners*. As I say, I was very much flattered at first by my wonderful excellence of speech ; but I almost rued the day, sometimes, when I acquired familiarity with the English tongue. And yet I ought not to say that ; for we did have a glorious welcome in America, and I would not have you think that I did not appreciate the kindness of my entertainers. O ! you American people ; you are the most hospitable and the politest on earth." This last sentence the Inspector uttered with great vehemence ; the words came from him with such sonorous volume that I was reminded of Dickens' description of the manner in which Boythorn once talked in the presence of Esther Summerson.

The number of private charities in Stockholm is very large. We have visited several, and among the most interesting is the school for feeble-minded children, at which we stopped one day while on a circuit of calls with Herr Meyerberg. Madame Rappe, a widow lady of titles, since the death of her noble husband has opened and taken charge of this asylum for these unfortunate creatures. At the time of our introduction, she had thirty-five pupils, ranging in years from four to nineteen. In the "System," all have their hours for work as well as play ; but it is with respect to their recreation that the most difficulty is experienced. In the principal workroom for the girls, nine children were gathered ; making lace of various kinds, and knitting stockings and bags. The degree of intelligence which many of these pupils indicated led us to inquire with a more curious and anxious interest than would have been otherwise excited, as to their history and the manifestations by which they were accounted deficient in intellect. All had been set down as incorrigibly stupid, before they were brought to this institution. Here, as before intimated, the great trouble was to induce them to play rather than labor. Colors and tidies of the most intricate designs were produced by them ; usually faithful copies of a pattern, but sometimes in all respects the original work of their own brains and hands. In some instances articles were shown that had been brought to table-cover perfection—(embroidered cloths)—from the wool and cotton, spun, woven and adorned by these girls on these premises—just as they themselves "took a notion." So said Madame Rappe.

But few of them looked up as we entered ; and no one of them vouchsafed more than a momentary glance during our entire stay, unless specially directed to do so by the devoted mistress. Their obedience was perfect ; and it was evident that they loved the lady with passionate fondness. One big, lubberly boy of about fourteen years—("here among the girls by his special request," said Madame Rappe)—who sat in a corner, engaged in heeling a stocking, gave us a sharp, reproving look when we spoke to him ; but when the Madame called him by name, he smiled,—in a half-idiotic way it is true, but in a manner that clearly indicated his great pleasure in being addressed in the tones of her voice. He laid his knitting on his knee and awaited her orders, with an expression that unmistakably signified anxiety to promptly do her bidding.

We bought some little specimen articles for household use —the product of the pupils. Hereupon one of the girls in attendance, who had been among the most industrious, rose and curtesied three or four times. We had selected from her box, and she had noted the choice by an "eye-corner observation," as the matron assured us. This acknowledgment and expression of pride and gratitude was from her own unaided thought and will. She had not been trained to observe and recognize a preference for her handiwork.

Here also is the slojdskola for the boys; and we witnessed nine or ten busily engaged in the shop, and apparently making as much progress as their wiser and wittier brothers and sisters in the basements of the public schools. And so we come to speak of the slojdskola, on which the Swedes lay some special boasting emphasis, when talking of their educasional training. Connected with all the primary and grammar schools of Stockholm and with the principal schools in almost every city and town that we have visited in the kingdom is a shop in which children are regularly taught to use edged tools. The instruction begins with the child of four, and may take in the youth of eighteen. Of course, there is a graduating point, and then pupils become teachers as well as master workmen. The beginning is with pegs; and from that up to the most complicated work-box there is a prescribed grade of pattern. Elaborate reports have been published respecting the utility of this instruction; and similar schools have been or are about to be started in Boston and at some other points in the United States.

On the article made is a record kept of the number—as No. 1, or No. 2, or No. 3, etc.—the age of the boy making the article, his name, and the time he consumes in the manufacture. As, for instance, I have before me a ruler, accurately shaped and handsomely polished. On it the label reads as follows:

Klara Slojdskola.
Nr. 7 Utfordt pa 3 timmar af,
Elis Larm,
12 ar, undervisad 1 slodj 26 timmar.
Godhandt,
Stockholm, 7-7, 1883. L. Anderson,
Vitso Roads————Slojdlarare.

A paper cutter and a match box, of superior workmanship, are on the desk on which I write; the former made in twenty-two minutes by Otto Peterson, eleven years of age, and the latter made in 262 minutes by Hugh Anderson, twelve years old—the tenth article of the kind from the same hands.

It is claimed for this instruction that it is useful and beneficial in many ways; that it must advantageously train the hand and eye to practical service; and that it is a fascinating employment for the youngsters, who would otherwise, in the course of nature, be engaged in sports or idleness. Care is taken not to trench upon time that ought, for the purposes of health, to be devoted to play. But, perhaps, as will be inferred without the saying, to many this is in all respects an industry which is the equivalent of games that involve much physical exercise.

A ready sale is found for such articles so produced, as are of creditable workmanship; and in Upsala there is a large store full of useful woodenware that is exclusively from the skilled hands of the schoolboys of Sweden. A certain proportion of the receipts for these wares is sometimes credited and ultimately paid to the ingenious pupil. The attraction to the youth that is found in this industry—always pursued in a regular class and under a special master, the same as in other matters of study—is perhaps sufficiently evinced by the fact that during this vacation time the slojd schools are full of lads, anxious to retain or improve their skill at carpenter and cabinet making—in the domain of the apprentice.

The law making attendance at public or private school compulsory was passed in 1842. In 1883 ninety-eight per cent. of the children of the prescribed age were recorded as pupils in the public academies or on the rolls of the ambulatory teachers, or catalogued as receiving equally careful instruction at home. The greater portion of the remaining two per cent. is accounted for by the lists of sick and mentally infirm.

The hospitals here are on "the pavilion plan." No man can be a surgeon or a medical practitioner in Sweden until he shall have attained the age of thirty; and then only upon strict inquiry and due examination. At least it is safe to believe that the doctor in this kingdom understands the anatomy of the human body, which he is called in to look at and prescribe for. But as I have overheard them talk and watched their operations in the performing room, it did not occur to me that these Swedish physicians and surgeons exhibited any more skill than the average of our American doctors, of ages between twenty-one and one score and ten. Of course, I am not competent to make a very important judgment in the premises; but I have had a considerable amount of layman-observation in this line, and I venture to pass my conclusion for what it is worth. (I believe there is a large amount of office practice in the cities of Sweden that is really conducted by those who are under the age fixed for open announcement as physicians.) I saw a woman's broken arm set and bandaged at a Stocholm hospital, and I have the audacity to say that I have witnessed a like operation more quickly and neatly performed by Dr. David Wooster of San Francisco, when he was a very young man.

There are just six large gardens with cafes or restaurants attached, in Stockholm. The principal ones are at Hasselbacken (Hazel Hill). At Hasselbacken there is the best cafe and restaurant in the city. There are completely enclosed and also fan-shaped and sounding board open-air music stands. There is the famous oak under which Karl Bellman wrote some of his most popular songs—a bronze statue of the poet being conspicuous in the garden. "Our Tom Moore," said one of our Swedish friends—pointing to the figure as we passed. The Stromparterre, is at one side of the bridge that leads directly from the front of the castle. The Mosebach, is on the Hill of Moses. There is good music at all of these in the evenings, and on some afternoons. At Mosebach can be had the finest view of the city and its surroundings; and an ascent to it may be made in an elevator that starts at a point on Glasbruk street, which is only a few feet from and above the level of the sea harbor. The scene from the tower immediately above the elevator landing, especially at sunrise and sunset, is magnificent. It is the popular photograph-album view of the capital.

At this date—in August—it seemed too chilly for outdoor or cafe enjoyment; but the people here to the manner-born are not of that opinion. They crowd the gardens every night, with the mercury low down among the fifties—as our thermometers would measure it; and they cannot repress a reproachful expression—by word or look—when we suggest that it is perhaps a trifle cool for perfectly serene delight at an open air restaurant table. "Do you feel cold? Indeed! You had better take a little pomerans, and eat some lax. Lax is warming!" Now lax is salmon; and it is brought

VIEW OF HASSELBACKEN, STOCKHOLM.

on these tables in a nearly raw state. And this is one thing that may sometmes somewhat reduce the poignancy of regret at leaving this beautiful land.

At the Stromparterre we saw a party of Fins, on their way to America. Herr Meyerberg knew them at once—knew their nativity, and their "classification," as he termed it. He conversed with them, and learned that among the five men there was over $8,000 in gold. They were going to buy land in Montana and send for their wives when they had built a house. "Some of them don't send for their wives," remarked our friend; "and that is a not infrequent failing with Swedes who go to America and leave their families behind them. A Swede is a very bad man when he *is* bad," added the inspector with that most agreeable smile, which, being interpreted, signified: "You see, I will claim superiority at all points." Hereupon a little child hummingly interjected an American nursery rhyme, about a girl that was very good when she was good, but when she was bad she was horrid. The great teacher was charmed with the appropriate quotation—as he repeatedly described it—and wanted to impress it on his memory; asking for its repetition, and himself repeating it for memorizing purposes, in a way that was full of humor.

The matter of gymnasiums in the schools came up again. "You see what a strong man I appear to be," said Herr Meyerberg; and he arose from his seat and stretched his arms in an Ajax-defying-the-lightning fashion. "Well, it was not always so. I have had my trials. My mother and a sister died of consumption under my care. I was predisposed the same way; but I went into regular training, and now you think I am a strong man? I have been a powerful man in my best years, and I am not a weak man now." From this the Inspector went on to describe the various methods of school gymnasiums; showing some of the mistakes that had been made in the way of overdoing and misdirecting, by exclusive practice with one set of apparatus, etc.

He suddenly changed the subject by saying: "You see those people coming down the stairs! They are what you would call, or what some other persons would call, of the Plebian order; the same as those Finish men by the railing yonder. Well, a few years ago there was a distinction made in the attendance at these gardens, and only those of the higher classes, as they are called, were permitted to come here and drink and sup. Not so now. We are as much on the social equality, as far as public gardens are concerned, as you are in America. This change has taken place within a comparatively recent period."

We spoke of our visit to Delecarlia and alluded to the practice of men and maidens from that section coming down to

Stockholm to work during the Summer season. "Yes, replied the Inspector, "it is of course a matter of great mutual advantage. We would be short of house servants if these strong and useful people did not put in an appearance. They are from our reservoir of help." "Do they often make their permanent residence here?" we enquired. "No, that is not a matter of very frequent occurrence. As a rule, they are most devotedly attached to their native districts. They generally marry one of their school fellows. They are often betrothed early in life, and their steadfastness to their betrothal vows is proverbial." "They give a stranger the impression of strength fully as much as of beauty," we remarked. "Yes, they can do the work of men the whole Summer through without seeming to tire under the strain ; and then they are such pleasant workers—so cheerful and even merry at their tasks."

We mentioned to the Inspector our suggestion about Swedish coffee houses with Delecarlian maids in costume to attend upon customers. "Aha! that would indeed be a good enterprise," he exclaimed ; " but I am afraid the partners in such establishments would have to keep up a regular procession of waitresses. For while these girls do not readily fall in love with our Stockholm boys, I am told that they are easily pleased with eligible offers of marriage from Germans and Americans."

Then our friend sprang up and walked over to the music stand and began a whispered conversation with the leader of the orchestra. He soon came back with a sad face and a shake of the head ; and saying : " He has not got the music." "What music?" "I wanted him to play the Star-Spangled Banner for your benefit, but he is very sorry to say that he has not the notes. I am going to have some of that music in his portfolio another season. I have given their conductor a hint about its being a good card for the garden, and I will speak about it in our paper, too. I am one of the stockholders in a paper that has as great a circulation as any in Sweden." "Will you also mention in your paper the desirableness of having an American flag displayed by the Minister and Consul of the U. S., in Stockholm, at least on the 4th of July ?" [Herr Meyerberg, at a subsequent conversation, quite agreed with us with respect to the bad policy of commissioning as Minister or Consul at any place of importance, a man born in the country wherein he was to represent his adopted nation. It would seem as if the impropriety of such appointments, except in rare instances, was too manifest to admit of occasion for regret or protest in the premises. I did think at one time, that I would introduce a Bill in Congress prohibiting the appointments deprecated.] "Why," inquired the Inspector, with evident surprise, "didn't your Consul hang out the banner of your country on the outer wall, last 4th of July?" We said that he did not. There was no American flag to be seen in Stockholm on that day, so far as we could notice, except in some of the back streets, where a soiled and ragged specimen bore the inscription of the Inman trans-Atlantic steamship line. "Well, you have no Minister here now." "But we have a Consul." "Well, he is a Swedish gentleman, who was a brave man in your wars. He lost a leg in fighting for the Union. But I will tell you something, that may in part excuse him, about this matter. We do not even observe the anniversary of our King's birthday here. We have very little anniversary enthusiasm about us. We have nothing like your 4th of July 'racket.' Still, I admit the propriety of his showing his colors on your great Declaration day. It must have slipped his mind." "If we are to have Consuls and Ministers Plenipotentiary at all," a lady in our party insisted, "and I confess I cannot see much if any use for the former, they should be men whose memories are not defective to such an extent on such a subject. It may in itself be considered a very small matter, and it may be indicative of much slothfulness or indifference, that is highly reprehensible." "You are right. I will have a flag out myself next 4th of July, and I will have this band play Yankee Doodle." The lady persisted: "In a kingdom that has hundreds of thousands of its children in the United States—some of them and a great many of them in the service of the country they have adopted—it certainly would seem natural to expect that in the great capital city the American flag would be seen floating from some house tops on our great anniversary." "True, true, and we will shame your representatives in Stockholm next year, if they don't hoist their national bunting bright and early on the 4th day of the memorable month."

There is an English church—a small but handsome edifice —situated at the North end of the city, and here we attended divine service one Sunday. The clergyman prayed for the Queen of England and the President of the United States. His congregation of about 150 persons was fully one-half composed of Americans, native and naturalized. There were three

ENGLISH CHURCH, STOCKHOLM.

or four Swedish girls in attendance, from whose conversation as they came out—which was necessarily overheard—we learned that they made their first visit to this church on that morning; their object being to see whether it would be of any benefit to them to regularly attend, with a view to acquiring a knowledge of our tongue. We were satisfied that they were playing truant from their own parish. They were of the opinion that they would still be in time to hear the hour-and-a-half discourse that is invariably delivered at Klara Kyrka on every First Day morning.

We note this as one among many indications of the widespread and increasing disposition to emigrate to America among the people of this kingdom. Even little maidens of twelve years are privately making ready for the voyage, by seeking and improving opportunities to learn the English language. There is abundant room and welcome for them. California ought to have a good proportion of the Swedish immigration of the next five years. By a little well-directed effort on the part of our Immigration Aid Society, California could call and receive many thousands of Swedish families within the decade—men, women and children, apt and accomplished in all the arts of agriculture; industrious, sober, trustworthy, and having a deep religious sense of duty.

The Royal Palace, which was consumed by fire in 1697 was reconstructed in 1753 by Nicodemus Tessin—at a cost of \$3,000,000 (representing then more than twice that amount, as devoted to materials and labor to-day). Its form is quadrilateral; length 418 feet, and width 391 feet. There is a portico to each facade, leading to the court-yard. The Northern facade, which fronts on the Norrbro or main bridge avenue, is approached by a double flight of steps, by the side of which, on granite pedestals, are two immense bronze lions. Hence the name—*Lejonbacken*. The palace is always open to visitors during the summer. On each floor, in each division, an attendant waits; anxious to show you courtesies and win your kroners. There are 583 rooms in the palace and 32 kitchens. To inspect them all you need at least five hours of time and you must fee nine flunkies. It is sufficient sight-seeing work for one day—is a visit to all the halls, apartments, bed-rooms, dining-rooms and kitchen range rooms that are exhibited. [I do not write at length of the Museum or of the Picture Galleries or of the Palace Castle itself; because I must suppose that most, if not all my readers, who have felt or are likely to feel any special interest in such matters will have already learned much about these places from other sources; and

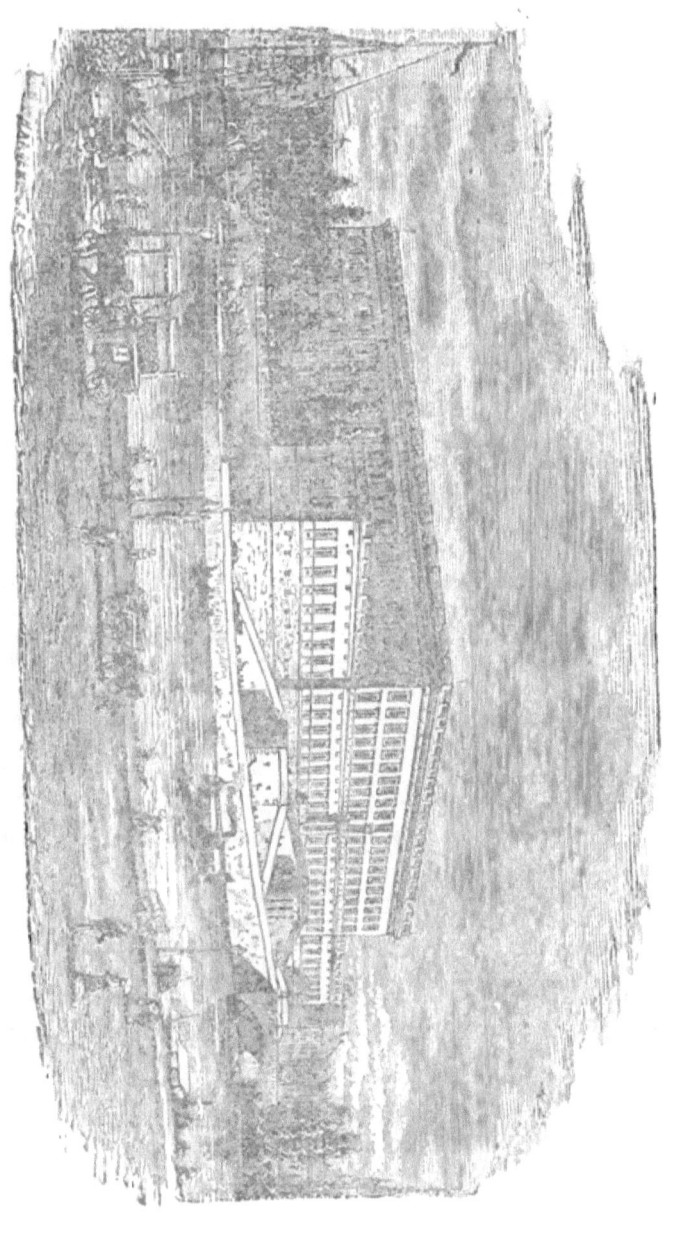

THE ROYAL PALACE, STOCKHOLM.

my descriptions might seem to be wearisome repititions before their eyes. Many inhabitants of Stockholm are or profess to be very much incensed on account of the arrangement by which each suite of rooms or each hall or set of lodging-apartments is placed, so to speak, on separate exhibition, at separate cost of admission. You will often be asked whether you have visited the Castle; and whatever may be your reply you will probably be told that in the opinion of your questioner the palace should be closed against "unofficial visitors" or else provision should be made for an attendance throughout the entire building at a fixed and reasonable sum. So that even with respect to this little matter, the people of Stockholm are in the habit of expressing their sentiments of justice and propriety, by due proclamation in private conversations.]

The ceiling of the magnificent Audience Room, painted by Foquet, represents Venus and Mars wedded by Love. Above them Hymen is dancing with his torch, while Cupids and Graces are strewing flowers. Summer, in the form of woman offers Mars a rose; while celestial giants are engaged in banishing the devils of war. The ornaments over the windows and other casings represent scenes from the life of Alexander the Great. Two candelabra, 29 feet high, are such splendid specimens of gilded and prismatic adornments, as of themselves to make you regret that the time allowed for inspection here is so brief. The grand gallery is 162 by 23 feet. You are requested to put on slippers, before you walk upon the tessellated floor. The massive doors are of carved oak, and are wonderfully attractive to all kinds of visitors. There are a great number of marble statues around the gallery, and several groups of sculpture by Bystrom. The allegorical paintings are charming. In the centre of the ceiling, in the Western gallery, there is a representation of Janus with Revolt breaking her fetters. On one side is a tiger and a blindfolded fury. On the other side is Bellona, mounted on a chariot, and pitilessly crushing her enemies beneath the wheels. Pity is represented as flying with one child in her arms and another by her side. Religion is represented as overthrown by war, while Discord and Jealousy, with torches and serpents in hand are frightfully conspicuous at the front.

We visited the study of the late King which is kept precisely as it was when he left it. There is a book, opened face downwards on one of his writing-desks,—exactly as he placed it with his own hand. A general idea of the magnificence of the Festival Hall is conveyed by the other name, that visitors have given—" The White Sea."

In the audience chamber and elsewhere, servants and artists were at work cleaning and refurbishing; and from all the attendants we heard the story of great expectations for the coming Winter's festivities.

The church of Riddarholmen, 192 feet in length by 60 feet in width, is of Gothic pattern. The old tower was struck by lightning and burned down in 1835; and in 1847 the new steeple, of iron lattice-work—302 feet in height—was erected. There has been no divine service in this church since 1807, except on the occasion of a burial of one of the royal family. Here are the remains of the great Gustavus Adolphus; in a sarcophagus of green Italian marble, that resembles in form the marble casing in which the great Lord Nelson reposes under the dome of St. Paul.

Near to the entrance of this Mausoleum church—on the left—is a vault in which there are a large number of coffins which appear to have been thrown in, on top of each other, without much reverential respect for the contents. Big and little, they lie upon and over against each other in a promiscuous manner, which suggests that they had "outlived their usefulness" as attractions on which the Swedish vergers could dilate, and were therefore thrust into this spare recess or cellar without conscience or ceremony.

Surrounding the coffin of Charles XV., who died in 1872, were a number of lighted candles; and a long biographical or genealogical account of the king's family, written in large and almost printed letters,—on one sheet—lay by the side of the inscription plate. Presumably this was to meet or satisfy the curiosity of inquiring visitors, who, it might be supposed —(perhaps experience had shown)—would otherwise torment the vergers by absorbing too much of their time in each instance, with demands for the information that is by this huge manuscript conveyed.

RIDDARHOLMEN CHURCH.

256 NORTHERN EUROPE.

The national churches in Stockholm very much resemble each other in structure and appointments. The interior of Jacob Church, which is shown by the accompanying engrav-

INTERIOR OF JACOB CHURCH, STOCKHOLM.

ing, will give not only a correct idea of the nave and altar of that particular edifice, but will serve as a "sample" for the city.

The great theatre is situated on the east side of the principal (Gustaf-Adolph) square; and a very correct representation of the view from the stage is herewith presented. It was erected by Gustavus III. in 1775-82. You will be reminded that it was here that Gustavus III. was assassinated in 1792. All the seats are eligible, for sight and sound; its acoustic virtues and its adaptability for spectacular pieces being topics for boasting on the part of the watchman who opens the doors and escorts the visitors in the Summer season. It will be remembered that here Jenny Lind made her first stage appearance—in the chorus.

A mere recital of the names of the Libraries and Museums in Stockholm, will sufficiently indicate to most readers the formidable and fascinating nature of the demand upon the attention of the intelligent traveller which this class of collections constitute. The Archives, the Belvedere, the Royal Library, [a large portion of the books being still retained at the Palace,] the Library of the Academy of Agriculture, the Library of the School of Art and Industry, the Library of the Conservatory, the Libraries of the Polytechnical School and the Academy of Sciences, the Museums:—of the Academy of Agriculture, of the Caroline Medical College, of the Zoological Department, and the Northern Museum (with First and Second Annex)—where the attendants are all dressed in the picturesque costumes of their respective Delecarlian Districts,—and, above all, the National Museum. In the Northern Museum, models of houses, and specimens of furniture, clothing, farm implements, domestic utensils and ancient and modern bridal ornaments, combine to make exhibitions of intensely fascinating interest. You will be drawn to them again and again—alternately prompted to re-read and re-visit; and trying to cheat yourself at your last hour in the rooms, with the promise that you will call once more! It is the same experience, in this nature, (although of entirely different tone, of course, that you have at Westminster,) at your farewell visitation.

The National Museum building is a splendid edifice, with Venitian windows and a magnificent doorway of green marble casings. It is situated on the Blasiiholmen, opposite the

KING'S THEATRE, STOCKHOLM.

Royal Palace. It has seven distinct departments :—Historical, Coin-Cabinet, Drawings and Engravings, Sculptures, Armor and Weapons, Picture Gallery, and Collection of Costumes. Statues of Odin, Thor and Baldur confront you with coarse but not unbenignant faces, as you enter. The Prehistoric Era and the Bronze, Iron, Mediæval and Modern Ages are represented separately by relics and selections that take you from where we can guess about our race as it once

NATIONAL MUSEUM, STOCKHOLM.

was on this globe down to the latest and best specimens of the mechanical and artistic skill of man. In the collection of Armor are pistols and swords that belonged to Gustavus Adolphus. "Now you have seen the most wonderfully historic sword in existence," remarked a Swedish gentleman to the little girl of our party, as we were looking at one of the great claymores. "Where?" "Why, right here;—right before you! this sword of Gustavus Adolphus!" "No; I have not, if you please." "You have not? Why, yes you have. If not, where is that most wonderful sword?" "I don't know where it is; but it is a sword that has a different name." "What name?" "The sword of Bunker Hill."

---o---

XXI

KING AND PEOPLE.

We were walking in the Djurgarden a few days before we left Stockholm, in company with one of our Swedish friends, when the King and a portion of his suite rode by, on their way from the Castle to one of his country residences in or near this great park. For be it known there are several royal residences in this vicinity; although there is one that specially bears that name. The King, as we were credibly informed, frequently "puts up for the night," with some of his relatives, who have princely mansions and gardens here and there in the neighborhood of the Capital. And so we came to personal talk about his majesty: his character and his manner of life, and the political and social relations which he bore to his subjects.

A Swedish friend, in a delightfully frank and suave manner, insisted that the kingdom was really more of a republic, so far as liberality and gentleness of Government are concerned, than the United States of America! He asserted that the King had less power than our President; and that if he should do many things, which it was said our chief executive had sometimes done with impunity, he would be "ostracized" to that extent that it would be almost tantamount to a dethronement! Of course all this was uttered in the very kindest of tones; and did not fail to meet with our answers of doubt if not positive protest. Could it be so! A King uncrowned by the contempt of his people, manifested only in the way indicated! Incredible, we ventured to intimate. Our friend persisted: "It would be intolerable to our Sovereign."

Unquestionably the present government of Sweden is eminently worthy of the study of the American people, and especially of those who in any large degree may be said to be representative men among the citizens of our Republic. For there are certain points with respect to the introduction and enactment of laws wherein Swedish people seem to exercise, as a mass, more absolute and immediate influence than is felt or recognized from the same or like source with us. Public opinion there, when it can once be said to have been formed, is speedily expressed in statute. And the King would never dare to interpose anything corresponding to a veto power against a measure of legislation arising in that way. If it be said that it is the same with us, I recall the messages of some of our Presidents; which certainly were in the face of the well-weighed and just desire of the vast majority of the people of the United States,—founded upon sufficient and honest reflection; I am reminded of vetos which were issued at the dictation of the Monopolists and amid the applause of the corrupt and corrupting agents and lobbyists at Washington.

Curiously enough, our friend went on to make another boast in behalf of his Sovereign, in comparison with our most distinguished General (for whom, as I write, the sympathies of our people are profoundly exercised, on account of recent and dangerous illness). And on this he laid a stress that at the moment seemed to me to almost impeach his intelligence. "Why," said he, "our king has a splendid physical presence; and what is more, he has a great big voice!" This he said with a rising inflection that reached the stentorian. "I was at your Centennial at Philadelphia, when the President delivered the opening speech. I stood next to some of the sailors of your Navy, who were ranged immediately in front of the platform; and several of them cried out at the time: 'O, go back to Washington, Father Grant, and take lessons in Elocution!' Now, if our King had been there, they would have heard him at a distance of full a quarter of a mile?'

We could not help but ask our friend if he was sure that our sailor boys used the word " Elocution ? " On his replying in the affirmative, we began to dwell upon the degree of intelligence and the advance in education which our people possessed over the majority of subjects in his kingdom !

I should like to see the Blue Book that would tell us how many uncles and aunts and cousins and grand-aunts—and relatives still more distant—are under liberal pension from the Swedish government. Turn where you may, and you will find some large establishment occupied by royal relatives, more or less distant from the throne. While the poor soldier receives a pension of about three dollars and seventy-five cents a year, some great-aunt of the reigning monarch is "provided for"—as the saying there is—by being given possession of a three-storied house, with thirty or forty rooms, with a retinue of servants, and a rent-roll of acreage in due proportion. It is not that there is anything absolutely unjust in making a provision for these good, ancient people ; but it is that they have a superfluity ; while the trooper who has been worn out in the service of his Majesty is left to starve in a hovel.

From every hill top in and about Stockholm, the view is beautiful. Of course, almost everyone who comes here and writes a letter hence, must needs dwell upon these sights ; and for that, if for no other reason, I should hesitate and decline to give my description in these premises. I mention this conceded fact—of city and landscape charm—as an introduction to my confession that at no point here have I had greater enjoyment, drawn merely from the vision, than when standing on the Norrbro, in front of the Castle, and looking down upon that other bridge,—a comparatively recent construction,—immediately to the east of the railroad crossing. It seemed to me as if I could not sufficiently feast upon the picture which those graceful arches presented. It is the second bridge from the Lake, depicted in the accompanying engraving, and is called the *Wasa*. I have repeatedly looked in volumes of engravings, with the purpose of comparing this structure with similar bridges in other parts of the world, which have received the eulogies of such men as Ruskin,

Bayard Taylor and W. D. Howells. But however you may otherwise compare or contrast Stockholm with Venice, etc. I put this one structure as of its kind a challenge against the world. I took my original liking and love for it, the moment I set eyes upon it. Afterwards when I drew the attention of friends, who had often passed by a good point of observation without making an admiring note of it (as we all will do), they agreed with me. And to this object more than to any other on the lower plane surface of this city, I direct the attention of my friends, when they shall make their Summer tour in this Northern land. To be sure, they will visit Moseback and Hasselbacken and some if not all the promontory towers of the King—one rising on the cliff by the side of his skating reservation and others in the Djurgarden the Kastellholm and Ladgarden-lander; but it becomes me to charge it upon them not to forget this minor spectacle. For as you stand on the upper granite crossing, and look at this new structure, letting your eye glance slowly from one bank to the other, you will seem to witness the actual process of the building. These arches do appear to leap over the swiftly running water that ripples beneath them. And there is altogether an indescribable beauty and fascination in their lines. The poetry of spanning architecture is here.

I have already spoken of the characteristically conscientious workmanship of the Swedish people. Of course there must be many unskillful and negligent and unfaithful workmen in the ranks of their mechanics. There are probably a large number of tradespeople who consciously do not always speak the exact truth, when "driving a sale." This is only going on the general average of humanity as it is to be taken and accepted, or expected, everywhere, and at its best. But whether owing to our good fortune or not, we have to say that in Sweden, as a rule, that has been rarely broken, the law of honesty has been scrupulously kept in our sight. When a Swedish merchant has told us that a certain article was the best of its kind, we have often had occasion by inquiry, or by accident if you please, to verify his statement. I could enumerate many manufactured goods which are proverbially of the finest workmanship; bearing that character with the Swedish name, perhaps, in every other civilized nation of the earth. The Swedish razor, and cutlery of all descriptions, when said by a Stockholm dealer to be of the most excellent quality may be confidentally taken as such. And in the market of perishable goods we have never been imposed upon. When we have asked the old lady as to the quality or freshness of her vegetables or fruit, we have invariably met with a candid and truthful reply. Not infrequently have we been told "the goose-berries are not very good this morning;" that they were a day stale in the stall, that they had had a long ride from the lower end of the lake, and so forth, and so forth. Of course this would be followed by a statement as to the reduction of the price on account of the inferiority, as measured from the standard of perfection or the line of the best.

Stepping into the fancy dry goods store of Froken Hultgren on Drottning-Gatan we inquired as to the price of a piece of ribbon for a little girl's hair; and when we had made the purchase we remarked that the cost to us was about twenty-five per cent. more than would be asked for a similar article in London. The reply was quickly made, and was noticeable: "It is nearly thirty per cent. as much more. But if you will allow us to tell you how much it costs us to get the goods here from France—inclusive of the cost of making a selection—and how much it detracts from the value of a bolt of ribbon to take off a piece like that, you will be satisfied that the additional charge is not unreasonable." This may seem a very small matter of illustration, as indeed it is; but it was of its kind one of those things that first surprised us. We have had heretofore so much sympathy excited in us for those people who are often "selling out below cost"—and have found that commiseration so often misplaced, that—well, let it be understood that we *were* astonished by this acknowledgement of the regular and proper average mercantile profit. There seems to be a single disposition and habit of perfect truthfulness among these small tradespeople of Stockholm.

A few nights ago we went into a store to inquire the price of a doll dressed in one of the Delecarlian costumes. The sum asked fairly shocked us on account of its largeness; and there was an exclamation by one of the party indicating this feeling. Whereupon the young lady in charge drew a pencil from one of the drawers and leaning over on the counter proposed to set down the exact sum paid by her employer for each and every portion of the mannikin, and the dress which lay before us. And she was vexed when we protested that it was not necessary; that we would accept her account of what the whole structure cost without going into details. She wanted to give us item for item and have us institute a regular committee of investigation to find out

GUSTAF ADOLPH SQUARE, STOCKHOLM.

whether it was so or not. Taking her figures the percentage of profit was very reasonable.

We have sometimes—not often—had occasion to hire a carriage in Stockholm. The terms have been two kroners or fifty-two cents an hour or three kroners for two hours and the reckoning has been scrupulously accurate. Nor have we ever seen our driver go out of his way to "make time," or purposely lag behind, that he might bring in an additional charge. A precise contrast with London experience. And as for the porters on the street,—who must never be confounded with the *portiers* at the gates or stairs-landing office of the hotels,—(a large number often assembling at the Hotel Ryder, corner of Gustaf Adolph Square)—they look to be as they are, embodiments of honest faith. You ask for a direction, and they will stand and give it to you by pointing, without appearing to expect a kroner in return. You must needs tell them that you wish to have them accompany you, if you want one of them to be your companion and guide. Nor is this owing to anything in the nature of stupidity or laziness.

With respect to the service which is rendered in the public houses to the strangers, whether by the girls from Delecarlia, who come down to the capital for the Summer season,—or by the regular attendants, it is most excellent in its promptness and sufficiency. There is no obsequiousness about it; such as you sometimes meet with elsewhere; there is no parade of activity,—nothing like that which we Yankees call "fussiness;"—but there is a quick answer to a summons, a patient and careful listening to a request or order, and an immediate obedience,—accurate and ample.

No wonder these Swedish girls are at a premium in New York City. When at Castle Garden, recently, we were told by the matron in charge that there were a dozen demands where there could be one supplied from the immigrant list of Swedish cooks or chambermaids.

It being necessary to have the services of a shoemaker, we stepped into the shop of the one located nearest to our hotel. Into a hall-way and into a handsomely furnished parlor—like a private dwelling in all outward respects—save for the sign over the window—went we in search of the Knight of St. Crispin. I don't know exactly how it came about, but we were using this very noble designation, when the door leading from the rear of the front room opened and barely afforded space to admit the master of the establishment. A giant in stature—not less than six feet, six inches in height; but having a most benignant countenance; with great lustrous eyes, that used to glow with an unmistakable warmth of good nature. It seemed, despite his obvious, remarkable pleasantness of disposition, as though we could not bring our courage up to the sticking point of asking such a powerful and distinguished looking person if he would be kind enough to straighten a heel and under-tap a toe?

But it had to be said; and with a voice as gentle as a dove, he to-be-sured us until we were impressed with his kind condescension to that degree that our sense of gratitude was painful.

On one side of his ante-room hung a life-size picture of the late King, and on the other a portrait of equal dimensions of his Queen Consort; and we naturally diversified our conversation by reference to the sovereigns that are and that were. Then it transpired that we were addressing the "Royal Bootmaker." Ah! we should never have thought of going into such an august presence with our little patch-work requisition! And giving some audible form to this sincere reflection, we had a good hearty laugh with His Majesty's skillful servant; and this communion without sycophancy and in all jollity! may be said to have been worth the price of the cobbling. A Jolly Giant indeed is this monstrous Sir Knight of the lap-stone.

Then comes familiar talk about matters and things in general. And finally it is mentioned that we hail from the Golden Gate State of America. "What, California? *California?* CALIFORNIA!" And immediately the Court shoemaker's wife is called into the room. "Here! here! These persons are from California!" And such a pleasant, hearty greeting as we then and thereupon received! "Why, we have a relative there, married to a jeweller named Engrist. Do you know her?"

We had the same experience at this shop as to faithful workmanship and candid statement as to the liberal but reasonable margin of gains to the workman on the labor profit.

A few evenings before our final departure from Stockholm, we took a walk around the Northern portion of the city and noticed the laboring people as they were leaving their places of employment. Two women who were cleaning the hods and covering the mortar beds in the vicinity of a building in course of construction, were saluted by us, and put under catechism. They made the mortar and they carried the hods. They were born at Stockholm; accustomed to rough labor all their lives; and for the last ten or fifteen years they had been at work during the Summer seasons as helpers for the masons. They received eighty ore a day—about twenty cents—and were assured of steady employment during the warm season at these wages. In response to our questions they said with a laugh—yes, with a laugh—that they believed they could do as much work of the kind of labor to which we have referred as any man; but they hastened to add that a man in similar employment would get twice as much in wages. Their hands were very hard and coarse, as you might well expect, but they were small, and had yet a feminine beauty about them.

One was a widow and one was a spinster; and they lived in a garret room, six feet by eight feet in surface measurement, with a sloping ceiling that ran from four feet to eight feet in height. This last item we obtained by giving them a small sum and accompanying them to their habitation; a lady in our party going into their room with them, and carefully noting the area in which they had their home.

We sat down in the little yard that surrounds Clara-Kyrka; and as one of the women that was engaged at a public wash-house approached, we bade her good evening, and questioned her. She was a widowed mother, with two little children. She was thirty-five years of age, and her eldest child was not yet five. She earned twenty-six cents a day. She was an expert in cleansing linen. She got twice as much wages as many in the same establishment who worked during the same long twelve hours. Her hands were "a sight to see." As we held one of them, we thought that it felt like a little bundle of cold lifeless bones; and it certainly looked to be just that. Here was an illustration of the familiar saying of working off one's fingers' ends. Literally, her nails were scrubbed from her finger tips. When some one in our company gave her a little silver money, she sank down on her knees and thanked God for the benefaction.

While in this church-yard we saw four men come rapidly through the North gate, bearing a box covered with a pall. It was a corpse, which they laid on a bench in one of the low houses—like our country meeting house sheds, with perforated doors prefixed, with which the Southern end of the yard is bordered. The funeral will take place in two days. Meanwhile the remains rest in this church-yard vault; in which, at this time, there were no less than five bodies awaiting interment.

Of course it is claimed that there is a free press in Sweden, and especially in Stockholm. It is so called; and in many respects

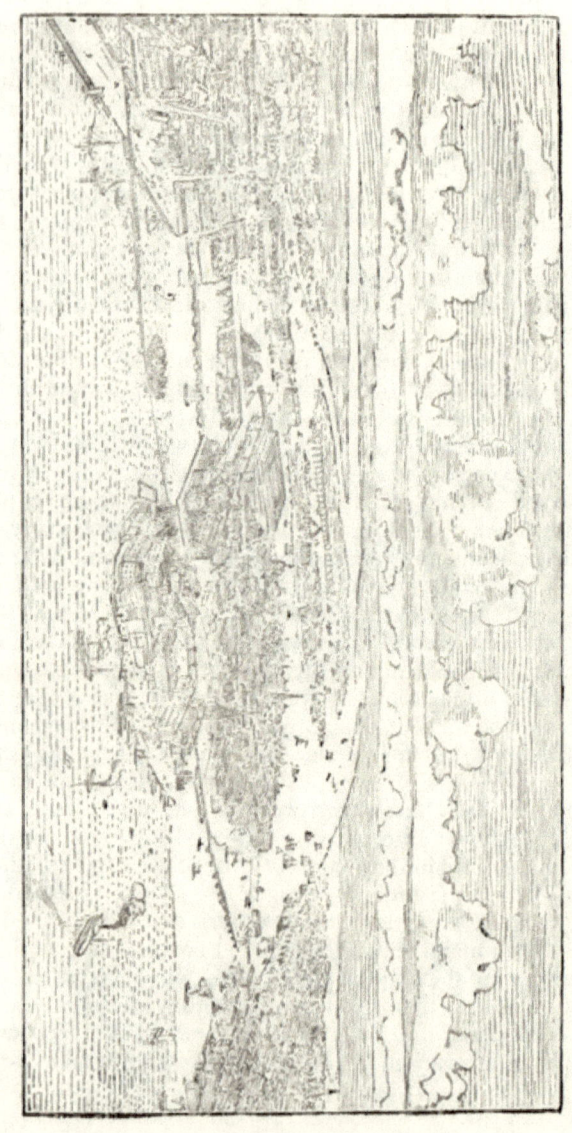

VIEW OF STOCKHOLM, FROM LAKE MALAREN.

it is eminently entitled to that name. And yet there is a species of censorship which we would cry out against very severely if we believed it existed in America; although there is with us an espionage and a tyranny from a different source, which is quite as reprehensible,—quite as much to be deplored. If you wish to criticize any of the officers of the Royal household, or any of the Commanders of His Majesty's army or navy, or any of the Superintendents of His Majesty's estates, you must do it in a very round-about, gingerly manner, or the communication will not be accepted. But precisely by this indirect method, by the "damnable inuendo," there is much of censuring comment upon public men and upon public affairs that are immediately connected with the Royal household. I had several illustrations of this. One in particular was in reference to an alleged false weight that was maintained by one of His Majesty's officers at the Superintendent's yard, at Stromsholm, in the midst of a large government farm. The newspaper of the neighborhood would not call the offender or the offence by name. But in a round-about way the grievance was complained of through the Press, and forthwith there was a sharp attempt to ascertain the name of the writer. But the identity of the correspondent was successfully concealed, and for the unjust balance an honest set of scales was soon substituted.

With reference to a division of the people of Sweden into political parties; the lines seem to be somewhat vague. But there is certainly a party of the Town, or, as it is sometimes called, a party of the Nobility—because the Nobility as a rule belong to it—and a party of the Country. But many eminent men in the cities sympathize with and are allied to the party of the Country. The party of the Country insist,— as I think I have before intimated—that the farmers shall no longer be compelled to provide in their several districts, for the household of the soldiers that are enlisted or drafted into His Majesty's army. And generally the party of the Country is the Liberal party,—though there are no sharp terms of distinction such as mark the boundaries between our political organizations.

The Capitol or Riksdagshuset,—the front of which, as elsewhere noted, can be seen depicted on the left of the engraving in this volume that prominently presents Riddarholm Church—is a very plain five-story building. We were told by the janitor or sexton at the Ridderholm that it was impossible for us at this Season of the year to obtain a look at the Chambers of the two Houses; that visitors were never admitted except during Legislative Season time; that a request for such admission was never heard of before, etc. But we marched through one of the open doorways of the edifice and up one flight of stairs, past a telegraph office, and into a room where a woman and child were sitting, both engaged in needle-work. We asked for the janitor or custodian. We learned that he was the husband of one and the father of the other of the two persons before us; and within five minutes we were introduced to him and on our way to the Halls of Legislation! How came this about? When we first made our request, the reply was "Impossible!" But when the janitor appeared and we informed all persons present that we were from California, and that we had a special reason, which we named, for observing how the Legislators were grouped together before their presiding officer, the inner doors were opened. Again the same refrain: now something of regular expectation. "O, from California; O! O! that is another matter."

The Members sit upon narrow benches that are ranged in close proximity,—in fact you might say that they were crowded together. There is less room, I should judge, than is usually afforded for such proportion of the Members as can or do sit on the benches of the English House of Commons, —taking into consideration the average size of the Swedish legislator. We were told that there was frequent complaint because of the lack of those facilities which our Representatives in our several State Legislatures and in our Capitol at Washington enjoy. But it would be impossible in these Capitol halls to put the 130 members of the one House and the 200 members of the other, and give them desk-room.

The benches are placed on a rising floor or a series of steps, having about the same ratio of elevation—from step to step— that is given in the orchestra portion of the California theatre

—almost as steep as in a Medical College demonstration or clinique hall.

At the Castle there is a room in which the Members of both houses assemble to meet and consult with the King. There the benches are of similar pattern,—the Lower House sitting upon one side of the single and central aisle, and the members of the other House occupying the opposite series of seats.

At the Capitol as well as at the Palace Council Chamber, where King and Legislators officially face other, in the Summer season, all is in dust and disorder. The benches in both Houses are made of pine, and are of the flimsiest construction. They are covered with a close baize cloth, with a little green fringe around the edges.

Adjacent to the Chambers or Halls of Legislation in the Capitol are sitting-rooms for the Committees, and long corridor apartments where the Legislator may promenade or may sit down and refresh himself at wine and card tables. Our guide—none other than the head janitor himself—told us that, on many occasions he had to provide for the removal of some noble Legislator early in the morning, by hiring a couple of stout porters to carry his lordship down the stairs and place him in a carriage.

The view from some of the windows of the Capitol, looking out upon portions of the city and the Malar, is almost equal in splendor to that obtained from the top of Moseback itself.

The appointed Members of the upper chamber of the Swedish Parliament must be over thirty-five years of age; must pay taxes on $20,000, and have an annual income of not less than $1,200. Their term is nine years; and there is no salary attached to their office. The members of the Lower House are elected every three years from the different districts without regard to property ownership, and are paid about $3.00 per day.

That was a sad night for us, when we parted with Herr Meyerberg, at the Hotel Kung Karl. We invited him to a little sexsor, which we ordered spread in one of our rooms; and when he came we all remarked with less emphasis than was really justified, that he looked exceedingly well. Indeed, what a splendid-looking man he is! No wonder that his Philadelphia and Baltimore audiences were so delighted to see him and hear him talk, that they made unreasonable demands upon even his strength for protracted utterance. No wonder that we often heard strangers inquire as he passed by, " What Nobleman is that ? "

Sure enough the days are growing shorter; for we have candles brought in just before the School Inspector arrives. And a little girl in the company says that the table must look very bright this evening : for it is " A Fareweel to our bestest friend in Stockholm."

He brings Wellin's Poems,—producing the large volume from under his arm as he enters the supper room, and in his own grand way he reads the apostrophe to George Washington! It is a reading such as Longfellow long ago interpreted for us, " Not from the grand old Masters, not from the bards sublime * * * But from some humbler poet." And we have the glorious "music of his voice." He must needs rise from the table, when he comes to the final comparison and appeal. He has the last verse by heart ; and the conclusion is a thrilling recitation. His declamation is for such an occasion the perfection of art. What could be finer in touch of intonation, or more delightful, appropriate and impressive than the waving gesture with which he signifies the amplitude of the glory that belongs to the name of our great heroes and patriots ! Wasa and Washington ! It was oratory and it was song !

Farewell, dear friend ! We would not speak this word to you on that night of supreme felicity in companionship— when most we enjoyed your society. We kept the fact of intended departure and such mournful reflections as were begotten of it carefully locked in our aching breasts. We can be partly, nay, largely satisfied and consoled by the pictures of the beautiful city that we shall take with us to America, but—as with respect to a few scenes in nature, on our journeyings—we do not now personally regret that he refused to give us his photograph. Our memories shall hold that best ; and let not recollection be disturbed or anywise distracted by the picture of his face. Alas! How imperfectly, with much larger opportunity or indulgence, could I hint as to the extent of our obligations to you. How many have been your thoughtful kindnesses. How excellent has been your guidance, conversation and counsel on every possible occasion for your hospitable attendance. Fortunate, indeed, have we been in forming your acquaintance, and gaining an access of intimacy to your sympathies and good-will. Fortunate will we name and number those who may come after us, to sojourn a little while in this kingdom, if they shall have your greeting and your good offices of friendship and esteem.

---o---

XXII.

FROM STOCKHOLM TO MALMO.

The sum total of fares, from place to place on this route, amounts to very little over the cost of a continuous-trip passage. The Government does not make a practice of issuing stop-over tickets.

The distance from Stockholm to Malmo, by Nassjo, is 383 of our miles. The express train makes the through trip in 18½ hours. The ordinary train as it is called, stops over night at Nassjo, which is about half way between the Capital and the Southern city of Sweden. The charges are respectively for first, second or third-class fares on the ordinary train, 52 kroners, 33 kroners, and 22 kroners. On the express there are two classes,—the first and the second: for which the ticket price is 52 kroners and 37 kroners. The second class accommodations are fully as comfortable as the first class cars on our Central Pacific; although there is not so much gilding and the cushions are of a brown, instead of a crimson color. There is really not a great deal of difference between the second and first class compartments. The great majority of Europeans travel in the third class compartments; even on the few roads where the seats are uncushioned, but where the conveniences and comforts otherwise are equal to our best.

The first town of importance through which you pass after leaving the Capital, on the road indicated, is Sodertelge; a watering place of which I made mention in describing the canal route from Gottenberg to Stockholm. The road passes in the rear of the principal town or city, and you have in part the same views of the place which are afforded from the canal, and also

NORRKOPING PUBLIC SCHOOL.

entirely different pictures of the town itself, and of the surrounding country. The city proper is bustling and thriving, while the "watering place" adjacent, with its great hotels for invalids, is a picture of quiet repose.

The next town of importance, is Norrkoping. This is a seaport city—close enough to the Baltic to be so called,—of 30,000 inhabitants. It is located at the mouth of the Motala, at its confluence with the Bravik ; and is very handsomely situated. It claims an origin dating back five hundred years : having had the honor to be sacked and plundered several times, by the Danes and the Russians. It is a modern looking town ; many of the houses giving evidence of having been constructed by or under the direction of an Architect who had studied our American styles! The grammar and commercial school—(*Hogre Elementarlaroverkets-Hus*)—is a splendid edifice ;—the first structure to which the local guides are accustomed to conduct an American.

There is an enormous water power here, which is afforded by the Motala ; and the advantages of Norrkoping's location for manufacturing purposes could not well be surpassed. In this respect it is another Lowell. Here are a number of iron bridges which are well worth an examination. Indeed it is claimed that the origin of iron and steel bridge construction as a separate and distinct business,—as something of speciality manufacture,— should be credited to the foundry-men of this town.

There are not only a large number of iron foundries and steel making furnaces here, but several factories for the weaving of woolen and cotton goods. And at the door of two or three of these establishments, we were proudly informed of the fact that Norrkoping was distinguished abroad by bearing the name of the "Swedish Manchester." When we suggested that the more appropriate phrase, considering the tide of emigration, etc., would be the "Swedish Lowell," the inquiry was earnest as to the reason for this remark. And I was afterwards assured that the substitution suggested should be made and observed in all future communications from our guide—to strangers coming from America.

Then comes Linkoping, the capital of Ostergotland. This is a city of about ten thousand inhabitants. It is connected with the Gota Canal by the river Stanga, which has been dredged out recently and coffer-dammed, so as to be navigable for large boats. The water passage for its commerce is made *via* Lake Roxen, of which I have hereinbefore given a description.

This is a cathedral town, and boasted of a Bishop as early as the 12th Century. There are a great many interesting historic "memories" connected with or located in this place, including

LINKÖPING CATHEDRAL.

the "Linkoping Blood Bath," where Sigismund and some of his principal followers were executed by Duke Charles,—nearly three hundred years ago. The spot where the execution took place is now surrounded by a circle of stones.

The cathedral church, the construction of which was begun in 1150, and completed in 1499, is of the Romanesque pattern, with an elegant choir, in pure Gothic. In the choir the windows are of stained glass and are of exquisite beauty. Above the altar is an immense figure of Christ, with Faith, Hope, and Charity represented on three sides.

Nassjo, where the ordinary train stops over night, is at the highest point on the railway between the Capital and Malmo. Though it is very eligibly and handsomely situated on the borders of a little Lake, it does not seem to have been a place of any importance, until the construction of the railroad. It is what we would call a Railroad town. There are, as might be expected, at such a junction and stop-over locality, five or six Hotels, all claiming through their advertisements and runners to be the best. There are also a number of private houses at which strangers are lodged and supplied with breakfast and the incomparable Swedish coffee on very moderate terms. And for the purpose of gaining information, we chose an over-night residence in one of these dwellings.

Matilda Gustafen was the name of the Lodging-house keeper who solicited our patronage, on the platform of the Nassjo depot, at five o'clock in the evening,—and got it. It was a walk of about three blocks which brought us to the door of her house; and better accommodations, in any particular, we did not have in all Sweden.

It was raining at the time of our arrival at Nassjo, and it was very sloppy inside as well as outside of the covered station. The roof was leaking, and the whole structure was undergoing much needed repairs.

The town of Nassjo contains about a thousand inhabitants; but unless some new enterprise is started in the vicinity, it will soon fall off one-half in its population. Our hostess says that now many of the heads of the families of the place have to go elsewhere to get work, during the Summer season; and there is a great deal of talk about "emigration to America." We sought and obtained introduction to five or six men, who were recommended to us by our hostess, with a view to set before them the advantages of California as a home for Swedish emigrants. It is not only that the people here are lacking in em-

PROF. VICTOR HUGO WICKSTROM, OF LUND.

ployment, and dissatisfied with their situation, to a great extent, but it is on account of this being one of the principal junction points, that it was eminently desirable to make a stop here, and improve the opportunity to the uttermost;—to educate representative persons with respect to the superiority of our California climate—that truly glorious climate—our fruitful soil, etc , etc.

The train leaves Nassjo for the South at a quarter to seven, A. M.; and we arrived at Lund at little after twelve.

Lund is the second University town of Sweden, containing about twelve thousand inhabitants, and being not far behind

LUND CATHEDRAL.

Upsala in the number of its students. Upsala and Lund are the Harvard and Yale of Sweden.

Here is also a famous cathedral—that of St. Lawrence—a venerable structure, 271 feet in length and 72 feet in height. It is claimed that the perspective of the interior is the finest of any church in Northern Europe. The building is larger at the

Western end than at the Eastern extremity, and the floor rises towards the centre nearly two feet, producing a singular but pleasing effect upon the beholder. The pinnacles in the choir symbolize the *Crown of Thorns;* and although this portion of the building was reconstructed a hundred years ago, there was no alteration made in the pattern of this section of the interior, as it was originally designed. The organ is the largest in Sweden, having 3,070 registers. The organist began a rehearsal while we were in the church; and though distant from him nearly 200 feet, we at once felt the force of the muffled trumpets; their voices producing a crawling, magnetizing sensation in our feet! When the full musical peals came on, they "filled the aisles and shook the sashes!"

There is what in Lund is commonly called the Subterranean Church—a huge crypt, in fact and fashion. According to legendary story, this was the work of a giant, named Finn, who contracted with St. Lawrence to construct the Cathedral at the price of the Sun, or the Moon, or the two eyes of the Saint. But it was the privilege of the Saint,—his chance, as we would call it,—to avoid this enormous planetary payment for which he was bound on this cruel alternative, if he could discover the name of the giant. The Saint accidentally overheard the name of the Monster pronounced by the giantess, and so escaped the loss of his organs of vision. This enraged the giant who endeavored to destroy the cathedral, which he had erected, and in this unholy scheme he was aided by his wife, through whose inadvertence his name had been ascertained. But the good Saint Lawrence (or Laurentius, as they have it here) uttered a prayer at the right moment; in response to which the giant and his wife were instantly transformed into stone. The two enormous stone images in the crypt are supposed to be their petrified remains?

The subterranean church is 126 feet by 36, with a height of 20 feet; being supported by twenty-four pillars, and lighted by ten windows. Here also is a spring, throwing up the purest of water; a miraculous fountain, like that adjacent to the Cathedral of Upsala, but not so abundant in its supply.

A little distance from the Cathedral and in front of the house of the Academical Society, is a splendid brass statue

CRYPT OF LUND CATHEDRAL.

of the poet Esaias Tegner—which we were informed was much inquired after by Americans, doubtless on account of the translations by Longfellow.

In the University House, which is North of the Lundagord, is a Library of 100,000 volumes; of which about 10,000 are in the English language.

There is a very rich collection here of manuscripts; including celebrated letters of *Cicero*, which were printed on

NEW UNIVERSITY HALL, LUND.

parchment in Venice in 1470. Here is also a manuscript Virgil, and the oldest manuscript-records of the Kingdom of Denmark.

In one of the histories of the time of Gustavus Wasa which I glanced at, in this Library, I observed the subjoined sentences—reading according to my translation as follows: "The noble and rich men of those days often could not read or write; but they had private secretaries to do their reading and writing for them. People were accustomed to rise at five or six o'clock in the morning, dine at ten and take supper at five. Plates were not changed at the meals, and the invited guests at a party had to take their knives and forks and spoons with them to the house of their host. The family hour for retiring was nine o'clock. The beds were fastened in the walls [as, indeed, they now are, in the houses of the lower orders of the peasantry of Delecarlia], and the sleeping places were arranged one above the other; sometimes four shelves on one floor. There were no such things as carriages; everybody had to travel on the narrow and rough roads on horseback. *King Gustavus considered, very wisely, that all the land originally belonged to the realm, and that it was only held as a trust by the landholders; as, indeed, their name implied. He, therefore, followed a maxim: that whenever a husbandman did not properly cultivate his land, but allowed it to deteriorate, he should be expelled from his possessions, and the land should be transferred to more faithful hands.*"

In the Historical Museum, among other very remarkable objects which are shown to visitors, is a chemise of the Holy Virgin which, if the ancient chronicle, which is recited by our guide with great distinctness and delicacy, is to be believed, possesses a miraculous virtue in promoting easy confinements.

Here also is the house of the poet Tegner,—indicated by a stone on which is written—"Here abode Tegner." All within and without is kept, as nearly as may be, in the same condition in which it was left at his death. The desk on which he wrote is shown; the bed on which he slept; and the very pen with which he wrote "*The First Communion.*"

It is a distance of only about ten miles from Lund to Malmo. We stop at the Kramer Hotel; literally close to the extreme Southern boundary of the Kingdom. The sense of regret which we have been experiencing with growing emphasis, ever since we left the Capital, now rises into a sharp pain as we realize that in a few more days we must bid farewell to Sweden!

Malmo, the official residence of the Governor of the province of Skane, is a city of about 40,000 inhabitants, and is located diagonally opposite the Danish Capital, and distant two hours' ride, by steamer,—variously put down at from twenty to twenty-five miles. Bædecker states the distance at sixteen miles, but this is contradicted by every inhabitant with whom we conversed with respect to this little geographical measurement. The difference in estimate of distance is probably owing to intermixed calculations of separation between Copenhagen and Malmo and Copenhagen and Landskrona, etc. However that may be, and singular as it may appear, this is a quietly mooted point—on the wharves of the Southern metropolis. One sailor told us that it was "all according to the shoot [or shute] you took when you made for the opposite shore;" a combination of sailor and landsman vernacular which needs accounting for by itself—probably explained by the amphibious nature of the speaker.

That we are on the border line between Sweden and Denmark is made apparent very shortly after our arrival here. Going into the dining-room of this hotel, we hear the unmistakable vowel distinctions between the two nations; the discordant distinction between the two languages being noticeable across almost every table in the spacious hall.

Kramer's Hotel is situated at one corner of the Stertog, on which also face the Hotel Gustaf Adolph, and the great hall of the city,—the Radhus—and also the residence of the Governor of the Province. It is about the size of Sinclair hotel, in New York, or the Montgomery corner of the Lick House, in San Francisco; and the spacious rooms are rented at from five to seven kroners a day.

Malmo began before the date of the earliest existing record of its people's lives to be "an important point" for herring fish marketing—so tradition speaks of it. It is absolutely "historic" only since 1259, when it was where it now is not. That is to say, it then was a little at one side—at a place now called *Sodewam*. It is like Gothenberg in this respect: Having shifted its base a few miles—(as notably ought to have been the case with our California city of Sacramento, in 1852). It never was much of a town to boast of, until one Frans Suell, in 1775-78—"a wealthy and public-spirited merchant"—actually created a harbor; by running out long piers and cross-ways on the Northwest side of the town.

At the extreme end of the main pier or break-water, or more properly sand-break —which extends a distance of half a mile from the main land—there is a tall lighthouse, while a shorter tower is set midway between it and the main tower dock. The lamp at the Point has a colored glass, and is revolving; and by its situation and appearances altogether it strongly suggests the picture presented by one of the well-

MALMO CASTLE.

known scenes in the opera of Olivette. I feel sure that the original idea of the setting of that piece was taken from actual observation of the lighting of the harbor lamps on the edges of the pier of Malmo.

Of course Malmo has a castle, or a fortress, so-called. And of course it was built upon the foundations of another castle, or on the same site at least. The present structure is dated 1537. It is now used as a jail for the province of

Skane. It will be remembered that Bothwell, one of the husbands of Mary Queen of Scots, turned pirate after his expulsion from Scotland. After his capture on the high seas he was imprisoned in this fortress; and visitors are permitted to visit the door-way of the dungeon in which he was confined. The entrance to this damp and narrow cell has been walled up; of which there is so much complaint on the part

MALMO CITY HALL.

of visitors, that it is said that the authorities are seriously considering the proposition of complying with a general request for unsealing and re-opening.

It is written that visitors may see in the Governor's house the room in which the late King Charles XV. died, on the 18th of September, 1872—while on his way back from Aix-la-Chapelle to Stockholm. We rang and knocked at the outer door of this Executive Mansion in vain. No one came from within to let us in, or to do us the kindness to tell us to go away. Finally a passer-by—kind, courteous soul: may his immense shadow never be less—stepped up to the inner porch, where we were pulling bell-knobs and thumping with audaciously increasing racket, and informed us that the new Governor was a—mean man. He had re-arranged the furniture in the room where the popular monarch died, and had closed out the show business, from which theretofore the porters had derived a modest and honest kroner, *per capita*, etc.

But could we see the interior of the Town Hall? Our chance acquaintance and adviser didn't think we could. But being in an exasperated condition of mind, collectively speaking, our company resolved that we would make an effort to get within. The exterior of this edifice is very handsome. There are oriel windows, and rich copings and attractive features in sandstone. We learned that the custodian was in the court room trying a case! But a lad told us that he would "come" presently. He does put in an appearance in a very short time; allowing for his having "a long term of action in hand,"—as another kind informant told us, in a determined effort to speak English. A slim, solemn-looking man of fifty came forth, very nicely dressed. (What if the prancing boy at Upsala had seen his coat! Would he not have been excited to a communistic pitch? So we simultaneously suggested.) We offered this gentleman a gratuity with fear and trembling. But he took it with a complacency that was—well, it was worth the money, to see how a man of his mien and deportment could take our offering. There was a kind of magnanimity, of condescension about it, that was deserving of study and eulogy.

The stair-way is of granite, with highly polished green stone balustrades. The frescoing is emblematic of commerce and agricultural industry. The first hall is adorned with pictures of Swedish monarchs and queens, ladies of the court who are distinguished as beauties,—together with a few landscapes and two or three battle pieces. The second and larger hall is where the great dancing parties trip—[and visitors are always saying that it must be dangerous to limb and neck to wheel rapidly about on these waxened floors]—and both grand apartments are of the pattern observed at the Palace at Stockholm. The smaller hall is used for a dining room, on festive occasions, and will seat 500 guests. 100 couples join in the mazy dance in the principal chamber.

The Kockumska Hus, erected fifty years before Columbus

ST. PETER'S CHURCH, MALMO.

discovered America—is in a good state of preservation. Here lived the "warlike burgomaster," Kock, and Suell, the wise and patriotic merchant before referred to.

At one of the churches we gaze upon a full length picture of Martin Luther—which does not represent him in an amiable mood.

In the vestibule of the Church of St. Peter is a curious

KOCKUMSKA HUS.

poor-box, eight feet long and four feet in both width and
height—said to be four hundred years old. It has four separate
slits, for church, hospital, widows and orphans respectively.
It is only patronized now by strangers; the usual
modern method of collecting being by bags or boxes held at
the doors after service. After the announced manner of all
"charitably disposed visitors," we dropped in a few ores, and
listened to the somewhat singular cavernous echoes.

At the great Malmo machine shop over 1,500 men are employed.
Just now the work is centred upon the machinery
of a huge steamer, which is to carry loaded cars across the
sound, between Malmo and Copenhagen, after the manner of
the Jersey City and Brooklyn, and our San Francisco and
Oakland and "Solano" steamer transfer. She is to take
freight-cars that will travel from Denmark stations to all
points of railroad connection in Sweden, and return.

Here the machinist gets from seven to fifteen kroners a
week—working by the piece; according as there may be
work for him in his particular line. The moulders get as
high as seven kroners [$1.82] a day; depending of course
upon their skill and experience.

The eccentric on the main shaft of the big ferry-boat was
being cut down to the proper diameter, while we were taking
observations; and we were told that it required a month of
labor to construct the machinery by which this stupendous
piece of business was being performed. The immense shaft
was held in the jaws of mammoth pincers, and its revolutions
in the face of the paring chisel were guided with mathematical
exactness by a single lever in the hand of one man.
This man had this twenty-two tons of iron under his thumb,
in the most literal sense that you could imagine. He seemed
to be playing with the whole arrangement. But in point of
fact he was not. He had a drawing before him; and he was
peeling that big bolt to a hair's turn. So he said, in a
quiet, confident and rather confidential way; and we believed him.

But to us an equally interesting section of the great establishment
was in the moulders' department. Here, in a build-

ing 300 feet long by 200 wide—an immense barn of space—
a hundred men were squatting literally on the ground floor;
digging in the soft black sand with their hands, or carefully
covering up an earthen image, which signified an ultimate
propellor or cylinder top, or boiler-head or bed plate. In

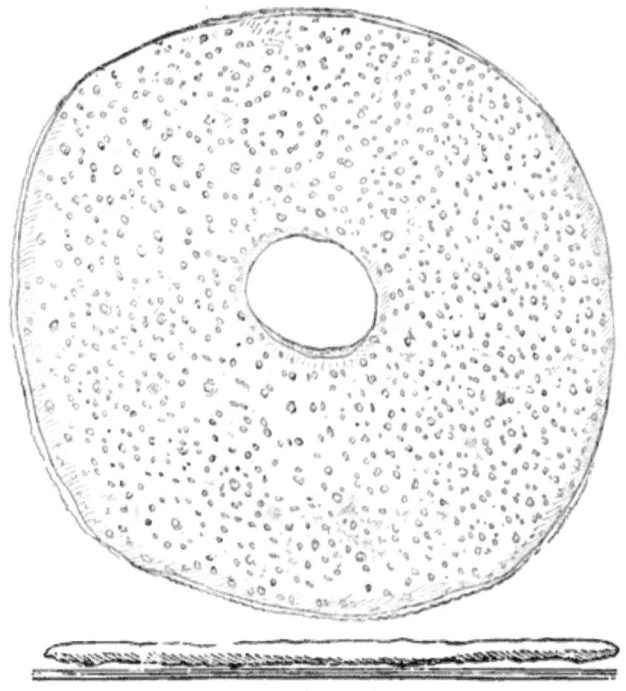

FLAT AND SIDE VIEW OF SWEDISH BREAD.

what august stillness these gnomes pursued their vulcanic
labors! The natural gloom of the building—with its comparatively few windows located high up, near the roof—
seemed to be deepened by the color of the earth which these
dumb delvers and fashioners were paddling or tossing about
with their naked hands. With finical nicety did one old man

scatter some white grains at the edge of one of his oblong, flattened boxes. Then he took a whisp broom and swept off the few particles that clung to the wood. "Was all this precision necessary?" was the question that went the rounds. Of course, it must be; and it was because of his skill and faithful scrupulosity in this department that this old man—now over seventy, and now worth in his own right over 40,000 kroners, the fruit of a long life of incessant toil—received seven kroners a day for his services.

Some of the elders in our party were indulging in the utterances of various economic propositions and sentimental suggestions and reflections, naturally allied, when a youthful companion—who had been remarkably silent for some time—gave a deep, loud sigh, and met the many inquiries as to the cause of her depression by the one exclamation, "O, what a place to make mud pies!"

We agree in favor of a social sexsor, on the night before we bid farewell to this beautiful land. What shall be the main articles of luxuriant repast for our delectation on such an occasion? We take another ballot: and lo, there comes forth a unanimous vote for—what think you?—Swedish bread and coffee! Aside from these, of course, let there be the best attainable variety of edibles for our guests.

How many times have you and I, dear reader, pitied those poor sailors in the United States Courts, who have been compelled to face the unnecessarily sharp cross-examinations of the attorneys for the defense, in a case of alleged cruelty on shipboard—how often, I say, have we pitied them, when they confessed that they never had tasted anything but brown or black hard bread, until after they left their native country. Why here we are, mourning our departure from this same kingdom of cracker loaves, because among other afflictive deprivations we shall no more taste this all-crust, brittle but delicious article of diet. And here we are delivering to one another our best emphasis of wonder, because at least in such great cities as New York and San Francisco there are not genuine Swedish bakeries (as well as Swedish coffee houses) to meet the wants of a large Swedish population,—as well as

COSTUMES IN SKANE.

to gratify the cultivated tastes of wise men and women of American parentage and Yankee, pie-biting table appetites. We have everywhere abundance of imitations of that—at best—unpalatable, indigestion-breeding oat-meal porridge or mush. Let us import an every way preferable article of diet.

But we are destined to have our plans in the last respect broken in upon. This comes in the form of an invitation to take a good-bye dinner at the house of a relative of a gentleman—Mr. Rasmus Parsons, of Boulder, Colorado—whose acquaintance we made while crossing the plains of America. Seven miles out of the city, to the house of our entertainers, we go. We pass several beet-sugar plantations on the road. The raising of this vegetable in this section for sugar-making has after many failures proved a success. We pass many wind-mills, that are turned about to meet the wind; the whole building being swung around so as to present a fan front to the prevailing breeze. We pass several honey-making establishments. Rows of bee-hives that number as many as fifty on a bench. We pass a great dairy owned by an Austrian gentleman; who has expended many thousands of kroners every year in valuable experiments on breeds and methods of milking and bestowing the cream. We see that every household has one or two window shelves ornamented with flowers; and notice that the myrtle grows here in luxuriant strength and spreading fulness. We overtake a small wagon loaded with brooms; and are informed that they come from America, along with the sewing machines and the petroleum. We hear again that the same Singer and Wheeler & Wilson's that cost our folks $45 are sold here for one-third those sums. We see a woman washing in a stream; and inquiring what that green treacle is with which she daubs her clothes, we are told that that is the genuine Swedish soap; that that which we call soap is unknown by such a name in this part of the globe. And thus we become communicative not to say confidential; and inform our Scandinavian friends that in the United States we have also two kinds of soap: one used for cleansing purposes, and the other, it is confessed, used by political saints for the purpose of carrying doubtful States at or immediately preceding a Presidential election. We are not thoroughly understood by all hearers, perhaps ; but we intend to be beneficially instructive. We meet two boys driving one ox before a two-wheeled vehicle filled with potatoes. We see a woman in a field milking a sheep ; and ascertain that she is proprietress of a small cheese factory.

Arriving at the house of our host and hostess, we are welcomed with enthusiastic demonstrations that apparently only stopped short of hurrahing ; and it would seem that there never could be again such heartiness and cordiality ! And such profusion of novel delicacies at a "greeting repast !" spread for our refreshment at the moment we enter the house. After four hours spent in delightful conversation—sitting within or walking round about—we are summoned to the great dining-room, for a Swedish dinner. Well, so far there have been approaches and approximations. But now we are to understand—as experienced ones in the party announce—that we have got the perfection. Seven courses, exclusive of Smergorsbord; with a central pivot of fruit-soup. And such dishes ! Who can abide these things? Is there no way out ? It is bidden that at least we must taste, to the end of the catalogue ! I know not what French cuisine may be awaiting us ; and I do not care. I am prepared to give in my verdict now, without any further evidence in the premises.

We do not need to be admonished that we shall often be called upon, if gratitude survives, to remember our most hospitable hosts of Skane :—Seppa and Margareta Manson.

No wonder the initiated traveller seeks to secure the services of a thoroughly educated Swedish cook. Here they are : a whole family of them (including—alas !—one beautiful girl, who has just fallen ill with incurable hip disease.)

"Thank you very much !" So say we all. For once we deferentially acknowledge, by an exact observance, the custom of the country, and audibly and fervently join in the formal sentence of thanks to our entertainers, on rising from the table.

Then we are shown the garret of this big house. A regular

OUR MALMÖ ENTERTAINERS.

old-fashioned New England garret. Here is a cradle that was made in 1742; just as good as the day it left the cabinet-maker's shop. In it have been rocked five generations; and unless future parents in the same line are converted to the idea that the motion is not good for the infant brain, what is to hinder five more generations from becoming occupants of this capacious lullaby edifice? Here is a rag carpet in a loom; and a ball of tape half completed. Here is a secretary over 300 years old; made in Denmark before Christian I. was born. And here comes a huge cat, calling to her kittens; whose cozy bed close to the eaves is a type of domestic comfort, and soon presents a picture of matronly fondness, pride, and bliss. (O, how Starr King would have enjoyed this garret!)

We ascend a hill a quarter of a mile distant from and directly in front of this mansion of Swedish hospitality. From the summit we descry Malmo, Lund, and Copenhagen, with five outlying churches on this side of the Sound.

---o---

XXIII.

COPENHAGEN.

THE Malmo-Copenhagen steamers make four round trips each day; the passage occupying from one hour and a half to two hours. The vessels are about the size of the Dover and Calais boats; and they very closely resemble each other in their model and accommodations. But this passage, although nearly the same in distance, is usually by no means so tempestuous or chopping as the North Sea Channel crossing; and in summer and early autumn it is as smooth sailing, from Swedish dock to Danish harbor, as it is in either the New York or San Francisco Bay in the pleasantest weather.

Denmark now comprises about 15,000 square miles of territory,—a little more than the lake-water surface within the boundaries of Sweden,—and has a little over 2,000,000 inhabitants, more than one-tenth of whom reside at the capital of the kingdom. While so insignificant in acreage and population, it is a great factor in international marital heraldry. England, Russia, Germany, Sweden, and Greece are all closely allied to Denmark by wedding-rings; and a popular sentence or phrase of gossip, that is often uttered with great seriousness, is to

the effect that Prussia will, or must, forbear from swallowing up the little left after the Schleswig-Holstein conquest, on account of existing and future demand and supply for eligible matches among the royal houses of Europe.

The first close view of Copenhagen touches the light-house and the fortress,—around which the steamer swings in its entrance into the straits which separate Seeland from the Island of Amager. The great dome of the marble church—(foundation laid in 1749; now nearly completed)—is a conspicuous figure from the water, as we make our approach; a fact to be more particularly noted now, because when you have once arrived at the city's edge you lose sight of this prominent object altogether, and wonder in what direction it bears from your wharf.

The landing of the Malmo steamer is at the corner of Hannegade and Charlottenborg; in close proximity to a line of custom-house sheds, of small dimensions, in which the baggage is temporarily stored for inspection. The examination by the custom-house officers is of the most trifling character. In fact, the practice is to look the passenger amiably, but "officially," in the face and ask him if he has anything to "declare." If the answer is in the negative, in nine cases out of ten the baggage is passed without unlocking or opening.

We had resolved to try an experiment at Copenhagen in the way of selecting a hotel; and we have to report a successful venture in this direction. Instead of naming any one of the inns recommended or pointed out by the various guide-books, we engaged the services of a porter at the wharf, and told him to take our luggage and lead our party to a quiet, unpretending hotel, in some street not far distant from the centre of the city—if such a place there was, to his knowledge. We were taken to the Prinds Oscar Hotel, 13 Kongensgade, Frants Jörgensen, Kjöbenhavn; and I respectfully, but cordially, recommend it to those who may come after. The entrance is "unpretending" sure enough. You might call it mean and contemptible, for a "hotel." It is a narrow doorway, from whence a short hall,—not more than ten feet in length and three feet in width,—leads to the stairway. But when you have arrived at the upper landing, you find excellently furnished suites of rooms, with good ventilation and outlook, and the attendance comes nearly up to the Swedish standard of perfection. We had occasion to visit friends at houses where the charges were more than twice as high; and we observed that we were, on all accounts, better seated and served in this modest hostelry. It is less than fifty feet from Prinds Oscar Hotel to the King's New Market or New Square—so that we could not well be more centrally situated. I speak of this inn location, because I do not know of any greater service that any person could do to me, as a traveller, than to give his conscientious judgment and recommendation with respect to such matters. And I have met so many travellers from America and from England, who have complained of extortionate charges and poor accommodations, at one and the same time and place, while stopping at what were called first-class hotels, that I am induced to make it a frequent practice to commend, in this volume, such reasonable and well-conducted inns as it may be our good fortune to patronize. I have already the thanks of one of the authors of one of our most popular guide-books for the trouble I have taken in the way of informing him as to our experience in the particular indicated, along our line of journeying.

From the King's New Market, thirteen streets take their departure. Immediately in front of the centre of this square, is the great *Hôtel d'Angleterre* (recently, I believe, renamed *de l'Europe*)—the principal edifice of the kind in this city, and capable of accommodating five hundred guests. In the centre of the Square, and in a small enclosure,—(in an oval space, not more than fifty feet in length by twenty feet at its greatest breadth, surrounded by an iron fence),—is an equestrian statue of Christian V., cast in lead. It is not an impressive figure, and it is not on a sufficient pedestal elevation. On the west side of the square is the palace of Charlottenborg, where the native artists exhibit their paintings, in the months of April and May.

On the north-west, as you stand before this great hotel, you have a view of a number of old-fashioned Dutch or Flemish houses,—with their long, sharp-sloping and many-story roofs; the pictures of which, long ago, formed most attractive features in the books printed for the entertainment of our children. We recognize at once the fact of the copyings of these structures, that were made in early times in our city of Gotham and vicinity; and we note the imitations, with modern architectural improvements, which are to be seen in newly-constructed and in nearly-completed buildings, in the northern portion of our great Atlantic metropolis. These quaint old houses give me a glow of tender recollection and a present satisfaction, which it seems as though every American traveller should feel on first sight, and often thereafter vividly recall.

I believe I can truly say that we omitted, in our visits, no building or point of importance or interest, in Copenhagen, pointed out by Baedecker or Murray or the local guide-book authors. But I can only refer, in these pages, to a very few of the places which I have seen and examined, and, as a rule, I have sought and shall endeavor, with respect to them, to note here only such things as are not spoken of or described in detail, by the writers whose volumes are convenient to have and to handle in any of our ordinary home or knapsack libraries.

But before speaking further descriptively, I will say one thing with respect to the guide-books which the traveller will be inclined to purchase on his arrival in England and before his departure for the Continent. So far as I am able to judge from my stock on hand, they are all written with a conscientious endeavor to tell the truth. Even Murray's, which is loaded down with advertisements,—giving a suspicion of partiality from that very fact,—can usually be relied upon for correct statements with respect to the accommodations that can be had in different localities, the prices, and the probabilities or danger of imposition, etc. But I must repeat, in the interest of justice: Baedecker's is the best. It is more compendious; it is more accurate. It has mistakes, but they are none of a very serious nature. And I happen to know from my own communications, that there is an anxious desire, on the part of the publishers, to keep up with the times in their information, and to render their pages as exactly correct as it is possible to make them. I believe there is a scrupulosity about this—amounting to anxiety—in the Baedecker establishment, which does not exist elsewhere. But even Baedecker did not name the Prinds Oscar Hotel! He must enlarge his volume by another line.

One of the most curious sights in Copenhagen, and one that strikes the observer almost on the instant of his arrival, is the tower of the Church of the Redeemer, which rises to the height of 286 feet. It is situated in what is called the Christianshavn quarter, and is a conspicuous object as you near the

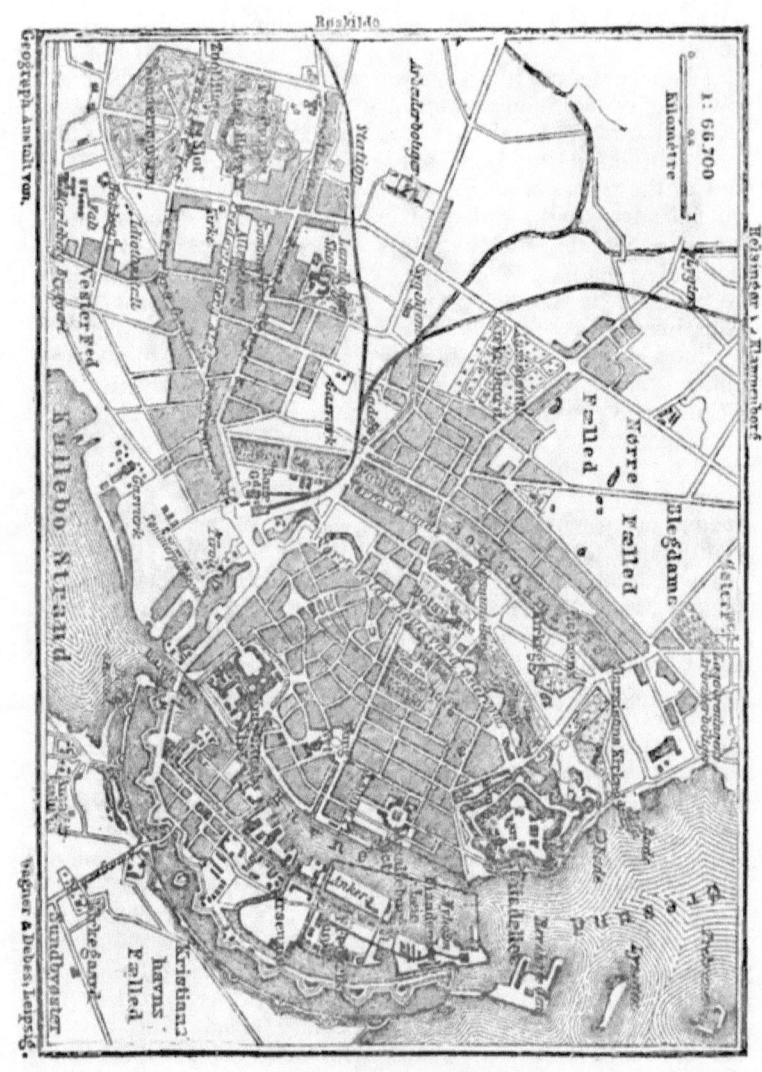

PLAN OF COPENHAGAN.

harbor; being discernible, on a clear day, from the Swedish border. The tower is surmounted by a figure of the Redeemer. By means of a spiral staircase, on the outside, you ascend to the summit. The figure has that appearance which suggests to the visiting children the idea of a watchman constantly on the lookout for fire. And I should say that, on all accounts, it was not calculated to inspire reverential ideas,—whether on a distant or a close observation.

Of course, we visited the museums, and not to mention Thorwaldsen's would be an unpardonable omission. For though it has been described a thousand times, a passing notice must at least be tolerated in this sketching. Taking the descriptions, as I read them from the authors with whose writings it is probable that nearly all my readers are familiar, I should say that such representations belonged to the early years of this edifice. The series of scenes in plaster on the exterior of the building, have been considerably defaced by time and weather; and, altogether, they present an unpleasing picture. There should be a well-directed appropriation for repairs and retouching.

Not less than three hours must be devoted to a walk through these corridors and cabinets, so closely lined with sculpture and painting. Taking the amount of labor of love that must have been expended upon these verified products of this master-hand, there is signified such industry as amazes and confounds the beholder. How is it possible that he could have accomplished so much! And all these but a fraction of the labor of his hands!

The galleries are well arranged, in this respect, that after you have passed before all the works of art here exhibited, under the usual leadership or direction, you arrive at the room which contains portraits and busts of the great sculptor, and articles of furniture which were in his household use. You are ready there, indeed, to sit down and gaze upon the features of this wonderful man. And you experience grateful and other delightful emotions when you are permitted to take into your own hand a few of the articles which belonged to his personal outfit,—as one of his watches, some of the pens with which he wrote, the glasses which he wore, and the like.

From this scene the natural order of visiting names The Church of our Lady, where Thorwaldsen's Twelve Apostles are to be seen.

The Museum of Northern Antiquities contains 40,000 specimens of implements, weapons, musical instruments, trinkets, coffins, etc., and their arrangement is better than in the larger institution at Stockholm.

Between the hours of ten and two you are permitted to ascend the round tower, which is attached to the Church of the Trinity, and which projects into Crystal Street. This tower is 120 feet in height, and is ascended by a brick causeway, which is fully twelve feet in width. The ascent is very gradual, and carriages could be taken to within eighteen feet of the surmounting cupola. In fact, Catherine of Russia and Peter the Great did "make the trip" with carriage and four horses, in 1716. The grade is about twice as steep as the highest on the Central Pacific Railroad, but the fare—for the privilege of walking up—is no greater than you have to pay for transportation over the same distance on the railway line that is owned and controlled by our great monopolists. In the inner cylinder of this tower were placed the treasures of the University Library, during the English bombardment of 1807. From the summit is an excellent and comprehensive view of the city and the vicinity,—the tower being situated very nearly in the centre of the populated district.

Copenhagen can undoubtedly boast of possessing one of the most attractive amusement gardens in the world—The Tivoli. It is situated on the Vesterbrogade,—just outside of the thickly-populated portion of the town. It is reached by several lines of tramways and omnibuses. Admission is usually 35 ore, or about 9 cents; but on great occasions, 50 ore, or $12\frac{1}{2}$ cents, is the charge for a ticket.

In this garden there are three music stands, with covered space for listeners; one of these stands being at the end of a very handsomely constructed amphitheatre. There is also a small but beautifully laid-out garden, and a series of conservatories. There is a theatre which is an entirely inclosed building. And there is a stage for out-door theatrical performances; that is to say, one of the stages is located at the foot of a gradually sloping hill, so that an immense audience can gather round in front of it and enjoy a good view of the performance.

There is a central railed inclosure for tight-rope performances, balloon ascensions, bicycle races, etc. Every afternoon during the summer season, four or five balloon-figures are sent up from this point,—causing extreme delight on the part of the assembled multitudes of children. There is a lake, fully a quarter of a mile in length, in which boat-rides can be had for a nominal sum; the width of the surface of the navigable water varying from twenty to thirty feet. There is also a merry-go-round for children; the tossing ships on which are moved by steam, to the usual accompaniment of an execrable hand-organ. There is no charge for the enjoyment of this trip, and the crowds of boys and girls that are put in line under the courteous and very cautious and watchful superintendence of the officers of the garden,—waiting in turn for the privilege of a ride,—are worth the price of admission to see. Here, also, is the original lightning-grade, dash-around railroad,—now so extensively copied in the United States. There are over 4500 gas-lights, circled with various-colored globes, in and upon the buildings, and around and over the arches at the Tivoli Gardens. When the illumination is entire, the effect, as may well be imagined, is very beautiful. On the second night after our arrival, and on the occasion of a benefit for some charitable establishment, there was such an illumination, with befitting accompaniments of performances. All the music stands were occupied, both theatres were running, and balloons and fireworks were sent up from the central platform. It was a scene of enchantment. The long, winding lake bore upon its breast a thousand lamps, and at every prominent point, and at many unexpected turns for observation in the grounds, revolving lights, with most brilliant playing-glass and phosphorescent effects, were displayed. The music, on this occasion, to which we listened, was not only exquisite in point of execution, but was well calculated to mingle with our other sentiments the thought and love of home. For, again, the old familiar tunes,—made familiar by the frequent operatic representations to which we have heretofore alluded,—were interspersed with the classical pieces that found most favor in this cultivated community; and at the open-air theatre we witnessed the performance of athletes whom we remembered as contributing towards the entertainments in our own California theatres several years ago.

The colossal gold-bronze statue of Hans Christian Andersen—the incomparable fairy-story teller—is surrounded all day by groups of admiring women and children.

In one of our evening walks we passed through the ancient gate which was constructed in 1664, and visited the barracks that are situated just outside. Here, in Denmark, in a nation of 2,000,000 of people, there are 65,000 soldiers,—many thousands more than are required for the maintenance of peace and good order in the United States of America. Here are barracks and other buildings connected with the great military establishment, which in the point of accommodation for numbers and magnitude of warehouse room, probably equal all the facilities possessed by our nation at the largest rendezvous.

And here were companies of soldiers, in a hollow square, listening to the catechising questions, and the oft-repeated instructions of a petty officer. We stood and listened. It chanced that we heard the fundamental inquiry:—"What is the first duty of a soldier?" And then the questioning went on, as to the extreme to which obedience must go:—to the putting of one's hand into fire, at the command of an officer, etc., etc. The "Yah, yah" of the officer, with which he greeted a correct or satisfactory reply, sounded very coarse and harsh, as compared with the softer pronunciation of the same word by our Swedish friends. But somebody said there was a military hoarseness which was appropriate to the occasion.

We tried to look into a long hall where fifty men, with wire gauze head-coverings, were engaged in bayonet and sword practice; but were politely warned off from the sidewalk adjacent to the door of this building, by a little unarmed sentinel. We apologized: and he said that he was sorry, very sorry, but he had his orders. We said that we were grateful to him for his courtesy, and thankful that we were not made the objects of any warlike demonstration, on account of our intrusion. He said:—"Not at all; only too glad; but don't come again."

Here we first see, and have the pleasure of riding in the two-story omnibuses which, we are told, are to be found in all the other cities on the Continent. And it naturally enough sets us to wondering why similar accommodations are not provided on the horse-car lines through the level streets of New York and San Francisco? For really, in anything like pleasant weather, the upper seats are preferable; although in Copenhagen there is an extra charge for riding below.

The postal arrangements of Copenhagen need a little reformation. Here there is one set of wall chests for the reception of letters destined for the city, and another for country and foreign despatch; and every stranger is almost sure to make a mistake,—which is apt to be fatal to the entrusted correspondence, in the selection or application of his stamps, and the depositing of some of his letters. It is difficult to understand why, in a city that is frequented by so many visitors, who are entirely ignorant of the language, or understand it but imperfectly, this miserable and ridiculous distinction in boxes should be made. If you put a local or city stamp upon a letter, it is not sent out of the kingdom. And if you put a sufficiently and properly stamped letter addressed to a person without the kingdom, in one of the local boxes, it is almost certain that it will be delayed twenty-four hours. But here, as elsewhere, throughout the civilized globe, save on our North American Continent, you can send a twenty-word telegraphic dispatch from one end of the nation to the other for 25 cents.

We realize that we are approaching English and American borders when we enter a barber's shop. There is less division of the duties of the attendants; and here and there we observe on the signs of the hair-cutting establishments a notice that some one within speaks the English language, and can attend to patrons on the English or American plan. The great business street of this city is known as Oster Street, and some of the shops are very large and elegant. There is a larger proportion of clerks of the masculine gender than in

the Swedish establishments of a similar character. And in
the city and vicinity we also remarked the fact that there is
less labor, proportionately, performed by women in the shops
and in the streets and in the fields, than in the more northern
cities. We are also reminded of our separation from our
Swedish friends and their jurisdiction, by the difference in
the cooking, and more especially by the difference, on the
downward road, between the bread and the coffee that was
and that is.

Most of the steeples and towers in Copenhagen, and many
of the roofs of private edifices, are covered with copper, and
when they are viewed from any eminence, they present a
striking and curious contrast with the adjacent rows of vari-
colored tiles.

Copenhagen is situated at such a low level that it is very
evident that naturally it would be subjected to epidemics on
account of lack of sewerage, if the greatest care was not taken
to clean out the rubbish and the refuse. During all the morning hours the great rattle of the dust-man, as he makes his
way through the streets, seems, to the stranger, to come from
every direction, and it is interesting to note the scrupulous
care with which the police regulations respecting cleanliness
are observed. Every particle of paper, as well as every scrap
of dirt in the literal sense, that can be gathered from the
pavements without, or the yard-floors within, is put into a basket or barrel, by the landlord or tenant, and set on the curb-
stone—so soon as, and not before the cart of the clattering
scavengers arrives at the line of a given block.

There are no less than 9,000 vessels entering and passing
out from the harbor during the year 1884. Steamers of 2,000
tons burden and upward run regularly hence to London.
There is direct steam connection with every large Swedish,
Norwegian, German, Belgian, and British seaport. Evidence
is given on every hand of prosperity in fair degree, for merchant and mechanic and laborer; and the people here have
all the appearance of contentedness which we observed in
the capital of Sweden. Here there is fully as much general
interest expressed to learn the condition of affairs in America,
but not in one case out of ten do we find among our new-

made acquaintances a disposition or thought of emigrating to the United States. In this respect there is indeed a marked difference from the prevailing sentiment and desire on the other side of the Sound.

Yesterday morning we observed a large crowd collected in front of the Hôtel D'Angleterre, and although that point was on our line of regular promenade, we made haste to learn what attracted such a multitude. We arrived at the front of the court-yard gate in time to see the Princess of Wales, seated beside her brother in an open carriage. She was greeted by a general hat-doffing and occasional bows from those who may be presumed to have had some personal acquaintance with some distant relative of hers, but there was no cheering. She was dressed in an olive-green suit, with a flat-backed bonnet that ran up to a point in a mitre shape. She bowed graciously on either hand, as her team was driven through the lines of the waiting populace, along the centre of the Square, and thence down the Bredgade to the military headquarters.

We heard that there was to be a family gathering of the children and other near relatives of the Danish Monarch, within a few days, and that the Princess of Wales was here, in advance of all other royal comers, as an elder child should be, to officiate as one of the royal home-welcoming party.

―――o―――

XXIV.

FROM COPENHAGEN TO STETTIN.

In the little steamer *Uffo*, at three o'clock in the afternoon, we take our departure from Copenhagen for Stettin; leaving at a wharf about 400 feet north of the landing-place for the Malmo Steamers. Our vessel is between 40 and 50 tons burden, and its arrangement so suggests the space-economy of the canal boats of Sweden, that we are not surprised to learn that its regular trip is from Gothenberg to the German coast, touching at the capital of Denmark. The accommodations are excellent, and the fare for first-class passage is about a cent a mile.

The steamer moves up and out of the little narrow strait which divides the mainland from the island of Amager, and swinging round the lighthouse, gradually heads down towards the lower end of the Baltic Sea, getting fairly out into the tossing billows at about nine o'clock in the evening.

The objective point, as we are informed, is Cape Arcona, which is to be sighted at one o'clock in the morning. "Will we sit up and watch for the lighthouse?" The officer would be much pleased to have our company. We will not sit up. The waves already lift and fall in a most exasperating and withal prophetic manner. We will take a recumbent position, and we are glad that the liveliest portion of this trip is made in the night season.

The Stewardess wishes to know if we will change from the cabin assigned to us, and take the largest one, in company with a number of children who are going on a school excursion trip? We are glad to agree to this proposition; for by this new location we obtain a great deal of valuable information with regard to localities, etc., from the free chat of the little ones. And this is to be noted: During the school vacations every school child is entitled to ride free upon all public conveyances in Denmark, going into or out of the Capital, or going short distances out of the Kingdom.

At four o'clock in the morning we were aroused by the sudden stopping of the machinery, and, looking out of the cabin window, we saw on our left a tall lighthouse surmounted by a fixed and brilliantly scarlet light, situated near the end of a long narrow peninsula. On the other side, as we soon discovered, was an island on which was located an Arsenal and a custom house, and adjacent thereto a town of considerable size. Slowly the little steamer pushed its nose up the contracted and shallow channel. We are navigating *Swine Strait;* and there is a desperate attempt on the part of some of our fellow passengers to be witty or, as they perchance imagine, aggravating, by indulging in the audible suggestion —in proximity to our party—that no American pork can come through this channel. We stopped about midway in this strait, which lies between the Baltic and Kleines Grosses Hoff,—at the frontier District Capital that bears the name of Swinemünde.

Here were a number of custom-house officers in waiting— seven or eight in all; and of this number we took at least four distinguished looking personages on board. They wore tall caps, with three red tape lines round about them, about equi-distant on an entire ascent of five or six inches. Their dress otherwise had what appeared to us a Polish cut; their coats being long, and flowing from the waist. When we inquired of some of our new-made German acquaintances, why so large a representation of the German custom-house force took their place on our little deck and really inconvenienced us by their presence, we were jocosely told that the Kaiser had grown suspicious of American visitors since the disclosure of the dynamite plots in London. Thereupon we acquiesced in the reasonableness of this apprehension, and I noticed that some of our company assumed a very grave and important, not to say a mischievous, air when they chanced to come face to face with one of the outlying messengers of the Berlin Government.

From this capital of Usedom the vessel turned to the left, and soon entered what we should have supposed to be an artificial water-way if we had not been explicitly told to the contrary. On this point of our passage we met a large number of boats capable of carrying a full half ton, which were loaded with vegetables, and which were rowed entirely by women. Sometimes there were as many as twelve oars to the boat.

Now, on our right there are a number of cultivated forests, as they are called—wood growths from saplings that have been regularly planted on the low levels where there were never forests before. It is said that in fifteen years from transplanting date, these trees are of sufficient magnitude to answer the purposes to which they will be appropriated. When we expressed doubt as to this alleged rapid maturing, we were told by one of the tide-waiters, to wait and see! (No heavy German about him; on the contrary, quite sprightly.)

Near the mouth of this strait, a great work of dredging and

break-water construction is going on; and our boat arrives at this point just in time to afford us a sight of a small army of laborers in procession on the line of the embankments— marching to the places where their fourteen hours of labor is to be applied. We remarked that there appeared to be very little sociability among these workmen; but we were told that the principal cause for this, probably, was the fact that they were recently brought together, and had not as yet had sufficient time to make intimate acquaintance.

It takes two hours to cross the little inland sea known as Grasses Hoff and reach the town of Pollitz. Thence it is half-an-hour's ride to the city of Stettin. On our route along the Oder, as we proceeded from Pollitz, we passed, to our right, four or five beer gardens, neatly and tastefully laid out and arranged, whose proprietors obviously enjoyed a large patronage. A great number of servants were at work cleaning up the grounds, washing the tables, etc., indicating in each instance that there was a big attendance of patrons on the previous evening.

We met four small passenger excursion boats of peculiar pattern, heavily loaded down with passengers. These boats were about sixty feet in length by twelve or fifteen feet in width, having a double deck with an awning stretched over the upper floor. The locomotion is by a screw, but the speed is not near so rapid as that of the little lake cutters of Stockholm. They do have, in fact, the appearance of old-fashioned stage-coaches put into ship-shape,—as you might say. All the little children on board the *Uffo* joined at once in a chorus of exclamations of delight, when these small puffing boats came in sight and passed us by. One of the little girls on board forcibly suggested the idea of toy-construction, by expressing the wish that she had one of these little vessels for her own special amusement. Here, also, we met scores of long canoe-shaped coal-boats, over one hundred feet in length, with bows reaching up from fifteen to twenty feet.

The landing at Stettin very much reminds one of his disembarking at Copenhagen; and there is the same good-natured pretence of custom-house inspection. This latter surprises us. After a custodianship, lasting four or five hours—under the immediate inspection of four or five tall and stalwart custom house officers from the coast—is this the frivolous pretense of an examination which our luggage must undergo? While we had not been wholly deceived by the remarks of our German friends, which we have before quoted, while in point of fact we took them in proper jocose phase and interest, as already indicated, we were led to expect from our personal surrounding, that here there was to be a sifting of our little luggage, fore and aft—in obedience to a general rule of authority and caution. We saw but one trunk opened; and as to that the owner had loudly "declared" that he had a box of fragrant Havannas. The case he confessed was conspicuously placed in the top frame, but the officers chose to dive a little deeper; and they brought up four or five packages of the dutiable article—much to the amazement of the candid gentleman from Verona. It is strange how petty smuggling everywhere seems to prevail most in the tobacco line.

Stettin is the Capital of the Province of Pomerania. The governor's building is a new and elegant structure, from the windows of which there is a magnificent view over the water and the plains which surround the city. The population is reported to be 81,000; but here, as at Gothenberg, we are at a loss to understand how so great a number of inhabitants can find a comfortable domicile within such a limited builded district. We are told that there is no crowding, and that the French system of residing in flats, which is here largely adopted, enables a very great number of people to live, with ample elbow-room, in one tall edifice.

The Province of which Stettin is the capital at one time belonged to Sweden, and it has given its name to a pungent appetizing drink which is to be found on every "Smörgasbord" in Scandinavia; although, in point of fact, the liquor is no longer manufactured in this district for exportation to Sweden and Denmark.

Here there are a large number of manufacturing establishments, including great beet-sugar refining houses. There is some ship-building and sewing-machine manufacturing, and

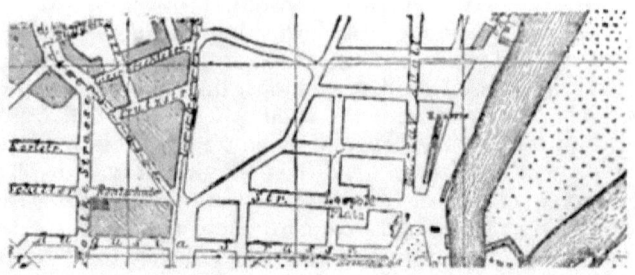

there is now and then an unmistakable flavor of chemical laboratories, as we pass along the suburbs on the headlands.

At several turns made by our coachman, we were brought upon eminences which afforded us excellent views of the surrounding country, and so presented the landscape as to make it at first glance appear an entirely new picture:—appearing as if it did not embrace many or any of the features which belonged to the preceding view,—although, of course, in point of fact, it must have done so.

---o---

XXV.

A GLANCE AT BERLIN.

FROM Stettin to Berlin is a distance of eighty-three miles, which the express trains run in two hours and a half. The fare is ten marks, or a little under three dollars. The accommodations for this money are in all respects equal to, and in some particulars better than that furnished by our poor Central Pacific Railroad proprietors, who have been charging as much as seven cents per mile for inferior facilities.

We were fortunate enough to have for our companion, in this passage to Berlin, the daughter of a Chief Councillor and *ex-officio* Keeper of the Royal Garden at Potsdam. She was a young lady, about twenty years of age, and gave evidence of great culture and refinement. She spoke four different languages, exclusive of English, which, she said, she was only just beginning to learn. But we found that she knew more of our own native vernacular than the great majority of those in this nation who profess to be proficient in the use of the English tongue. Our lady friend was very glad to meet us, and gave us a cordial invitation to visit the Royal Gardens at Potsdam. While we were hunting in the guide-book for a map of the route between the two cities that we were spanning, she drew our attention to a card that is placed in every compartment on the German railways (a most excellent idea) on which the route—together with the names of the important stations—is indicated.

There are nine railway stations in this city of 1,200,000 inhabitants, but at each one of them there are the same regulations with respect to city transportation. And, while we may regret that there is not a central house, and may boast of our great New York and Chicago depots, where many railway companies unite in side-tracking their trains, we ought to recommend the method by which the traveler is introduced here to his particular cab-driver. There is what is called a controlleur, at the main door of every railroad station, who gives the newly arrived passenger a metal ticket with the number of a cab upon it; the kind of vehicle, whether first-class or second-class, or luggage-cab, being first inquired about and designated. Then the passenger selects a porter, who takes your ticket and your baggage checks, and "consigns you altogether" to your proper vehicle. The ticket is not given to the driver until the seats are occupied. There is, of course, a specified rate of fare for cab transportation; and this is not only conspicuously posted up, but you are told by the station porter what your fare will be. When you arrive at your hotel the *portier* there inquires as to what station you come from; and again you are informed how much you ought to pay.

The Kaiserhoff, at which we stayed during our sojourn in Berlin, is a large building of nearly, if not fully, the size, in ground dimensions, of the Palace Hotel, San Francisco—a standard building for measurement and comparison, it will be perceived?)—lacking, however, one story in height, in comparison with our great San Francisco tavern. It occupies one entire block and is supplied with all modern conveniences, including a "lift," or, as we would call it, an elevator, which runs up and down semi-occasionally at the rate of about two miles an hour.

The rooms which look into a covered court, on the ground of which a line of restaurant tables is set, should be avoided, as Baedecker suggests, by travelers, who desire to do any substantial sleeping during their stay; for the clatter of the platters, rising with increasing volume of reverberating echo, is worse, as a disturbing racket, than than would be the hammering of a closely adjacent boiler factory. As we were located in outer apartments, I speak of this matter only as something brought to my commiserating attention.

Here you pay five or eight marks for rooms of a description, in location and furnishing, equal to those that you would be required to pay fully twice as much for in New York, or in any other one of the principal cities on our American border.

Here, as at every other large hotel in this Capital, there is a *portier* and a set of waiters who profess to be able to speak fluently in the English tongue. They have, as a rule, ac-

KAISERHOFF, BERLIN.

quired the smattering of our language, which they possess, by virtue of a few months' sojourn in Great Britain—having been domiciled there for such a length of time, as servants in some gentleman's establishment. In their anxiety to get the extra wages given to English-speaking attendants on the Continent, they take their departure from the British Isles at much too early a date. It is not only because their stock of words is limited, that we complain—not so much that ; but they possess that sort of education which enables them, in four instances out of five, to absolutely misinform and misdirect. Some of them are shrewd enough to impose considerably upon a good-natured English patron, and more especially upon the proverbially amiable American traveller, by cross-examining him, on every available occasion, with respect to the meaning of this or that word, concerning which some dispute naturally arises. The amount of gratuitous instruction which I have given to some of these flunkeys would aggregate a whole series of conscientious lessons in short-hand; and I have been casting about in despair to know how I am to get even with the German nation on account of this enforced pedagogic labor.

No more patronage for a Berlin shop by any of our little company, when there is a staring sign in the window that says, "English spoken here." Talk about English and American pretenders, who assert that they possess a fair degree of acquaintance with the German tongue! There is no sufficient ground for comparison with the frauds who will stand behind the counter in the capital city of the Kaiser and deliberately and audaciously shout "Yah, yah!" when you meekly inquire if English is spoken in this particular establishment. I will give one fair lady shopkeeper the credit which is due to her for her reply in German, when this question was put to her in English by a stranger from Yankee-land, "Is English spoken here?" "Yah." "By whom is it spoken here?" "Principally by strangers."

Well, Berlin *is* a beautiful city; with most of the streets laid out at right angles—so suggestive of most of the great cities in our dear land—and with most of the buildings on the principal highways of modern construction, with elegant fronts and in every way pleasing interiors. There is no institution or point of interest designated by the Guide Manuals, as located in Berlin, which is not well worth the seeing and the examination. It is not so elsewhere; we should have said quite to the contrary with respect to all other cities; and we would advise consultation with local guides before you map out your city's trips in many other places. But here the galleries and the museums and the monuments appear to us to be better than they are described in the letter-press of our chosen companions.

Only in one thing were we disappointed, and that was with respect to the Linden Avenue. If you carefully examine the measurements given in the guide-books of travel, of course you will be informed as to the length and width; but the general impression that Americans have as to the size and beauty of this avenue and its adornment at either end, considerably exceeds what you will realize on absolute personal observation.

One of the great sights of Berlin, certainly, is a beer garden on a holiday or at twilight, or at any time, during fair weather—in "the season"—in the evening hours from six to twelve. Such immense crowds of good-natured, and withal, industrious people! Here is *pater familias*, with his book or his paper, and, of course, with his pipe and his mug. And here is mother and grandmother and little children, all nimbly at work knitting or crocheting or embroidering. What a race of working people! And how orderly! What excellent deportment! Why, there is rarely any loud talking, even in the sense of noisiness; and not a sign of intoxication did we see in Berlin during our sojourn.

The great Blondin is advertised to walk the rope at the New World Promenade Grounds. We are in attendance. The great Blondin himself stands near the outer gate and distributes the programmes; answering the inquiry as to the price by "What you will; what you will!" The great Blondin ascends to his lofty perch precisely at the appointed hour; the beginning of his ride up the inclined rope on his saddled eagle being announced by the sound of a cannon. There is but one Blondin! All others are wretched imitators. May he "walk his chalk"—as a German advertisement wittily expresses it—for another decade! for we shall not see his like again.

Here, at the New World Garden, is a locomotive, driven by an electrical engine, and the patronage that is given to the cars on this little circular tramway, on every trip, is lucrative to the last possibility of a foothold.

Of course you meet soldiers at every corner. They are, to our American judgment and disposition, altogether too plentiful. They suggest the great unrest of Europe. They compel us to wonder where the civilians will be when another half million is added to the standing army—as is already proposed. But the uniforms are very handsome; and they who wear them are very courteous. Generally they are very good-looking and in every merely personal respect pleasant to behold—these soldiers of Germany. But it is a heart-felt expression of gratitude, when we detect ourselves thanking God that we live in a nation of fifty millions of people which does not need to put a large minority of the population in permanent military training quarters.

The office of the American Minister is directly opposite The Kaiserhoff. He is not "in residence" at the date of our visit—being reported to callers as sojourning in Paris. His suite of rooms, for business purposes, is appropriately and elegantly furnished, and his secretaries exceedingly courteous and obliging. We learn that Bayard Taylor was thoroughly appreciated as a master narrator of travels and a charming poet, by the *literati* at the German capital; but in general popularity it appeared that he had no advantage or precedence over Mr. Sargeant. However much the latter may have provoked the official displeasure of Prince Bismarck, it was evident that he was held in high personal esteem by all with whom he here came into political or social relations.

Just before reaching Unter de Linden—with which my readers will be presumed to have a general knowledge—the great historic Frederick street suddenly takes a switch-angle to the north through one block of three hundred feet; having a glass roof over the enclosed side street, which is about twenty feet wide, and which is called the Kaiser Gallarie. The shops on either side are mostly small, largely devoted to the sale of porcelain and bronze articles and furnishing goods. In the matter of the line of brass and bronze pieces for use and ornament the artisans of Berlin and vicinity confessedly surpass all others. Here and at the Architects' Union, in Wilhelm street, one may profitably, and in a condition of entrancement spend hours, as did we, in looking at the utensils, furniture, ornaments, and toys of the unrivalled German moulders, carvers and glass-stainers. We tried the famous coffee which is dealt out in deep glasses. No! it will not bear comparison with the one supreme consummation of Scandinavia. Of course it is infinitely preferable to what many London inn and lunch-room keepers audaciously—I was going to say atrociously—call by that name; but "Weiner" restaurants in America give their customers a vastly superior decoction than is here dispensed. Perhaps you will be inclined by this time, dear reader, to suspect that I am or have become a "coffeemaniast." Not so, I do protest. This matter only came to my attention, and was emphasized upon my notice, in the common course of events. I do declare, that on this I write *pro bono*.

The Weiner establishment is entitled to the word "grand"—which is prefixed to it on sign-board and guide-book. The fittings up outside and the fittings out inside are resplendent with mirrors and gilt and plush, and massive with marble. It is another sight to see—an Aladdin's palace at the head of the Linden avenue side of the street-divided block. Railed off from the pathway, but in an open space, with tables set closely, is room for a hundred persons. I have seen nearly that number taking refreshments there at one time. Within, there appears to be space duly appropriated and set apart on the second floor for twice that number of guests. In the pleasant season many stand without—promenading, perhaps, a little in front of the establishment—where they wait ready to take the first vacancy in the line of seats or tables.

Another attractive resort under the archway near the great avenue is the wax-works exhibition, or panopticum. Not so large a stock as Madame Taussaud & Sons, of Baker street, London, but in some respects a better entertainment—so to call it. The rooms are most conveniently arranged, and the "effects" are heightened by methods that are novel and fully as ingenious as any to be seen at the admittedly greater collection in England. A series of halls or galleries, with small, intervening rooms or vestibules, have been converted into exhibition walks; and it is a process of initiation that would be sufficiently vivid for an ancient Knight Templar, that is experienced in passing unwarned along the prescribed visitors' route, from door to door. Let me mention a few "items," as you may overhear them called by one of the attendants.

A soldier lies on an ambulance near the entrance. He is supposed to represent a dying Zouave. As you approach him you note his breathing, and mark the spot where the fatal bullet is supposed to have entered his breast. This is nothing more than you might have expected; but as you gaze on him he opens his eyes and turns them full upon you. This you had not seen before, and perhaps this may give you a little twinge of—well, of sympathetic emotion. But presently, as you move up by his side, he raises one of his hands in a feeble, uncertain way, and apparently tries to place it in one of your hands or on your person. By this time, in all ordinary human probability, you have seen enough of this life-like mockery.

You start to go up-stairs. Your wife, perchance, notices—for no man would be apt to notice anything of the kind, particularly—that a lady leans over the banister and nods and smiles at her. She is apt to imagine—your wife is—that it is an attendant, who is appropriately stationed at this particular point to welcome strangers and indicate in what direction they are to turn when they shall have mounted the flight of steps. I observed several persons returning this wax-lady's most courteous and most natural (not overacted) salutations. Then a number of people unwittingly or unconsciously contributed to this delusion by posting themselves at the landing above, or rather alongside of the show attendant, and smiling down upon the up-coming multitude in expectation of (or at least in the witnessing of) new victims. It is good —very, very good.

There is one chamber in which is represented an ancient tap-room of three centuries ago. Three men are playing at a game, and the oldest of the trio, who nearly faces you as you enter a distant door, has a peculiar way of nodding his head, half in meditation and half in negation, which is exquisitely true to life.

Here are two scolds, put in pillory, face to face, with hands locked in almost touching distance, with such devilish malignancy depicted on each countenance that it is no wonder a youthful visitor cries out in the shock of the first glance and just as they are made to rattle their wrist-holders: "Mamma, they are going to spit at each other."

You approach the fourth or fifth hall or gallery, far within which you think you can see some unmistakable human bazaar sales-women standing behind a show-case. You are attracted and beguiled by this picture until you come close to the threshold, when an old gentleman sitting near by the jamb, points with his thumb over his shoulder, directing you to enter the apartment referred to. You show your manners by audibly thanking him, and in a moment's flash you feel as if you could knock the stuffing out of the bald-headed old impostor. Still, I have seen worse on platforms at public meetings in San Francisco. Then, as you look up—having advanced a few paces—you observe a young lady, all radiant with smiles, nodding at you. You return her agreeable expression of countenance; you smile back at the artful piece of mechanism with an "Excuse me—not this time" sort of complacent sentiment; when lo! this loving, lovely damsel approaches and desires to sell you a gold pen (made of brass) for "less than you could make one of the same kind yourself." All this while you are getting your money's worth.

You begin to be suspicious of everything and everybody, and you have a right to be. The handle of a weapon which you are by express word of notice allowed to touch—an old-fashioned battle-axe—suddenly turns in your grasp. A set of armor of striking pattern, at which you have been gazing for half a minute or so, wondering if you knew anybody large enough to fill it, suddenly is occupied; and the eyes of a diabolical Saracen are glaring at you from under the visor. An old lady sitting in a low chair, on being too closely approached, quickly drops the knitting which she had been intently examining and stares at you with a look of amazement and almost reproof.

Things get to be uncomfortable before you have gone half the rounds or inspected the chambers of horrors at all; and as for the scenes in the prison and on torture-beds, murderer's gallows and beheading-block line, why, having made up your mind (as you 'thought you had at the outset—but you had not), that they are all ancient relics or masked straw and sawdust, with a little machinery connected with the floor or railing, you rather enjoy them, or give your personal attention considerately to other people who, viewing these extra tragedy scenes immediately on their entrance upon the upper floor—without your experience—seriously shudder and exclaim: "This makes me nervous," "This is frightful!"

The Old Museum, the New Museum, and the National Gallery, with all their sub-divisions, offer and comprise attractions which alone call for a sojourn extending through many days; and a week of admission-time in them barely suffices for either a satisfactory glance, or one that may be called creditable on any traveller's printed record. Let me mention at least the Mural Paintings by Kaulbach, on the walls of the New Museum, by the side of the splendid staircase, in the middle of the building. You are advised by the catalogue that "these six paintings represent so many of the most important epochs in the history of mankind." They are respectively named: first, "The Fall of Babel;" second, "The Prosperity of Greece;" third, "The Destruction of Jerusalem by Titus;" fourth, "The Battle of the Huns;" fifth, "The Crusaders before Jerusalem;" sixth, "The Age of the Reformation." The first picture has King Nimrod for the central personage, surrounded by the children of Shem, Ham, and Japheth. In the second picture, Homer is represented singing to the children of Greece. In the "Destruction of Jerusalem," a high-priest is represented as killing himself and family, while Ahasuerus, the "Wandering Jew," is escaping. A Christian family is also seen in flight. "The Battle of the Huns" represents a desperate struggle; the malignancy of the combatants being such that during the night the slain rose and fought in the air. The portrayal of this legend is exceedingly vivid; and you lose your first feeling—that it is absurd—in the interest and excitement which the picture engenders. The painting of "The Crusaders" represents Godfrey de Bouillon offering the Crown of Jerusalem to our Saviour. The name of the principal figure is of course sufficient to arouse great expectations, and you are never disappointed. A large number of amateur artists are engaged in copying this magnificent painting. The colors are more than you are promised, or than your imagination would anticipate from the reading of the official guide-book.

Again I say: if never before, economize your time by a thorough preliminary reading about what there is to be seen. I have heard bitter regrets expressed because of a failure to do the wise thing in this particular with respect to the "sights" in such a city as Berlin. It is a great metropolis, and, like London and Paris, can only be "visited" in so short a space as ten days or a fortnight, with any satisfaction to the studious traveller, after special preparation and selection made immediately prior to reaching the place. If this counsel hits and controls any one who comes after me on this trip, there will be remembrance and thanksgiving in my behalf.

When you consider that there are four public libraries, six palaces, nine large picture-galleries, thirteen museums, sixteen theatres, a score of large gardens, over fifty churches with attractive interiors—to all of which your attention is particularly invited—you can gather some faint idea of the work in hand for the intelligent and ambitious tourist. And this, of course, is leaving out a long catalogue of attractions, well worth the time and labor of a visit.

The Post-office is admirably arranged. (The office of the Chief Postmaster-General, and the Post-office Museum, are situated some distance from the central public delivery, and many travellers fail to visit the museum because of the misunderstanding about locality that is here indicated.) There are sixty-two branch offices. In the same proportion, there would be at least ninety branch offices in New York, thirty in Brooklyn, and twenty in San Francisco. Twenty words, exclusive of address, are telegraphed to any part of the kingdom for twenty-five cents. It costs the German Government more to send a telegraphic despatch from one boundary of the kingdom to another than it costs our great telegraph monopoly to transmit a like despatch from New York to San Francisco,—although we have to pay four times as much as the European postal establishments ask, and realize a profit from, in this department of mail facilities.

In every civilized nation, save on the North American continent, there is a Postal Telegraph,—which means the absolute ownership and control of telegraph lines connecting the post-offices of the country, and offering telegraphic postal facilities at a low uniform rate. The rates in Germany will soon be greatly reduced—as is also the promise in Great Britain. A weekly newspaper proprietor in one of the smallest towns of Germany that is capable of supporting such a publication, can, in proportion to his patronage, get his news despatches from any place in his country, as cheap as the most influential and widely circulated journal published at the capital.

ROYAL PALACE, BERLIN.

Post cards and unsealed letters are sent between all postal stations in Berlin through a system of pneumatic tubes. This rapid transit might be commended to our own Government, for adoption in our large cities?

The royal palace is a building 650 feet long, 380 feet wide, 100 feet high, and contains 600 apartments. It is surmounted by a dome 250 feet in height. An excellent view of its front

is herewith presented. It is a treasure-house of art. Over
1000 paintings are here. The picture gallery is over 196 feet
in length; and in many other halls and apartments the walls
are lined with the choicest productions of Watteau, Camp-
hausen, and Schluter. In sculpture, it seems to me that
nothing from the hands of modern genius can surpass the
force and beauty embodied in marble by Rauch and Shadow.
"Victory," a sitting statue by the first-named artist, fairly and
firmly and even thrillingly—albeit there may at first seem to
be here some contradiction or incongruity of terms—impresses
and inspires you with a sense of the majestic composure of an
assured and perfect triumph.

Around the city is a line of railway (Ringbahn) six miles
long, with fifty stations. The fare is six cents. Shorter distances are traversed at proportionate prices. The trains start
every five minutes, between six A.M. and ten P.M. At many
points you get an excellent view of a portion of the city, on
the one side; suburban or country landscapes on the other.
And it is very easy to form "chance acquaintances" on this
trip. The characteristic reserve and exclusiveness of the average German—who by our experience is recorded as far less
sociable than the Englishman, though we had notable exceptions—seems to give way before a realization of the fact (as
familiarly proclaimed to me by a native, shortly after we took
our seats), that "most of us are out on a lark." How did he
learn to speak our English so well? This wonder being audibly expressed, there followed answer and question, and instructive and delightful dialogue and companionship—during the
entire ride. He knew that we were from the States—right
away—he did. He had been there himself. Well, he should
rather say so. He went there when he was a lad. He
brought back a passport. No "gobbling him" for the next
war in Europe. He had "fit mid Sigel." He had his army
discharge papers also. Did not he love to see a Yankee?
(This remark was entirely voluntary and unprovoked!) Well,
he had lived in Boston. He liked the people there when he
he was a boy and when he was a man. He knew what it was
to eat beans and brown bread. He was in Europe on a
year's visit; had been to his birthplace and seen his brothers

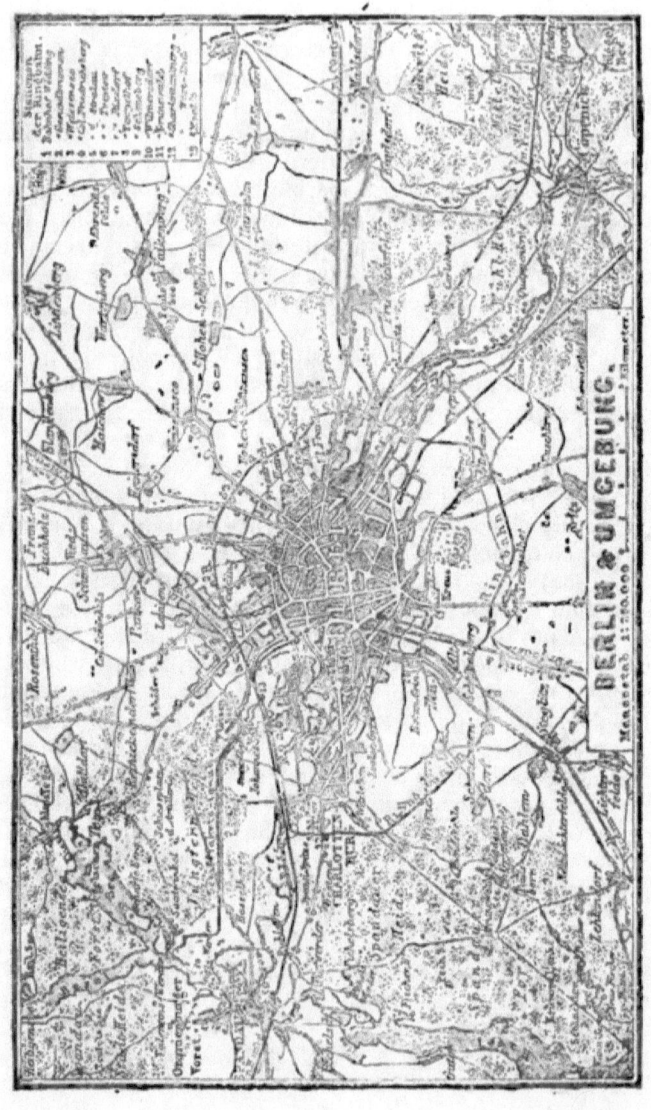

and sisters. He was going home next spring. [This was said with an intense emphasis on the word *home*.] Then he would point out for us and describe on the one hand and the other—giving himself up to our service from the moment of mutual introduction. Exchanging cards. Shaking hands twice. Introducing us to others in an interpreting fashion. Drawing our attention to the fact that his freedom of manner and general cheerfulness and hilarity were not greater than that of our neighbors in the car, who had not had that which he proudly called his American education. After each description of building, estates, manufactories, etc.—suggested by objects brought to view on the circuit—he suddenly exclaimed, in a very earnest manner, "Now look at that fellow standing on that platform! You see how his face is all scarred from his chin to his forehead. What do you think that is? Do you think that young man was in any of the battles with the French? He was hardly away from his mother's apron-string then—when that racket was going on. He is a student at one of our universities. You have probably heard about their duelling. You probably know their rules—not to cut below the face or below the breast. When a severe cut is given the surgeon stops the fighting. Now will you please to tell me what sense there is in that? What do these goslings want to fight for? And what makes him so proud of his scars? Has he fought for any principle? Is he any more of a man than he was before? And what sort of authorities are those that do not put a stop to it? Or if they are going to allow that kind of thing, why don't they let them kill each other outright? That, I think, would put a stop to it. Then the parents would generally be calling for a 'constitutional amendment'—as we would say in the States—that would make these fellows outlaws."

We parted with unaffected sorrow at the Landsberger-Platz, —he waving his hat as our steps turned in different directions, and shouting, "We meets again! We meets again! On those Pacific shores! We remember. Now you 'shust remember.' 'Ring-around-a-rosy!'" This last exclamation —attended by a flourish of his handkerchief as well as a toss of his hat—was more particularly addressed to the little girl in our company. "I wonder," said the child, after we had walked a little distance from the station without speaking, "I wonder if that man is not a brother of that other funny man we had with us on the Gotha Canal?" (After another period of silent meditation.) "I think he must be a cousin-German, at least."

---o---

XXVI.

BERLIN TO DOVER. A FEW NOTES AT DRESDEN, COLOGNE AND PARIS.

The express train from Berlin to Dresden makes the trip in three hours by one route (by the most direct) and in three hours and a half by Juterburg-Roderau. The fares are about the same, the difference being a little less than two marks in favor of the shortest line. For accommodations equal in comfort to those given by our "first-class" trains on the Central Pacific routes, you pay twelve marks, or about three dollars. The distance is about 120 miles. Here are also what are called ordinary trains, which make the trip in four hours, and in which the fare for good accommodations, in cushioned compartments, is as low as a cent and a half a mile. At a distance of about fifteen miles from Dresden you perceptibly enter the valley of the Elbe, which alternately contracts and broadens to your view from the train as you approach the city.

Dresden, it may be well to remind my readers, remains the capital of a kingdom. Saxony may still be said to boast of a king; but since the grand coronation and royal salutation at Paris shortly after the taking of that city by the German forces, Saxony is as absolutely under the dominion of the Kaiser as are any of the provinces of Prussia proper. And the unity of the German Empire is as much a matter of prevailing congratulation and pride in Dresden and throughout the kingdom—so far as we could judge from conversations with representative men—as in Berlin itself.

The population of Dresden and the immediate vicinity,

taking the number of inhabitants within the bounds that are reached by the omnibuses and the tramways, is just about the same as San Francisco—or 350,000 souls. The population of the city proper is set down at 212,000. As the maps will tell you, the city lies on both banks of the Elbe; but as you will not be otherwise informed by any one of the many books descriptive of the place, which I have seen, let me tell you that the portion called the "old city" appears, for the most part, to be quite as new as that section which has the special name of being most recently constructed. The adjective is historic—states the fact as to date of settlement—but for its application you must draw somewhat on your imagination.

As we pass down the valley on the flying train, the visions presented from the window give us, in contrast, the plain which is receding from sight and the mountain lines which at first seem to be approaching at an even angle on either side. We realize at once how it is that the pictures and photographs which we have seen, which purport to give a correct idea of the appearance of the country immediately north of the capital of Saxony, really impart a very erroneous impression. We should not have recognized our location from the photographs supposed to be taken near the points we pass—photographs which we had recently and carefully examined at Copenhagen. The fact is that the view is always shifting, almost completely changing the general outlook at every half or quarter-mile post on this end of the route. It suggests the very same peculiarity to which we referred when speaking of the totally different aspects of the country from the several heights of Stettin. It is dusty to the degree of uncomfortable on this short trip, and you have to comment upon the change from the cool and even chilling atmosphere of the Swedish capital, which we have so recently left behind. Now it is so warm that the people are walking in linen coats and covering their heads with Panama hats, and eating iced creams, and even plying their fans in the streets.

At the station where the Berlin train draws up there is such quiet that we do not know of our arrival until the guard snarls, with peremptory accent, that we must "All out! all out!"

We are reminded of our almost noiseless entrance into some of the London stations. There are the same excellent ar-

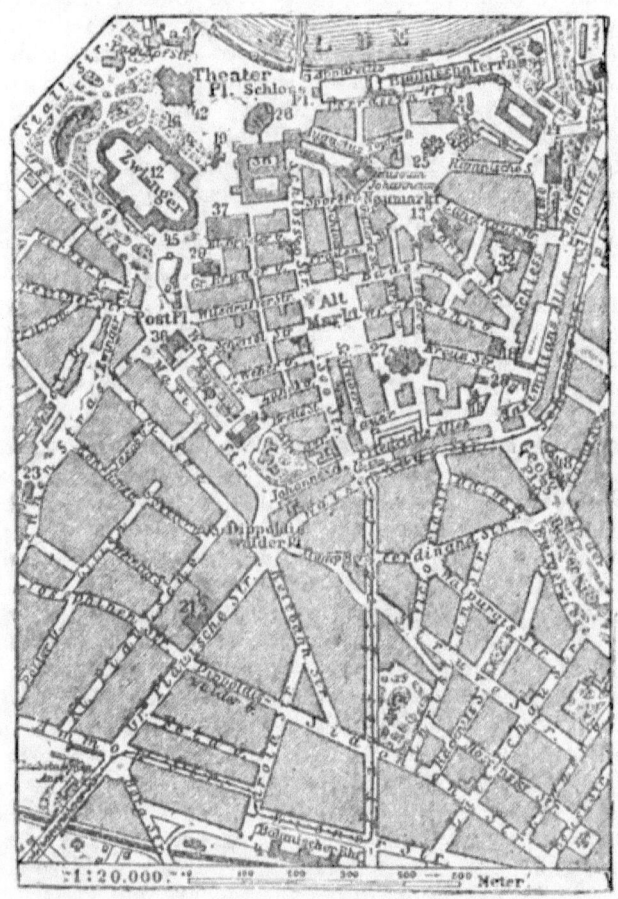

CENTRAL PORTION OF OLD DRESDEN.

rangements with respect to checking for baggage and procuring a cab that we noted in Berlin. At an upper station, where there is a momentary pause—just before reaching this city—a little boy comes along and hands into each compartment in which it is ascertained that there are any foreigners, a copy of a little pamphlet of 40 pages. It is entitled "A Dresden guide for the use of foreigners, by the association of Dresdeners and strangers, for the protection of their mutual interests." The information contained in this valuable document is printed in German and English in parallel columns. It appears that the association was started in 1875, and that its purpose was to "strive" against the many inconveniences which at one time made themselves felt; and afford strangers, during their stay in Dresden, every possible assistance in word and deed. There is a list of the principal places of interest, the museums, galleries, churches, etc., and there are six or seven pages devoted to the names of physicians, apothecaries, bankers, printers, booksellers, and merchants of every sort; and boarding-house keepers whom the management of the association doth recommend. To this latter portion of the pamphlet there is a convenient index. At the end there is printed "an order of arbitration for the association of Dresdeners and strangers, for the protection of their mutual interests."

It appears that prior to 1875, and during more than ten years before that time, there had been frequent complaints of extortion on the part of merchants, and, on the other hand, some of the principal dealers had been obliged to bring suits in the courts against strangers who had ordered goods and refused to pay for them on one pretext or another—generally on the ground of alleged overcharge, or bills for extras not included in the terms of purchase. And it was also a matter of complaint that the keepers of "villas," who entertained strangers for a consideration, were in the habit of suddenly raising their prices after the first week of sojourn, especially if there was an unusually large influx of visitors at that particular time; so that when an Englishman or American supposed himself located for the season in comfortable quarters at a satisfactory sum per week, he was liable to receive a surprise-notice to the effect that his rent was doubled. We were told that this sort of "business" proceeded to that extremity and was of such frequent occurrence, that the society of which this little pamphlet is the proclamation was organized. It is claimed that it effectually put a stop to the class of impositions to which I have referred, and we can well believe that it has produced improvement; for during the time we were in this city we made comparisons with respect to our reception at shops and the prices charged at the stores, which are favorable to the place, and which confirmed the statement of Consul Mason,—to the effect that as a rule shopping, especially for ladies, can be done here at a less draft on the family purse than in the city of Berlin. But impositions are still practiced by the shop-keepers; in making bills exorbitant, or beyond agreement. and in selling worthless articles by means of indirect misrepresentations. *Caveat emptor!* And, by the way, I must even here note our surprise at finding the American Consul at his office—a most agreeable gentleman, attending to his business. Four consuls present out of nineteen on our routes so far; four only, at post of duty, sober and civil!

The Elbe, which divides Dresden, is at this point about the width of the Hudson River at the city of Hudson, or the Sacramento River at Rio Vista, but it is shallow and does not probably contain a greater volume of water than flows in front of the California capital city at mid-water mark.

I wish to recommend the selection of my time for a visit to the Central Bridge. With me it was a matter of accident, but it was and will be accepted as being worthy of design. Starting from our hotel, the *Golden Angel* (a most excellent house), just after nightfall, and making a Hawthorne dive into the city, it so happened that I passed around the Central Square, at which the tramway cars do congregate, and crossed through the archways of the Zwinger (the palatial buildings now devoted to the exhibition of paintings and casts and museum-collections), and came out by the cathedral. Passing round the front of the cathedral, you are suddenly brought face to face with the noble flight of steps leading up to the BRUHL TERRACE; and you are then adjacent to the old city terminus of the Central Bridge. As you walk from the Court Church diagonally across the street until you strike the sidewalk-wall just below the bridge, a scene of enchanting and fairy-like beauty bursts upon you, and from many quarters the music of magnificent orchestras salutes your ears. Immediately in front of you, at the very first turn, are the brilliantly illuminated steps of the Bruhl Terrace, with the great, gilded groups of statuary representing night, noon, and morning rising on either side. As you pass along, the lights upon the long Central Bridge, and then the line of lamps on

BRUHL TERRACE.

the lower crossing with their reflections in the water, and the mirroring shadows of the lamps on the embankments, rise and flash upon you. O, it is a vision of transcendent loveliness, on a clear, starlight night, in the month of September, in the city of Dresden! Keeping on your prescribed walk along the great bridge, you have a charming, ever-changing picture presented at each new angle; touching for central or pivotal lines, the shores on the river at some illuminated point, not fully discerned or not observed as prominent save at a particular alcove. Be it known that at every few rods there is a semicircular projection from the sides of the bridge pavement, giving sufficient room for a score of persons to sit and two score to stand without interrupting the tide of rapid passers-by. A little way from the first abutment you have a full view also of the Upper Bridge, with its tiers of lamps and its own shadows and fire-flashing reflections in the flowing stream. The views in the daytime from this same promenade are not devoid of beauty. They have an

HELBIG'S RESTAURANT.

added excellence in some respects, taking in, as you then do, the sweep of country all around about. But I beseech you to begin your visitation to this place at this appointed time.

Immediately on your left, as you step away from the bridge in the old city, is a long building which has only one story above the pavement on the square, at the side on which the cathedral is situated, but which has three stories on the side facing the river. These three stories are open, like unto covered balconies, during the summer season, and the refreshment tables on every floor are surrounded by closely sitting patrons; most of the companies having the appearance of family kinship. Moored near to this large house of entertainment—known as HELBIG'S RESTAURANT—in whose corridors a thousand people can be fed at once, is a long, low barge, resplendent with the light of lamps that are upon it, and that are placed upon the surface of the water about it; in which barge are seated some forty or fifty musicians, the strains of whose instruments fill the space all round about to

THE BELVEDERE.

a distance that may be measured at not less than one-third of the line of the bridge itself. On the new city end of this crossing, and immediately to the right, is situated what is known as the Wiener Garden, where there is also excellent music to be heard every night, and where, three nights in the week, an extra performance is announced, which includes recitations by a band of one hundred musicians or more. At the farther end of the shaded Bruhl Terrace, a distance of a quarter of a mile, perhaps, from the cathedral, there is another garden with a great orchestra—the BELVEDERE—the voices of whose many reeds and trumpets make the night musical during the pleasant seasons of the year. And when you shall have visited this bridge on many an occasion and accustomed yourself, as it were, to the delights of the vision and the charms of the musical performance, you will be able to detect, in what may appear to be the pauses of the cornets and drums of the great companies on either side of you, and in close proximity to the river banks, melodious sounds that come from afar off—from the other city gardens, above and below and distant on either hand.

One thing I desire to note, as a proper remark from an American born and bred;—the writing being suggested also by the frequency of one comment (I will not call it criticism) which musicians educated in our country, but of no mean quality in any respect, have frequently made in my presence. It has been a complaint—perhaps that rather than anything else—that the German music as heard in the United States— the music of German orchestra—was too loud and harsh; and especially has this been a comment with respect to musicians coming from Prussia; the performers from Austria having a gentler disposition, so to speak, while producing the same pieces. One needs to come to Germany to observe the excellence of similar companies of musicians—the superlative beauty of their performance—in the great gardens and on the high places where they are accustomed to sit and discourse. Then the vast and strong volume of sound is, as one may say in homely language, absolutely needed for distinctness of articulation; then it no longer appears that there is a hoarse blare of the bugle or a rough bang of the kettle-drums, but by the same token there is an emphasis not only appropriate but delightful. The all-encasing air takes up and takes in these mighty symphonies, and sheds them abroad upon the senses of the comparatively distant auditors with effects that cannot be described; they are of such fascinating power and such entrancing sweetness. The "little German band" or the great German orchestra placed in a cubby-hole theatre or music-room, or in a little yard of a garden, or between the walls of a narrow street, is sometimes an unqualified nuisance—as we know either of them in America, and as we undertake to regard either of them from an humble layman's standpoint of judgment; but a small company of German harpists and flutists and violinists in Dresden, or a gallery crowded with orchestral artists in one of its gardens —ah! there is all the difference in the world!

In the new city of Dresden, and distant half or three quarters of a mile from Weiner Garden, is a shaded enclosure where there are seats for over 1500 persons, and where, on one evening in each week—during the season—there is a display of fireworks. The rockets and the wheels are set imme-

OLD BRIDGE AND CATHEDRAL, DRESDEN.

diately in front of the orchestra-stand, within a space not exceeding twenty-five feet from the foot-lights. The pyrotechnic display is very fine and lasts fully half an hour. But the spectators are unquestionably in danger from their proximity to the pieces, and on the occasion of our visit a number of children were somewhat injured by the explosion of the bombs; while there was an unnumbered concert contribution from crying babies, from the beginning of this section of the performance to the close. I would not repeat such a visit.

But the exhibition met with great applause, and is so popular that the crowds which seek admission are not more than one-half accommodated by the chairs and tables that are provided.

The cathedral, or Roman Catholic court church, to which I have already referred, situated nearly opposite the old bridge, has fifty statues of saints on the parapets and fourteen in alcoves near the entrances. As one of its familiar names implies, it is here that the King of Saxony attends; and a visit to the interior is generally sought during high mass hours, that in addition to the view of the paintings and sculpture the royal household may perchance be seen. The guide-books are particular to inform you that "strict order is preserved during divine service." This naturally leads you to expect that there there will be no walking about while mass is being sung or the preacher is speaking. In point of fact, there *is* a great deal of promenading at this very time; there being, on the part of many glancing visitors, a shameful disregard of the solemnity of the place. There is even less decorum here in that respect than in St. Paul's or Westminster, in London, where, as many of my readers know, the frequent disobedience of the injunction of silence, which the Dean has conspicuously printed and posted, is something which is at first very surprising to reverential minds. The altar piece is a fine picture of the Ascension, which, you will be told, has been in times long past very much overestimated. What praises have been bestowed upon it you are not likely to know without special search, but it is certainly deserving of a high place in the catalogue of art. As viewed from the extreme opposite end of the edifice, it is full of strength and beauty. The loud prattling of gossiping girls and dames from—yes, I grieve to say—from the United States, is hushed when, with their week-day license or in their inconsiderate and irreverent attendance on a Sunday morning, they come suddenly in sight of that magnificent scene. When we attended on a Sunday a a young man delivered the sermon. The preacher could scarcely have been twenty-eight years of age. His text was, "Be ye therefore reconciled unto God." He displayed so much ability in the way of elocution, admirable articulation, and most appropriate gesticulation, that, taking his sermon altogether, matter and manner, I have set him down prophetically as a Bishop; and I am going to watch the catalogue so long as I live—if I do live after his arrival at the eligible date—to know precisely when he assumes the mitre. If he is not made a Bishop when he becomes of prelate age, I shall be inclined to think that the Pope has not been duly informed. And as for the chanting! Here again is a revelation of possibilities in sweetness and power. Here indeed,

"Heavenly music seems foretold,
And pours its floods o'er shrines of gold."

The Green Vault is the name of a series of rooms in the Palace, but more particularly it attaches to four in the order,—there being eight in the series. The walls of the Green Vault room are of the color which gives the adjective, and contains vessels of gold, silver and crystal, and a jewel casket made over 370 years ago, and not equalled in workmanship of its kind since it left its master's hand. The eighth apartment is the most interesting, not only as containing the court jewels, such as the box with 662 diamonds and the largest onyx in existence, seven inches in height, but also as containing historic rings. Here is one that was worn by Luther, another that belonged to Melancthon, and others that belonged to kings and electors of renown, the "seal of splendor-loving Augustus," circles and bracelets worn by his wife, and the like.

A few rods distant from the Berlin station, in old Dresden, there has been erected a round panorama building in which is now exhibited a painting of the Battle of Sedan. This style of single picture gallery, so to speak, has found great popular favor all over the continent, and imitations are now being constructed in a few of the cities of the United States. Something similar was to be seen in 1874-7 in New York City, but that lacked the realism of this latest encircling "scenorama." You enter on a level with the ground and pass to the centre of the building, which is probably seventy-five feet in diameter. You then ascend a flight of twenty steps, which brings you upon a circular rail-enclosed platform, that is immediately in the centre of the edifice, and which is about twenty feet in diameter. Above you, perhaps twelve feet above you, is an inner roof or awning, umbrella shaped and of a blue-brown color, that extends full to the edge of the platform, and, perhaps, projects over a little. Your vision is thus confined to a given space on the surrounding walls, determined by the elevation of this false ceiling. There, on the walls, the painting has been placed—that is, so much of the "paint" as is painting. But just below your feet, and coming close up to the side of the stand, is unmistakable earth, sod, rocks, cannon, broken accoutrements, deserted camp-grounds with tents and utensils in disorder; and here and there are the bodies of dead soldiers, with perhaps the figures of sympathizing comrades leaning over the form of a dying dragoon. Now, where the tableau ends and the painted picture begins, is often something that it is difficult to discover; and it all makes a vivid presentation of the stirring scenes of the battle. Of course there is claim here for historic accuracy, which may well be conceded, inasmuch as certificates of French as well as German officers support the advertisements.

A dispute arose while we were paying our second visit as to where a line of fence ceased to be real and began to be a matter of canvas and black pigment. So close and neat are the divisions on this line that a portion of the same dismounted cannon is on the land and a portion on the wall. There is no available trick for illusion left untried, and there is in this ingenious deception alone an attractive force that brings many visitors to the rotunda, again and again. We are told by a French guide that he was once offered two scores of shares in the smaller panorama of the city of Paris, which is situated near the Champs Elysées, in the French capital, for a thousand dollars, but he laughed at the proposition. Had he accepted the offer he says that he would be well-to-do to-day on that single investment. The enterprise has proved a great success, as without addition or alteration it has continued to draw immense patronage from day to day ever since the hour when it was thrown open to the public.

At the entrance of the cemetery in Dresden there is a large horseshoe-shaped edifice with a pillared corridor that affords standing room for a thousand persons or more, who can there, to use the precise expression of one of the gardeners— used in the most solemn manner—"welcome the corpse." The rule of monuments here is unobtrusive. Most of them are so modest in dimensions and inscription, that they form a pleasing contrast to the catalogue of superior and now unapproachable virtues which, times innumerable, we have all seen recorded elsewhere in similar places.

At several points in our divergent walks in the old city we came flat up against fragments of ancient walls, and were dis-

GROSSE GARDENS, PALACE AND LAKE.

posed, if not forced, to cry out like the old clerk in "*Great Expectations*": "Halloa, here is a church!" or "Halloa, here is a museum!" as we found one or the other adjacent to, or enclosed in part by, these ruins.

The Grosse Garden, or Royal Park, is situated about a mile southeast of the old city, and in its three hundred acres is a palace in which is a collection of ecclesiastical antiquities, and also a museum of casts and models, and a zoological garden. There are two broad avenues dividing the park, with convenient outleading and intersecting roads. Children are allowed to play on the grass, by the same signs, often, that bear on their faces the mild suggestion that they had better not get too near the cages. The domestic and wild beasts and fowls on exhibition are widely separated—have plenty of room themselves—while abundant space is allowed for spectators before and around each distinct species of animals and birds. Books on natural history are for sale on the grounds, and children were seen by us reading from them in the immediate, august presence of the Royal Bengal tiger himself, and again studying the same volume while standing on the outside of the warm cottage appropriated and set apart for the flannel-lined cages of the anacondas. There can be no mistake about the accuracy of the illustrations. The small side gates of exit to the zoological grove are closed at sundown, and then—on Sunday nights especially—there is a gleeful hurrahing of picnic and school parties hastening along the winding walks, lest the darkness cover some lone and lost little ones in the labyrinth of paths. Grown people have been known to wander here in bewilderment many hours, until they were forced to confess their condition at a keeper's lodge, and pay liberally for the services of the laughing guide who led them out. It is said that some secret societies are accustomed to appoint a preliminary promenade in this park for their blindfolded candidates for initiation.

The hills on the south (the " line of mountains," they are called) have their summits not more than a mile distant from the edge of the city proper, and we walk up to them and along the ridges almost every day of our sojourn, with the double purpose of gaining the outlook and conversing with the peasants whom we may chance to meet on the road.

The harvest of hay and grain is being carried in. Most of the workers in the field are women. Many of them are bareheaded; all of them are barefooted. They are glad to make a mark, or twenty-five cents, a day; working from daylight to dark. They have no idea of hours for their labors; at least those with whom we conversed would not give a direct answer on this point, but simply said that they worked from morning till night.

The crops hereabouts are reported as of more than average

excellence in quality and quantity—a great contrast to the fields a few hundred miles to the north. The farm boundaries here are small, but we were told that (as elsewhere throughout the civilized globe) land-holding in vast area is again becoming the rule in the German Empire.

In the suburbs of Dresden there are a large number of houses with long sloping roofs, which give two or three stories at the gable end above the main floor. Through these roofs, along the line of the separate floor divisions, there are dormer window-openings of an eyebrow pattern, which suggest irresistibly the thought of an actual outlooking on the part of the structure itself. The little children, who are strangers to such a sight, exclaim in surprise and delight at this architectural phenomenon; and are provoked, not to say disgusted, because they cannot make their temporary playmates who are to the manner born appreciate the fact that these roof portholes are "very, very funny,"—as the London street singers would describe them. "O, look at that house!" one and another of the five-year-olds would fairly scream out. "Look at it, looking at us! It has got six eyes!" And I have seen children of seven years of age, whom I have credited with possessing very good sense, literally lie down and roll in the grass in a paroxysm of laughter on beholding these queer orifices with their fan-like shades.

As we were nearing our hotel, after a long walk, some of our party remarked that it would be very refreshing to meet with a person direct from San Francisco. Just at that moment—remarkable coincidence!—we simultaneously looked across the street and saw a sign on which was painted in flaming yellow letters these words: "E. Kamminsky, formerly of San Francisco." Now, Kamminsky, as appeared by other and detailed notices of modest dimensions, was and is a shoemaker; and he offers his goods at the lowest price: with special discount to strangers from the Pacific Coast! All this being a matter of due exterior record and publication, and our sentiment of homesickness and yearning for home fellowship being as above indicated, the necessary result was a literal race across the street and a dive into the shop of "E. Kamminsky, formerly of San Francisco." His store is at the corner of a street (I have lost or mislaid his number), having a show-window on two sides. About 12 by 8 feet are the floor dimensions of his establishment, but his walls are all lined with cases which are packed with goods ; and we infer that he must do a large business, from the fact that he has two fine-looking lady clerks, while he is himself fully capable of serving at least three customers at the same time.

Glad to see us! Why, he said it was no name for it. He did not want to sell us anything—not he. The sight of a face that he felt had been bathed in the fog of San Francisco within the year, did him more good than to sell one hundred dollars worth of manufactured shoe leather at 33 per cent. profit. We desired to believe him. We would have been inclined to believe almost anything that he told us—notwithstanding the natural and inevitable suspicion respecting trade protestations—for we were really glad to see Kamminsky. His identity as a man who had lived in San Francisco and San Luis Obispo was unmistakable. At once he fixed *that* beyond a peradventure ; not only by mentioning names of streets and prominent houses and the like, but by giving us indisputably correct characterizations of people and "sets," as he called them, in our metropolis.

Well, of course, after the first outburst and several repetitions of the hand-shaking operation, he wanted to know what we thought of Dresden, and we—well, we returned the inquiry. *He* must know what ought to be thought of the country in which he was born, and to which he had returned for business purposes ? We could only give some superficial observation and judgment. Let him begin! Nowise loth, he began, and he continued. We were listeners, and interested, amused and happy listeners, too, for about the space of an hour. I think I could come pretty close to reporting the whole of his oration *verbatim*, but of course I shall undertake at this writing nothing more than the transcription of a few sentences.

"What do I think of Dresden ? " said he. " I'll tell you what I think of it." And he settled or *posed* himself like a clergyman who had just announced his favorite text. "Dresden *is* a beautiful city; and it is full of art galleries and museums and monuments and what-not; and it is beautifully located on the Elbe; and we have plenty of beer gardens, and wind-instrument players till you can't rest; and there is a fiddle in every garret and a trombone in every basement; and you cannot stand in your front door at six o'clock in the morning but some English girl will come along and put her easel on the opposite side of the street and begin taking your picture. But you cannot sell shoes here at half the profit you can in San Francisco. And we have got soldiers here till you can't rest. You can't wink between the soldiers that you see; and there is an officer on every corner, and you cannot safely 'sauce' them if they should run over you, because they would run over you again if you did. And we have got Dukes and Counts and Kings; we have got four or five Kings;—why, we have got a King of our own here! You can see him down at this cathedral next Sunday—if you want to. Blue-blood nobility is abundant; and between the nobility and the soldiers and the tax-gathering officials there is not much chance for a poor man. I am sorry beyond anything I can tell you that I left San Francisco. I lived down at San Luis Obispo awhile. That's about as nice a land as any man can put his foot on. Don't ask me why I came back. Don't you aggravate me!" shaking his fist at us in wrathful reproof for one interrupting inquiry, and then apologizing at some length. Then he continued. "If you want to say anything about that movement of mine, you kindly hire a man to kick me and then tell me that I have got my just deserts. Why don't I return to San Francisco? Well, now, it is not so easy to pull up stakes again and get out of this country with small change enough to set up business over yonder. I suppose I am built in here for life. I am very sorry for it. I don't think any man ever left San Francisco, who had lived there ten or twelve years, without wishing he was back; until his dying day—when he stopped wishing altogether. If you ever hear of anybody sailing over this way, for mercy's sake tell them to come and see me. Tell them I won't ask them to buy a shoe-string. Tell them

I would fire them out of the house if they proposed to patronize me at all. I just want to look at them. I have got a photograph of San Francisco up in my room. I have got it where I can look at it the last thing at night and the first thing in the morning. Sometimes when we have a good fog here I go down to the river bank where the mist is the thickest, and stand in it and shut my eyes until I can fancy that I am in San Francisco. Do you know I have got so I can appreciate that feeling among the Chinese, about having their bones carried back to the Celestial Empire when they die. I would like to be buried on the Pacific Coast, anyway."

Most of the marketing here is done in the public squares, and to these points for buyers and sellers of vegetables in the early morning there may be seen approaching processions composed of men, women, dogs and carts, or a man or a woman yoked with a dog in the traces in front of a two-wheeled vehicle capable of carrying two hundred pounds of truck. Some of the market women bring their produce a distance of three or four miles, in huge baskets which they carry upon their heads or balanced on the end of a yoke-pole.

Yesterday we took a stroll from the new city to the southwest, along the line of the river, a distance of two miles or more from our hotel. We had a walk in a circling path of more than a mile, in a dense wood; the trees being about thirty feet high on the average, and the underbrush reaching up one-half that distance. Then we came out into a more open forest, and crossing a stream-bed or gulch about five feet in width, with banks that slope down twenty or thirty feet on either side, we came upon a main road; and walking still in a southerly direction we arrived at the gate of a chateau which overlooks the Elbe,—the building itself having an elevation of probably 150 feet above the water. We were saluted by the keeper at the lodge, and asked if we did not wish to go in and see the beautiful grounds. Of course we were agreeably surprised by the suggestion and invitation, and we soon made our way around to the front of the building, which appeared to us to be about three times the size of Mrs. A. T. Stewart's residence, on Fifth avenue, New York City, or four times as large as Mrs. D. D. Colton's dwelling, on California street, San

Francisco, and bearing some resemblance to each one of these structures with which it is compared. From the rear end of the building there is a magnificent view of the Elbe valley; embracing the city of Dresden and a number of small villages on the river banks, to which pleasure steamboats to and from the city regularly ply. The chateau is set back from the river about a thousand feet, and winding walks that adorn the grounds lead to terraced levels on which there are huge temple-fronts with Corinthian pillars,—porticoes standing in front of the hillside, and affording large, separate accommodations for pleasure parties on festal occasions. We could well believe that when there was a grand social convocation at this regal establishment—as we were told there would be within a few weeks—the spectacle presented by the illumination of all these terraced walks and columns and cornices must be exceedingly beautiful. There were four broad avenues and landings from the foundation of the chateau to the level of the river bank, each one of similar pattern in its arrangement and adornment, yet each different from the other in some noticeable and pleasing particulars. From this point of observation we were shown the residence of a German noble who had sought and won his bride amid the beauties of Delcarlia, and we could not but wonder whether we had not seen at Bolange the father of the Swedish heiress, whose fair face and charming voice had captured the Count of Elbianissimo.

What more shall I say of the galleries and museums and churches of Dresden? I think it will be comprehensive to state that after a first visit to the picture gallery, ours will be accepted as a good rule:—to spend at least one hour of each day in that portion of the great Palace of Art. The youthful minister of the Scotch church here—a Rev. Mr. Scott—must needs continually inform me that the Madonna of Raphael does not equal the one to be seen in a gallery of Vienna, but as his predecessor, the Rev. Laurie Fogo, subsequently declared with pleasing simplicity, "It is satisfactory; he need not have mentioned any other." This wonderful picture—an altar-piece eight feet high and six feet wide—presents the Virgin and Child in the clouds, with St. Sixtus on the one hand and St. Barbara on the other. The two cherubs which

are beneath have been copied throughout the world, and alas!
have been sacrilegiously made to do service on theatrical advertisements and the placards of the pork-packers of Cincin-
nati. No doubt the criticism is just that declares the child to
be too large, but all else is perfect. In a room by itself is this
picture placed — a room probably forty feet square. On
three sides of this chamber there are seats along the wall.
These seats, during exhibition time, are always occupied,
and no one has a thought of audible conversation in that
presence!

ROYAL MUSEUM AND THEATRE.

There is another picture in this collection which especially,
and I should say painfully, impressed me, of which I do not
know that there is any particular description in any of the
Visitors' Catalogues. It is a picture of a company of German
emigrants about to leave their home, or in the act of departing
from the old farm-house. They are evidently going on a sea-
voyage, and from some indications it is probable that the intention was to represent them as about departing for America.

One little feature in this speaking canvas let me note. I think I can make an appreciative reader, by a very brief and simple statement, feel something of the thrill it sent into my breast. In a court-yard full of emigrants an old lady of more than three score years and ten has taken a little boy, twelve or fourteen years of age, to one side and is whispering in his ear. The grandam's countenance is partially concealed by the necessities of her attitude, but the boy's face is full upon you, and there is a partial revelation of the character of the injunction which the good old woman is giving as a parting

ZWINGER COURT-YARD.

sentence to the little child. It is evidently the mother of the boy that stands off at a distance of five or six feet and is watching her child's face. The old lady's right hand is lifted with the palm extended towards the mother, as though she had warned her off, and told her that what she was saying to the child must be its own secret burden between him and her and the Omniscient One!

Every morning I must go and see that picture.

We will say that it does not require more than a fortnight's sojourn in Dresden to satisfy an intelligent traveller that to any one of taste and refinement the capital of Saxony has such attractions that it is entitled to a first place in a summary of combined peace, comfort and luxury. No wonder that the millionaires of the old world and the new, who have gone the rounds of Christendom, centre and settle there, with the complacent announcement that they have found the spot which, taken all in all, is the serenest and loveliest of city homes. The first few days, the first week, does not bring you completely, perhaps, to this conclusion; but on the second week—the first six days having been presumably well occupied with sight-seeing—you will have this opinion. I have known persons to make a single season's stay in California—in San Francisco especially—and depart and remain away, with expressions of comparative dislike for the climate and the style of living, the society, etc.; but two seasons' or two years' sojourn with us almost invariably suffice to keep the testing residents, or to so attach them that their life ever after—in less desirable sections—is shadowed with regrets at their enforced departure from the Eden of the world, the golden commonwealth, the delightful sunset land—as you then hear them claim and describe their beloved California. Certainly, on your entrance, you are charmed with Dresden; yet you think you might prefer Berlin as a lifelong home; but with the period for making acquaintance with things animate and inanimate which I have prescribed, you appreciate enough of its own peculiar, incomparable fascinations to understand the reasons of the selection which thousands of artists and cultivated men of leisure of every sort have made: —their choice of a final resting point on this little planet, after having looked over and duly considered the "eligible places" on the globe.

And now I can take a short retrospect and find agreement with the judgment of all our little party—a unanimous vote being had—declaring that with a view to economy of "mere living" and advantage in purchasing the simple articles of dress, Dresden is somewhat preferable to Berlin, and by a considerable percentage better than Paris. And as to those things which more particularly affect the health of the stranger, the French capital is inferior to its little Saxon rival.

The water, the milk, the wines, the beer, the coffee—as by the average of purchase and test considered—are purer and more palatable in Dresden than in Paris; while for study in the fine arts and in some of the sciences, Paris has very little advantage or few added opportunities and facilities to speak about and proclaim. And all this without detracting from the force and unchallenged warmth of our chance acquaintance, who from his California standpoint was unquestionably justified in much of that which he amusingly declaimed.

Usually the journey from Dresden or Berlin to Paris is "broken" once or twice at least, by the American traveller; the most frequently chosen stop-over places being Liepsic or Hanover and the City of Cologne. From Cologne the custom is to go direct to the French capital by rail (a few stopping at Aix le-Chappelle), or via the river Rhine to Coblenz or Mayence, or beyond. It is called "one day-light journey" from Berlin or Dresden to Cologne; but as the trains from either place do not start until seven o'clock in the morning, the arrival at the great cathedral city by the regular express is appointed at nine o'clock; so that there is a margin of from one to three hours of night drive,—according to the season.

From Dresden, the road by which you are ticketed, on the horseshoe route indicated, runs first to Leipsic, the famous printing town of the world. Here Baedecker has his establishment; and if there was no other publication to give distinction to this place, for the travellers who are called upon to discriminate as to guide-books, this would be sufficient for a red-letter mark. But during more than a century Leipsic has been noted for its cheap publications of every description. At the present time the writings of the principal English and American authors are sent from the presses of that city at a cost to the purchaser of less than one-half the sum required in England or the United States. On the covers of these publications there is conspicuously printed a request not to carry the book into British lines; the assertion being that while English authors have been paid for the continental circulation, which their works will have from Leipsic, it is not in the contract to permit them to be deposited elsewhere. Looking over a shelf ten feet long, packed close with the

BERLIN TO DOVER.

paper-bound books of this description, I noticed among "*British* Authors," Bret Harte, W. D. Howells, John Burroughs, Mark Twain, and Mrs. Harriet Beecher Stowe. A copy of a most appetizing book on American Humorists, by

REV. H. R. HAWEIS.

our esteemed friend Rev. H. R. Haweis, of London, was also on the latest rack.

Mr. Haweis is one of the most popular preachers in London. His church (St. James, Westmoreland street, Marylebone, London) is packed at every service, when it is known that he is to occupy the pulpit. He is a charming writer, and an eloquent and inspiring speaker. He has been largely instrumental in drawing attention to the merits of American authors, some of whom would have had as yet a scant audience in Great Britain but for his happy paragraph or extended chapters of complimentary introduction. As editor and author, and as an English gentleman of great hospitality towards those of our people with whom he becomes acquainted, he is eminently entitled to the cordial welcome of large audiences in this country.

So far as our observation extended we found the statement of our Consul, Mr. John D. Mason, with respect to the accommodations on the Dresden trains from that city to the German border quite correct. For two and a half cents a mile, we had what we considered far better accommodations than are afforded on our California routes at Central Pacific extortionate prices. And for a considerable portion of the distance between Dresden and Cologne, we had a large and elegantly furnished compartment all to ourselves, although we were assured that it was what was called a busy portion of the year, with respect to passenger traffic.

Between Dresden and the first important station, we were fortunate enough to have for companions Mr. Charles M. Kinsell, of Columbus. Georgia, and his wife. One year ago they removed from Georgia to the neighborhood of Dresden; hiring a partly furnished house with the intention of there residing until they could make a proper selection and purchase of a permanent home. They had left the United States with the expectation of not returning; but in less than a year man and wife were endeavoring to conceal from each other the degree of their homesickness. Each resolved that the other should be the first to suggest that they should return to their adopted State. The firm endurance of the masculine martyr proved the stronger of the two; and on one Spring morning Mrs. Kinsell laid down her knife and fork at the breakfast table and said, "There, Charles! I have come to the end of my patience about one thing." "What is that, my love?" "Well, I have been waiting for the last two or three months to hear you say that, instead of buying a homestead here, we had better turn right around in the middle of the Elbe and go back where we belong. And I know that these have been your sentiments during all that time. But you are just that mean sort of a man that you would stay here a whole year, and do anything (except buy a place) to make me believe that you had no idea of being homesick; but you can't fool me." "Well, my dear, a candid confession is good for the soul, and productive of harmony in a small family; and since you have had the frankness to own up, I *will* admit that it did occur to me that possibly it might be a good thing for us to reconsider our original intention." "O, what a tantalizing way you have of getting around the fact! But no matter; *I* am not going to stay here. You can get a deed for three or four homesteads, if you like; *I* am going to take—if necessary in order to get home—a third-class passage back to old Georgia. Now that's settled. And it's only a question with me of a few days." "I told my wife," said Mr. Kinsell, in his bland and pleasant manner—rubbing his hands slowly—[I could see that his complacency must be exasperating at times]—"I told my wife," repeated Mr. Kinsell, "that if she would be patient till Fall, on the first day of September we would move out of our premises and start for the old plantation; and she can't deny right here and now but what I have substantially kept my word."

With this most agreeable introduction—so well calculated to put us on thoroughly intimate grounds—we improved the time very jealously in the comparatively short partnership portion of our day's trip, between Dresden and Leipsic, in conversation with our new-found friends.

We noticed along the whole line, from our starting point to Hanover and beyond, that most of the harvest work was being done by women, and that these women wore flaming red petticoats, and often had a checkered handkerchief on their heads; their whole costume amounting to a uniform reminding us forcibly of a spectacle so familiar in the Dalecarlian section of Sweden.

The railroad fairly runs over the grand old city of Hanover, and from the back you have only glimpses of portions of that long Avenue of Limes, which is said by the Hanoverians to be, as a drive and promenade, without equal for charms in all the cities of Europe. The station is a double structure, our train arriving in the second story, and having its complete suite of rooms for ticketing and refreshment upon that floor.

We arrived at Cologne between 9 and 10 o'clock; making the last 150 miles of distance at the rate of 40 miles an hour. By moonlight and gaslight we got our first glimpse of the historic and beautiful Rhine; and for two hours after our arrival we found ourselves, in company with many other passengers, sauntering along the streets that edge upon the water, or taking our views from the points of bridges and on housetops, to which we are escorted by active and communicative guides.

The principal hotel at Cologne is the Hotel du Nord, the court-yard of which is said to surpass in excellence all others of similar arrangement—(in immediate connection with or enclosed with the hotel)—both as respects the gardens and the corridors which surround it. The open space is probably 60 by 100 feet, and in the centre of a series of flower-beds there is a fountain of peculiar and very diffusive spray. The water, in shower and cascades, is illuminated by colored lamps, producing the effect of enchantment. Double tiers of tables for refreshments are set on the broad piazzas which border the enclosure. The rooms are comfortable, but with respect to furniture they will not bear favorable comparison with the accommodations of the kind furnished the traveller in other parts of Northern Germany or in the Scandinavian countries which we had visited. The charges are 25 per cent. more than in Berlin.

At peep of day we were up to see the cathedral, of whose proportions we could only gain a limited idea by our observations during the night previous. There was no bustle, no uproar in the city at the time of our rising, save that caused by the incoming and outgoing trains; but when we arrived at the cathedral we found that mass was being said in one of the chapels, and that not less than a thousand persons, mostly women, were kneeling before the Eastern shrine. Like other

visitors, who at this early hour had sought to get a glimpse at the great church, we entered one of the side doors. That appeared to be the only place for entrance at the time. No sooner was mass concluded, and we sought to make our exit by the same aperture, than we were surrounded by a number of would-be guides, and on our parleying with them, and at the same time walking towards our expected point of departure, we found that the door was closed! We must needs walk the whole length of the nave before we could escape from the importunities of these clamorous acquaintances. Of course the situation was one that a traveller of any experience would appreciate in a moment. The best thing to do was to utilize one of these young men immediately. Otherwise we would consume the entire time occupied in walking down the length of the church in listening to solicitations. Let us make the bargain now and take the benefit of companionship by way of direction, at once and forthwith.

I shall not attempt to describe the interior or exterior of this magnificent edifice. Its dimensions and its main characteristic are familiar to most of my readers. And I presume there are few persons of intelligence who are not aware of the remarkable fact that for several centuries this great building stood in a state of incompleteness, and that it is only within the last half century that steady work has been going on in the way of finishing its walls and rearing its majestic towers; and that within the last quarter of a century the famous crane which stood for over two hundred years on one of the towers was taken down, and work continued and completed from its ancient standpoint.

After you have looked at the building from the principal corners of observation, at the suggestion and with the counsel and descriptions of your guide, you are besought to enter the celebrated Cologne water establishment, where there is a model (said to have cost 12,000 marks) of the great church, on free exhibition. Engravings of the cathedral in its incomplete state—fifty years ago—are hung upon the wall. Certainly this pattern is worth a mark's profit on a bottle of the scented water, and you expect the hint will shortly be given

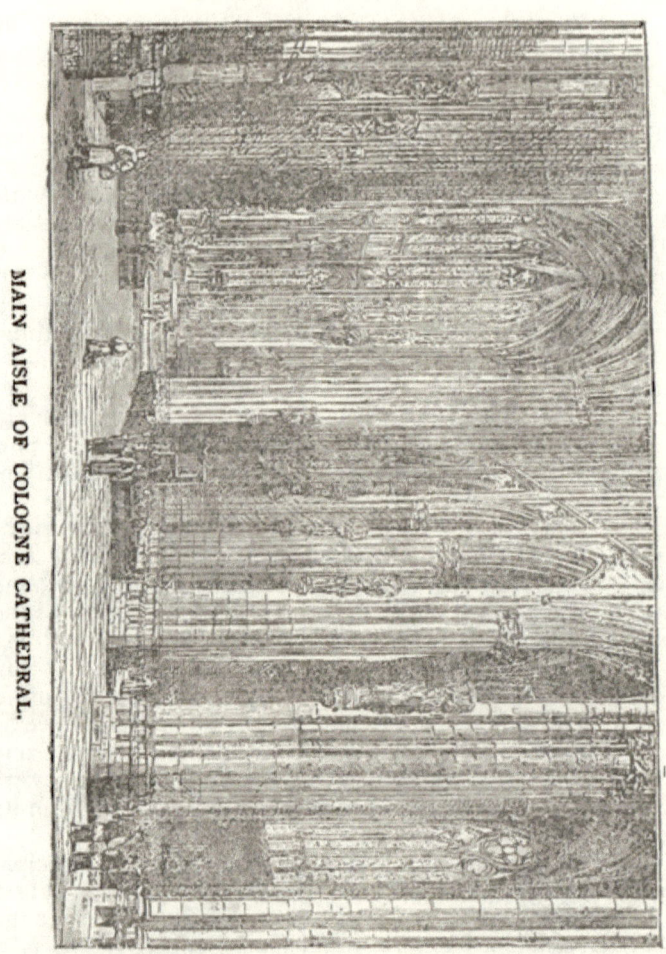

MAIN AISLE OF COLOGNE CATHEDRAL.

to make the purchase that is supposed to be equivalent for an admission price at the door.

It was yet early when we stood in front of this agency; the shutters had not been taken down, and our guide had to rap violently on the door in order to arouse the inmates. Two frowzy-headed, dirty-faced, altogether slovenly-looking girls came to the door, uniting their strength for the purpose of unbolting and unlocking. After we had passed around the model once or twice, the tallest of these slatterns came to the front of the little counter that runs close to the door, and between it and the room where the model is placed, and desired —through our guide—to know if we wished to purchase half a dozen or a dozen bottles, and how we would have them sent? When we insisted that we should confine our buying to a single quart, and that contained in the most convenient vessel she could exhibit, she did not hesitate to express her disappointment or disgust, whichever it was (or both), at our parsimony. It was usual for visitors, she said—especially *Americans*,— with great emphasis on the national noun—to buy a box. We protested that we were already overloaded with baggage, especially in the hand-satchel line; we sought to mollify her by a careful restatement of this fact; instructing our guide that our deep regrets be expressed because we could not take along with us a few hogsheads of this standard and incomparably delicious perfume. But all to no purpose,—so far as this lady of Cologne was concerned. She rolled up our little jug with an air of injured innocence, bit the string with which she fastened it as if she had our thumb between her teeth, and literally tossed the article into our hands; muttering something which we could not interpret and which was not clearly explained to us, but which we are strongly of opinion was in the nature of not wishing us to go to Paradise. We were glad to get out of this museum of models and samples.

We met at Cologne one of our Stockholm acquaintances, Fröken Emma Hultgren. We learned from her of a hotel in Paris—"modest and unpretending"—where Swedish and English are spoken by the landlord and most of his servants. So it happened that we came from the Rhine to the *Hôtel de Paris et d'Osborne*. This inn is located near the Tuileries Gardens.

On the evening of our arrival in Paris, there was a fête in progress at the corner of the public grounds, and closely adjacent to our apartments. While we were thus enabled at the outset to have a very lively view of the kind of entertainments which do most satisfy and enrapture the French citizen, we were far from regretting the hour—three days after our arrival—when the booths were closed and the harlequins folded their tents and moved away. Moreover, it seemed like a desecration of this garden-park to set such a tumultuous crowd of boisterous circus performers in any corner. But here was the French citizen surely. Not, indeed, the highly cultivated gentleman; not the artist or the scholar. But the common people do love these antics and do enjoy these exhibitions with a degree of ardor that amounts to enthusiasm. There is no mistake about this. I have stood in a group of persons, certainly not of the lower order, who were engaged in watching the somersaults of what I should consider a very ordinary leaper. But at every double throw of his body they became so wild in their applause (clapping their hands till it seemed as if the palms would be blistered, and rapping on tables or posts with their canes until their sticks were shattered, and shouting at the top of their voices) that it was some time before I could realize that what I saw in the ring was the only provocation for these violent demonstrations on the part of these native spectators.

In the first week of this fête there was given an entertainment for the benefit of the sufferers by the recent earthquake at Ischia, which I was told netted over 10,000 francs. On the Sunday after our arrival there was a fête to be given for the benefit of the poor of Paris, at which it was announced Madame Sarah Bernhardt would act and Miss Christine Nilsson would sing. As a part of the advertising programme, there was on Thursday an Announcement that Mlle. Bernhardt had committed suicide and a Denial in extras the day preceding the benefit. It happened that during the Saturday night previous a violent storm arose, which tore the canvas from the sides of the great theatre-stage which had been erected for open-air performances, and at which the two distinguished artists were to have appeared. Notwithstanding the fact that the wind continued at its highest rate of velocity during the entire day, not less than 15,000 francs were realized for the object specified; and the very fury of the tempest

ARCH OF TRIUMPH.

seemed to add to the enjoyment and hilarity of a good proportion of the immense multitude that crowded within the gates.

Twice each week, coaches call at all the principal hotels for persons who may desire to go the "rounds" of the city and "see the sights,"—so advertised in one English circular;—and on other days a four-horse coach, with competent guide, interpreters and messengers, leaves for Fontainebleau. The charge is very moderate, and the trip is worth taking as a preliminary or preface-sketching tour of observation. After that one may select the points that most interest him and go without hesitation—with the sufficient knowledge obtained in the run around—directly to his chosen places, without the intervention or cost of a guide.

The residence of a Nevada Bonanza millionaire is directly opposite the *Arc de Triomphe*, and is, perhaps, the most eligibly situated of any of the dwellings that from the five angles may be said to face this commanding structure. It was a matter of common gossip when we arrived in Paris that "a rich American speculator" had offered a hundred thousand francs to the city to be permitted, on an occasion of one of his parties, to illuminate the *Arc de Triomphe*. [Such little personal matters are often prominent topics of conversation in European cities, when there is not a word about them in the newspapers.] The host of the evening agreed to pay all the expenses, of course, connected with the fitting of the lamps, and so forth. But the authorities applied to, though said to be sorely in need of funds, declined the offer. There are four other wealthy persons who have their "grand home" adjacent to this crowning spot, and it was argued that if one was given the privilege it must be accorded to the others; and would it not eventually serve to bring contempt upon the structure, thus used as a beacon pile for the millionaires, whose parlor hearthstones were facing its columns?

In conversation with an officer in charge of the grounds and buildings of the Invalides, on the occasion of our visiting the tomb of Napoleon Bonaparte, as well as when talking to many of the crippled or infirm soldiers who stood about, we found that there was the same devoted love and admiration for the memory of Napoleon—if we could judge by intensity of expression—that existed two generations ago. Still he remains to the soldiers of France not only the most wonderful marshal that ever led hosts to battle, but the

TOMB OF NAPOLEON BONAPARTE.

noblest ruler, and, so far as they can judge or comprehend, the wisest legislator that the world has ever seen.

We sought to attend the funeral mass at the Church of the Bonapartes, as it is popularly called, sung for the repose of the soul of the late Comte de Chambord. Patiently we stood in line an hour and a half, in the vain hope of getting within the walls of the sacred edifice for the purpose of viewing the ceremonies and hearing the music. Three or four hundred anxious persons were our companions in suffering and pastime; and while we had to regret the fact of being barred out, and still more to deplore the personal effects of our prolonged standing in a broiling-hot sun, the attendance was not without profit. We opened up conversation at several points along the line, shifting backwards for that purpose to which there was no objection) when we found that it was certain that we could not enter. We opened up conversation with respect to the sentiments of the people generally on the royal question. Most of those in line, so far as we could ascertain or infer, were simply curious to see and to hear, without any sentiment of bereavement or any imperial affiliation or desires. But some of our chance-made acquaintances —French gentlemen, who became very communicative when we informed them, as we took great care to do, that we were Americans—were very outspoken and emphatic in their declarations of favor for a monarchical system of government, and some were unsparing in their denunciation of the administration of the Republic. All these gave utterance to one criticism on the late Count. They regretted his unconquerable obstinacy; because he would not take the colors and the arms after the enforced abdication of Napoleon III., on the acceptance of which he would have been enthroned. Some, who seemed to have been numbered among his more steadfast adherents, declared that it almost shook their allegiance to him when he persisted in this unwise and, under the circumstances, as they considered, absurd determination. As for the Prince de Paris, I did not hear a single favorable opinion. One Frenchman said, in a way peculiar to his countrymen—giving treble emphasis by a gesture—tossing the back of his hands upwards rapidly three or four times:

"He is light, he is light, he is light!" I felt inclined and even anxious to inform him about our western vernacular, wherein we speak of an individual being "very light timber." But I was afraid that the seriousness of the occasion would not tolerate such an explanation in the judgment of this gentleman of refinement and taste and, most evidently, intense imperialism.

As to some of the places to which everybody is said to go —much of the history of which is common learning—let me

PALAIS ROYAL, PARIS.

name for note one :—the Palais Royal. Here are a series of shops on the ground floor, in enclosed squares, and a series of restaurants above. The articles in the shop are priced at about 25 per cent. more than the same articles can be purchased for elsewhere, in this same city. The restaurants here are not first-class, while the tariff is often extortionate.

The best eating-places in the city, all things considered, for the ordinary restaurant patronizer, are the Duval establishments. There you are given a general diet and drink pro-

GRAND OPERA HOUSE, PARIS.

gramme as you enter the door, for one, two, three, four or more persons—as your company may number. This catalogue of the articles that are supplied at the table, you hand to the person who attends upon yourself or your party, and who marks upon it by tally points only the number of plates of any particular article which you may order. Included in this enumeration is the number of napkins which you use—five centimes for each. With his ideas of cash-arithmetic, the American who has not shaken off his home calculation tables, as he sees the large centime numbers increase on his list, is naturally inclined to be apprehensive of an immense bill at the conclusion of the entertainment, and is proportionately surprised when the aggregate comes out at a low figure in our dollars and cents. You pay to the lady who serves you; and she brings you back that programme or catalogue, stamped by the cashier, whose desk is at a counter on the floor where you eat. This paper you return to the auditor and door-keeper,—the same person who saluted you and ticketed you at your entrance. If you do not have this paper with you when you shall have arrived at the outer door, you will not be permitted to pass out until inquiry and ascertainment is made as to whether you have paid your bill! I am told the proprietor of this establishment (who looks very much like an ex-mayor of the city of San Francisco, now or lately residing in one of our southern California counties) started business in this place with less than 500 francs for capital, and that to-day he is the owner of not less than 500,000 francs, with "establishments" in every part of the city.

When we saw, by chance, at a distance from a shop at which we were purchasing some trifles, the name of Maison Dorée, over doors and on windows, we made haste to look at that building—the alleged model and pattern of a similar establishment on Kearney street, in the city of San Francisco. And on the following day—just for the sake of old memories and future retrospect—we dined at the Maison Dorée. It was an excellent dinner; but we shall dine there no more. If the prices at the Maison Dorée in San Francisco were in any wise approximate to those on the way-bill at its forerunner, I am

GRAND STAIRWAY OF OPERA HOUSE.

of the opinion that my friend Leon Dingeon would have a very limited number of patrons.

We attended at the Grand Opera House during the performance of *The Huguenot*. The advice is given from all quarters that if you have not time to make more than one visit to this magnificent temple of music, you had better sacrifice one of the acts—forego the pleasure of listening to the introductory, or second scene—for the purpose of examining the corridors and staircases. The advice should be repeated until it is known to every visitor. It will be readily accepted; the more so if, as on the occasion of our attendance, the performance be slovenly in orchestral accompaniment, and not more than fairly good on the stage.

The grandest thing about the opera house of Paris, after all is examined and said, is the grand staircase. If I were to give advice in the premises, I would say that, unless some great singer or some star company was engaged, the tourist who cannot spare more than one night to visit the building should donate most of his time to walking in the foyer and up and down that splendid flight of steps. I have seen the interior of many amphitheatres, which, although not so spacious, gave me just as much satisfaction as this concert-room interior; but that staircase is worthy of the extreme Parisian eulogistic phrase—as Carlyle translated it—"the superlatively superb." I was not surprised to hear it said, that artists and architects have been known to pay, for the second and third time, an admission fee, that would take them past the lower hall, for the sole purpose of re-studying this beautiful entrance, with all its "effects" under the artificial light that is ablaze during an Opera evening.

Whatever may have been the sum of his faults, political and personal, certain it is that no visitor to Paris can fail to experience a sense of gratitude to Napoleon Third, for that which is there unanimously credited to him by the native resident—for the great public street improvements chronicled in his reign;—and especially will this sentiment be large and throbbing in the breast of a traveller who has been sojourning for a shorter or longer period previous in the mighty metropolis of Britain. O, for a Louis Napoleon, with his

THE SEVEN BRIDGES OF PARIS.

Baron Haussmann, for one year only—if no more—in charge of the street-department of London! How they would push St. Andrews street plump into Ludgate Circus! How they would open up an air-line avenue from Trafalgar Square to the corner of Oxford street and Tottenham Court Road! How pitilessly they would by straight and broad street connections bring down St. John's road to the banks of the Thames! From the little I know of Paris, as it was before the days of Napoleon III. and as it is now, I believe that many sojourners have with intense power-coveting declared that they could revise the map of London, under the supposed road-monarchy, with immense satisfaction—to themselves, at least. And that too, without much, if any, destruction or impairment of the most loved "historic" street-corner localities.

It is a great comparative comfort to ride on the Parisian omnibus. But then, during the busy portions of the day, you must go to the starting points and obtain your ticket, or you will probably never get an opportunity to ride outside. In the pleasant months of the year it is "one grand recreation" for the Parisian himself, to mount his city car and take the full worth of a through ticket, day after day.

The inhabitants are very proud of their loveliest of cities; they seem never to tire of looking it all over; and as a rule—even as we found it in Gothenburg—they put aside all their avocations and duties. so far as possible, to inform a stranger, or to carefully direct him to the sources where he can best obtain full and perfect particulars. Even Boston has now no superior average of public-spirited citizens, in this respect and manifestation.

And what a contrast to the robbing London cabman is this most polite of hack-drivers. George Augustus Sala had led us to expect quite the opposite. (But that was in his letters written during the crowding of strangers to see The Exposition.) The Parisian "cabby" is not only courteous, but precise in giving you the time or distance, and explaining with accuracy what the fares are from point to point. With what perfect urbanity he listens to the broken French that you thrust at him; doing what he can to help out your speech or to make sure of your intentions, as though he had been a servant in your family all the days of his life. And if he hears you pleading for a special privilege anywhere — on account, for instance, of your mistaking about the hour when a public institution would be open to view, or the like of that—how quickly and strongly, and yet withal how deferentially towards you, he comes to your support! "Surely you must let the American gentleman in, if it is possible." Adding in an undertone: "The people of his republic are friendly to France." And if you ask him to be your guide, and lay the full responsibility and dignity of direction and appointment upon him, with a happy sense of the confidence reposed he picks up his reins and starts on the rounds; never missing a point in all his routes, or failing to turn about in due proximity to a gallery or a church or a monument or a panorama, and ask in his own way: "Monsieur has probably seen the ———? 'No!' Then we are close to it, and it is [or is not] worth Monsieur's time to step out and pay a visit to it."

O, most excellent of conductors and city coach and cabbox companions! No wonder that a famous German songstress could not forbear chanting thy praises, in a recent poetical epistle.

Now that we have seen *Notre Dame* Cathedral—the glories of its fretted arches and stained windows, and the riches of its ecclesiastical regalia, and the robes of its martyred prelates—have gained and enjoyed the magnificent view from the accessible tower, will we see "the ghastly sight?" He remarks that "Some persons, especially ladies, do not wish to see it; but as the place is convenient to the cathedral, perhaps we would like to stop on this route?" He does not even name the place. What a delicacy there is in this! But of course we comprehend at once that he means The Morgue. "Some will wish to see it,"—with true French inquiring suggestiveness. Only three bodies on this particular morning— old, middle-aged and young. The veteran was said to be over 70; a small, deeply-wrinkled face, but with a strong, thick shock of gray hair. The second body was that of a very large man, whose water-bloated carcass had evidently been much distended by a regular course of alcoholism before he tumbled into the Seine. Number 3 is a tall, slim youth of not more than 23 years, with an Irish cast of countenance and with a big mark of contusion on the left side of his head. Strange it is to observe a smile in the expression of his mouth, while his eyes seem sparkling rather than glassed in death. The clothes of the three are hung on a rack at one side, and all indicate that they are laboring men. There are but few persons in attendance—not over a dozen—and none who appear to be attracted by anything but idle or morbid curiosity. "Sometimes," our driver says, "it is very hard to hear the shrieking that comes from that little house. But,"—(he adds, in another tone, and with a characteristic French shrug)—"not more than one out of twenty that are exposed here are identified by anybody that has any special love for them."

Will we go to the Garden of Plants? The managerie will be sure to please the child. We go. In the crowd we can see less of the animals than at Dresden, and perhaps on that account think it is an inferior exhibition. But the garden proper is, of its kind, unsurpassed. Here the attendants get from one to five francs a day; from the boy that waters and feeds the pigeons up to the master of the tigers and the keeper of the elephants. The women who sell a drink that answers in insipidity to the Swedish *sept*—we are carefully informed—make more on Sundays and holidays than the wages of any of the men in charge of the premises, except the house-warmer and blanket-keeper for the snakes. The Anaconda Boss gets seven francs a day, and is not to be accounted among the ordinary workmen in the garden. He resembles Leland Stanford.

Most of the French children that we meet or see in our "rounds" seem to be not merely happy, but enthusiastically so. I will not say that they are unnaturally excited, as some have written, in effect, of the whole brood of Gallic offspring. It is natural with them to be very lively; but they are not any more boisterous than are our own young folks of similar ages and otherwise adapted for just comparison.

And observe how good-natured, to the degree of jollity, are

the majority of the laborers upon the public streets; where it does appear that the hardest work is done. We ask the driver to make an excuse and stop by the side of some of these men who are engaged in laying down a wooden pavement, while we venture on a little questioning. They get four francs a day; and, taking their habit of life and the cost of bread and meat and onions or garlic into account, we judge that in the matter of pay they are about ten or fifteen per cent. from a wages-par with laborers upon the public streets of New York. That is, when their pay and the cost of their living and the like are all duly considered.

Will we look in at the panorama of the Bastile? We have to wait a half hour before we can gain admission here, or at the panorama of the city of Paris—the number within being limited to threescore, and the waiting attendance being four times that number on our "circuit day" under this guidance. The arrangements within are the same as at Dresden, as hereinbefore described. A new rotunda, with central platform and umbrella and embankment margin and canvas walls—representing an ineffectual effort to dislodge the Germans from a forest in the suburbs of Paris—has just been opened; and we act upon the suggestion that we might desire to look in upon this also. You are not surprised to hear that many persons visit these paintings several times in the year—that is, those paintings which have been on exhibition long enough to test and establish popularity.

The people of the Arrondissement in which we sojourn will hold an election on Sunday. We attend at the polls to see the gathering. Our view is in a large hall; and nothing could, under the circumstances, be more orderly. Why, we have seen town meetings in staid old Berkshire County, Massachusetts, that were proportionately more tumultuous. I speak of demonstrations in noisy conversations, and the like. Of course, strong feeling is exhibited; but here again the politeness of the race comes in: this time manifested by all classes to each other, and from representatives of one body of citizens to every other class.

But "Did I not discover that the French are sore over their defeat by the Germans, and determined to avenge Sedan at the earliest practicable period?" Well, yes, many told me—speaking usually in what, for a Frenchman, might be termed a phlegmatic manner—that the time *would* come when they would get even; but most of these men defer the next war until the next generation,—candidly admitting that they were not prepared for it now, and probably would not be for the next 20 years. "But the time would come! Ah, yes: the time *would come!*" That would do for a legacy to their children; and their children would bear it in mind. And when we pleasantly and gently referred to the superiority in numbers of the German armies, we were told that France was richer than Germany, and would one day be more populous than that Germany which the Berlin monarchy could hold together. "See!" they would exclaim; "see! How rich France is! How quickly she paid off, or arranged to pay off, her indebtedness! It astonished the world, and well it might. But France, for its size, is the richest country on the globe." You will probably be told this many times, and with many substantiating details, if you open this line of inquiry and conversation.

They think that Americans should sympathize with them very deeply, now that France is a republic; and it was the understanding with most of those with whom I had communications on this subject, that our people, as a rule, do feel a special interest and hope in the future of the new Government. Often and long we talked of the origin and promotion of the Bartholdi Statue project, and the significance it already had and would acquire. In one company I quoted the lines of Oliver Wendell Holmes on "The Sunny Land of France:" —the paragraph where he describes how

> "The city slept beneath the moonbeam's glance,
> Her white walls gleaming through the vines of France.
> And all was hushed save where the footsteps fell
> On some high tower, of midnight sentinel.
> But one still watched: no self-encircled woes
> Chased from his side the angel of repose;
> He watched, he wept, for thoughts of bitter years
> Bowed his dark lashes, wet with burning tears;
> His country's suffering and her children's shame,
> Streamed o'er his memory like a forest flame.
> Each treasured insult, each remembered wrong,
> Rolled through his heart, and kindled into song.
> His taper faded; and the morning gales
> Swept through the world the war-song of Marseilles."

And from my English recitation, and an attempt to translate, I aroused such an interest in it—such a curiosity about it, I may say—that I am sure the lines are by this time worthily written in French hexameter. I wondered that there was no rendering of it long ago in their best frame-work of song. But let me be satisfied if I did not mutilate it, in the Gallic tongue, in vain!

Close by our little hotel was the Church of St. Roch, a huge building, with two great altars, so to speak—the one directly behind the other. The latter is not in a lady chapel;—for I should say that the rear church-room and appointments were too large to admit of that term. We remarked that the front of the church was draped for a funeral; some notable person was to be buried on one day of our observation. We went in and saw a bier placed high above the altar rails in the body of the church; but no one was near it. The strains of mournful music were heard proceeding from the farther end. We met a funeral procession coming out from the interior gates on the left-hand aisle, headed by a priest, who was chanting, and a trombone performer, who was sounding a dirge-accompaniment. The procession marched down nearly as far as the threshold of the great door—a distance of two hundred feet or more—and there the music ceased, and the coffin, which had been carried between four liveried men in a dangling and indifferent manner, was lowered to a stretcher which was brought up behind the weeping widow and her family train. Then all the gentlemen in the line—fully three score of them—shook hands with the widow and other relations of the deceased who were present; and all the ladies and many of the gentlemen in attendance embraced and kissed the widow with great heartiness, and I should say with vehemence that approached to violence. They smacked the poor little woman on each cheek with an intensity of ardor that was painful to behold—and to hear! And I could not help observing, after the ceremony was over and the marching resumed, that her face—the right side particularly, which received the first force of these strong consoling osculations, appeared as though it had been slapped or poulticed to the verge of blistering.

Going up St. Roch street a few evenings prior to our departure, I saw through an open window a very old man reading a newspaper to his wife, who could not have been much his junior. There was a crowd at the point on the narrow sidewalk, so that all must needs hear the passages, which in a voice expressive of deep emotion the old man was slowly making audible. It was the story of a poor girl who had been her mother's only support for years, suddenly thrown on a bed of sickness. There was an appeal in the paper for help, and before the crowd diminished so that I could push on my way, the aged pair within had put on their hats and made ready to go to the scene of distress. I marked the spot—a little thread and needle store—and went in there, the next day. After purchasing some trifle, I asked how the poor girl was whom they had visited the preceding night. What I knew and how I came to know what little (much, it seemed to them) that I did know about their going to that place, was a matter of tormenting curiosity to these good folks. They had not dreamed that any stranger in the wide, wide world was aware of their going; certainly they could not understand how they had been identified as charitable visitors at that bedside? But I got my information in reply to my surprising question:—which information was to the effect that they and others had supplied all immediate necessities, and that there would be no suffering in that garret if they could help it. And they *could* help it (this last said with great emphasis). But I was called back to be told that there was "a grand lady from America" whose "house-word" had been sent to this chamber of affliction before these old people got there; and I understood that it was expected, according to the message, that she or her immediate messenger would come on the following day. Word had been sent that no comfort for the girl or the mother should be lacking. With some difficulty, I got her name. It transpired that, whether she was in Paris or elsewhere, her instructions to take notice of private or personal appeals for help to poor families, made it certain that no such item as the one referred to would go unobserved by her home representatives.

When I listened to the Duke of Cambridge, in the British

House of Lords, uttering his arguments and denunciations against the Channel Tunnel—opportunely supplied with facts and figures by the then recent victor of Alexandria—I could not restrain a sentiment of indignation, which I fully expected would be revived and intensified when I had occasion—as occasion I needs must have—to cross that little, narrow division of water, which is so notorious, the world over, for its pitching perturbations! Would not every sea-sick passenger anathematize the Duke who so powerfully denounced the tunnel project? But I never thought of the Duke, nor of

STEAMSHIP CITY OF BERLIN.

General Wolseley—no, not for a moment—on the water section of the trip between the two great Capitals of Europe; for, while the day before had been so rough as to absolutely preclude the passage of steamers from Calais to Dover, at the time of our crossing the sea was as smooth as the Pacific Ocean in its calmest mood. Of necessity, with small steamers of such sharp build as make this trip for passenger connection, there will be rolling and teetering at the best; and, as the medical chairman of the Dinner of Poisons, in Dickens' celebrated tale of fashionable French suicides, had occasion to remark: "Some folks will be so provoking as to get a little

CLIFFS OF DOVER.

nervous and eructious before the proper time, when they know that they are apt to have actual cause in a little while."

From the proportion of passengers who are talking of their preferences for trans-Atlantic steamship lines, it is certain that a majority are old travellers; and we note the fact that the most experienced seem to favor the Inman Company's boats and management; many being very emphatic in their praise of the officering and accommodations on the City of Berlin.

Many passengers who make this trip for the first time, on the run from the Continent to England, will certainly feel inclined to put the inquiry of surprise to the typical John Bull, as that captain paces his central deck in command of the ferry vessel," Where are the *White* cliffs of Dover?" Not at this season of the year, at all events, does the color of the British headlands, as presented to the eye of the approaching visitor, suggest or justify this adjective. Cliffs, sure enough; and higher and more precipitous by far than the pictures or photographs usually represent them. And squarely against the breast of one of them, the keen-edged vessel runs its nose, when it slips up to the dock.

Before the passage across is half-way completed, you can discern, with the aid of your own or the vessel's sea-glass, the lower promontories,—the light-house and castle of Dover; and before you arrive at the landing, there is a good half-hour of clear vision—on a cloudless day—of the populated heights, and the great warehouses of the town. But think you that the new people on board are giving much audible expression to their thoughts with respect to these structures or their surroundings? Not a bit of it! But just as we cross the line of the castle's longitude, we are mutually surprised—a score or more of us—by a loud chorus of agreeing curiosity and anxiety,—the preceding *solo* of interrogation, coming from the youngest in the multitude that stood upon that deck;—about the probable location of the cottage which was once occupied by no less personages than Betsy Trotwood, Mr. Dick and David Copperfield? One set inquire as to its whereabouts, within what limits it necessarily must be; while, simultaneously, others, of the number indicated, have a positive judgment in the premises at once. Many separately exclaiming as they point, "*There* is where little David must have seen the donkeys on the lawn and heard his benevolent but irritable relative call out to Janet, just before he put in an appearance and identified himself, in the garden adjoining the cottage." The fact is, that at the place or point where Aunt Betsy's cottage once stood—of which a literally exact description was given by the great novelist—lodging-houses of a very expensive size and style are now to be seen. (Says Alfred Rimmer—the author of that delightful book, "*About England with Dickens :*"—" Miss Trotwood's house was not far from Dover Castle, which rises magnificently toward the sea at an abrupt elevation of between three and four hundred feet above the level of the water. The French coast is clearly visible at times from here, and whenever it is seen, rainy weather is not far off. Donkeys will always be found, and no doubt they trespass as much as the donkeys of Miss Trotwood's time did.")

And then again, we are surprised—or we should have been if we had not heard the same thing a few months before, under somewhat similar circumstances—we are surprised to overhear expressions of wonder on the part of English ladies and gentlemen—for such they undoubtedly gave evidence of being—with reference to our manifested extensive and intimate acquaintance with and love for the writings of the dead novelist. And some of these,—(perhaps you will say that they, for once, impeached their standing in manners by so doing), expressed their contempt for that "vulgar author ;" who—be it understood from them—was never permitted to circulate freely in first-class society in his native land! He was an author, they averred, who could not thoroughly "interpret" the "nobler classes" of the English-speaking race, as they were seen in all the higher walks of social life in Great Britain! Such was the substance of current remarks in the quarter indicated. It appeared as though our mild protests and our quotations of the British public's own words and deeds in opposition to this criticism, only served to focalize upon ourselves a personal judgment.

People of the United States should place at least one

more Memorial Window in England. This time, if such a thing be possible, it should be in close o'er-setting proximity to the body of the Benefactor, whom it might even thus seem—to some beholders—to honor defiantly, as well as in a most appropriate form of appreciation and gratitude:—a splendid, conspicuous and long-enduring testimonial, shining as near as Dean and Chapter will let it, above or adjacent to the grave of Charles Dickens.

SHORTHAND AND REPORTING.
A LECTURE BY

CHARLES A. SUMNER.

New edition; with a portrait; several pages of the lecture stereographed in phonography; a great body of notes; and a biographical sketch of the lecturer. 114 pp.

"One of the most instructive volumes, and certainly the cheapest book ever issued."—*Students' Journal.*

"'Shorthand and Reporting' is a valuable historical record, containing much information entirely new to me."—WM. INGRAHAM KIP, *Bishop of California.*

"I venture to express the hope that you may awaken a proper interest in the subject on the part of those who control our educational institutions. If you do, you will deserve to rank as a public benefactor. Your historical matter is admirably presented, and your practical suggestions are of the highest value."—HON. A. A. SARGENT, U. S. S.

PRICE 10 CENTS, POST PAID.

Published and for sale by ANDREW J. GRAHAM,
744 Broadway, New York City.

www.ingramcontent.com/pod-product-compliance
Lightning Source LLC
Chambersburg PA
CBHW032033220426
43664CB00006B/457